COUNTERFEITER

COUNTERFEITER

*How a Norwegian Jew Survived
the Holocaust*

MORITZ NACHTSTERN AND
RAGNAR ARNTZEN

Translation by Margrit Rosenberg Stenge
Foreword by Sidsel Nachtstern

LYONS PRESS
Guilford, Connecticut
An imprint of Globe Pequot Press

To buy books in quantity for corporate use
or incentives, call **(800) 962–0973**
or e-mail **premiums@GlobePequot.com.**

Originally published in Norwegian as *Falskmynter i Sachsenhausen*
This translation has been published with the financial support of NORLA

First published in Great Britain in 2008 by Osprey Publishing

Norwegian text © Spartacus forlag AS 2006
Norwegian edition published by Spartacus forlag AS, Norway
Published by agreement with Hagen Agency AS, Norway
English translation © Osprey Publishing 2008

First Lyons Press edition 2012

Every attempt has been made by the publisher to secure the appropriate permissions for materials
reproduced in this book. If there has been any oversight we will be happy to rectify the situation
and a written submission should be made to the publishers.

The views and opinions expressed in this book and the context in which the image of the crowd
of survivors at Ebensee (66290) is used do not necessarily reflect the views or policy of, nor imply
approval or endorsement by, the United States Holocaust Memorial Museum.

Text design: Sheryl P. Kober
Layout artist: Justin Marciano

Library of Congress Cataloging-in-Publication Data is available on file.

ISBN 978-0-7627-7988-8

Printed in the United States of America

10 9 8 7 6 5 4 3 2 1

TABLE OF CONTENTS

Foreword

    It Cannot Be Erased by Sidsel Nachtstern vii

    "The Norwegian Will Die Tonight" by Bjarte Bruland xi

    Block 19 and Operation Bernhard by Lawrence Malkin,

        author of *Krueger's Men: The Secret Nazi Counterfeit Plot*

        and the Prisoners of Block 19 xxv

Counterfeiter 1

Two Interviews with Moritz Nachtstern 237

Credits 239

Glossary 241

Index 243

FOREWORD
It Cannot Be Erased

THIS STORY WAS WRITTEN DOWN BEFORE I WAS BORN. MY PARENTS SAT together in the little apartment on Brugata in Oslo, the same apartment where my father had been arrested a few years before. He spoke, she wrote.

When I was born in July 1946, barely a year had passed since his own "rebirth": He had survived the Holocaust. Not long after he came home he experienced great happiness. He met Rachel and found love. Together they created a home and a family.

He was my storyteller. It was he who introduced me to the trolls and to Askeladd (Ash-lad—a Norwegian fairytale figure) and who transformed me into the Princess in the Blue Mountain. He sang about Lillebror (little brother) and the Teddy-bjørn (teddy bear), and taught me a German children's song, which I have kept among my treasured songs. I know that he was very proud of being the father of a small child, and he threw himself completely into the role of being a papa (daddy), which was unusual for fathers in those days.

When my brother was born four years later, I believe his happiness was complete. He had the family he had been dreaming about, but which he never thought he would have.

When I think back, he seemed to have managed to hide his past well, and when I was a child it was impossible for me to notice the changes in his disposition or behavior. Nevertheless, I remember the look on his face when for the first time I consciously discovered the prison number on his arm. I can still see the pain lying like a dark shadow across his eyes and mouth, when I asked him what it was.

Later I would get to know Papa's story well, with his nightmares time and time again and fear in the otherwise warm and calm eyes.

Outwardly Papa was a lively person who enjoyed playing games and having fun. His laughter was so contagious that one could not help but laugh with him. At parties he was often the storyteller, and he loved to entertain with songs and stories. He would get up and sing *"Mein Vater Spiel Viol"* ("My Father Plays the Violin," in Yiddish), while he swung the bow toward his imaginary violin with his whole body.

His body language was strong, and when he ate it was so fast that it was as though he was afraid that the food would disappear into thin air. He sat at the table as if ready to run, rarely leaning back and at ease during meals. Everything was done in a hurry. He somehow wanted to embrace it all, not to miss out on anything.

I can recall how much time it took for my parents to prepare the food for Pesach (Passover). They worked side by side in the kitchen: He chopped the liver for the entree; she cooked the chicken and soup with matzo balls and made the world's most delicious gefilte fish. Papa loved tasty foods, and he could go on and on savoring the flavor itself.

I suppose we were, in a way, a happy little family, but black clouds always prevented our lives from being perfect. My mother and her family had fled to Sweden, when the threatened arrests of the Norwegian Jews became a fact. Her father was arrested and perished in the Germans' gas chambers in Auschwitz.

Such experiences cannot be erased.

Before the war and until 1940, my mother was a member of the Communist Youth Organization, and she was always an active presence at their meetings. In 1942, after all the male Jews had been arrested, she dyed her coal-black hair red and moved among the Norwegians under the alias of Vesla (Little One). With the help of her communist friends she managed to get the rest of her family into hiding. Ten days later, at the start of December 1942, they crossed the border to Sweden and freedom.

My home was marked by the events of the war. I do not think we spoke much about it, but the war somehow shadowed our everyday life with a kind of nervous and indefinable disquiet.

Nevertheless, Papa was able to talk about his experiences, and when he did it was usually with a touch of humor. That is, he spoke little about the prison ship SS *Donau* and Auschwitz concentration camp—the most difficult time, when death was a threat every day. He preferred to talk about life in Sachsenhausen, which is described in this book. He always came back to the jocular tone among the prisoners, which helped them to get through the days.

His worst memories were revealed while he slept, and they manifested themselves in nightmares and violent weeping. One nightmare occurred again and again: the young man who stood in front of him in the tattooing line and begged to change places to postpone it a little, because he was so afraid of the needles. They were both typographers, and when the Germans needed printers for their counterfeit operation in Sachsenhausen, Papa's number was the last to be called up. Thus, Papa survived.

He never saw the young man again.

He tried to hide it in front of us children, but I can still hear his cries that woke us up at night: "I am so sorry! I am so sorry! I am alive, I am alive . . . but you are not!"

On the bookshelves of my childhood home there was a large selection of war literature, among them Hitler's *Mein Kampf.* Papa used these books for reference.

When I was twelve years old I removed one of these books from the shelf. It was the first time I found out something about the horrors Papa had gone through. He found me crying in my room, hidden halfway under the bedcovers with the book. I can recall how he held me and let me cry until I had no more tears left. Then we talked for hours.

Papa died as he had lived, quickly and without warning. We spoke together on the phone the night before. He was a bit stuffed up, he said. I asked him to take care of himself. The next morning he was gone.

Sidsel Nachtstern
Nøtterøy, April 2006

"The Norwegian Will Die Tonight"

By Bjarte Bruland

THAT WAS HOW CLOSE MORITZ NACHTSTERN WAS TO DEATH IN AUSCHWITZ. He was one of 771 Jews deported from Norway during the German occupation of 1940–45, and one of only thirty-four who came back. The manner in which his story is told is unusually sober. Death is present in his entire narration. During his relatively short time in Auschwitz, he was close to death several times, and could have easily been one of those who never came back, one of those who could never tell his story. Chance would have it differently.

But his story leaves no doubt that, even after he was sent from Auschwitz to Sachsenhausen, and even though he kept hope alive, he knew that he could be killed at any time. Perhaps this is why his narration is so full of humorous reflections, poorly concealed sarcasm, and extensive irony. However, it is also a story of human worth. In an apparently absurd reflection, he says that he would prefer to go to the gas chamber with hair on his head.

Why did he write his story as early as 1949? One can only wonder why he felt the need to tell it at a time when most of the others seemingly wanted to forget. In many ways Moritz Nachtstern went against the stream. He had a need to commit the events to paper. It was probably a way to deal with his experiences, to distance himself from them in order to continue living. In his original manuscript, he describes the arrest, deportation, and Auschwitz experience more fully than in this book.

If the narration in the book is sober, the descriptions in the original manuscript are even more so. But even from his raw manuscript it is evident that he had a great talent for storytelling.

Moritz Nachtstern was born in Warsaw in 1902 but moved with his family to Norway at an early age. Here he grew up in a small apartment together with nine siblings. His family was not rich, but his parents managed nevertheless to save up money to emigrate to the "promised land," the United States. Moritz was the only one of his parents' children who chose to remain in Oslo, where he had steady work and friends. Until the outbreak of the war he lived a bachelor's life in Oslo. His circle of friends consisted of both Jews and non-Jews. One of his best friends was Leo Løgård, who was deported together with him. Nachtstern later watched him being beaten senseless in Auschwitz because he did not follow one of the camp's absurd regulations. Leo Løgård was one of the many who did not come back.

It was Germany's invasion of Norway in 1940 that caused the Norwegian Jews to become caught up in what the Nazis described as *Die Endlösung der Judenfrage* (the Final Solution of the Jewish question) in Europe. For Adolf Hitler and the Nazis who came into power in Germany in 1933, the question of race was central. In their view, the Germans belonged to the Aryan race; the Jews were the exact opposite of this pure and proud people. They were the incarnation of everything evil, and they wanted to get the better of the Aryan race. Ironically, the Jews represented both capitalism and communism, crime and degeneration of that which was "pure." The fight against the Jews was the very essence of Nazism. The first anti-Jewish actions began shortly after Hitler had come to power.

The beginning of the anti-Jewish policy was slow. Jews were not allowed to occupy government positions. In the spring of 1933, the SA, Hitler's political troops, organized a boycott of Jewish businesses. Some Jews were arrested, mainly those who were communists. All this was bad enough for Germany's Jews. However, the Nazis' anti-Jewish policy then took a much more dangerous turn. In 1935 a new citizenship law was introduced that included a legal definition of the concept *Jew*. A Jew was a person with three 100 percent Jewish grandparents. The law also defined the concept of a "half-Jew" and a "quarter-Jew." The law excluded Jews from the state's protection, and they were no longer considered citizens. From that time on Jews could be prohibited from anything. Until 1941 one ordinance followed another: Jews could not visit parks, could not go to the movies, could not work as doctors or lawyers, etc. In a rapid series of laws the Jews were segregated and isolated. They had no rights. It was against this background that German troops occupied Norway in 1940.

Nevertheless, it was some time before the first anti-Jewish actions began in Norway, and here, too, it was slow initially. In May 1940, radios belonging to Jews were confiscated. Some Jews were arrested, but there were no systematic actions, no laws or proclamations. The Jews in Norway began to calm down. In September 1940, the Nasjonal Samling (National Unification party) became the only political party permitted in Norway. Occasionally anti-Semitic articles appeared in the press and on the radio, and at times the right-wing Norwegian politician and notorious Nazi collaborator, Vidkun Quisling, or one of his supporters, made speeches in which the fight against Judaism and Bolshevism was proclaimed to be the most important undertaking for the Nasjonal Samling. The Hird, Quisling's storm troops, painted anti-Semitic slogans on the windows of Jewish stores in Oslo.

However, in early 1942 a new era began. On January 20, 1942, the Norwegian police department announced that all Jews had to have a red "J" on their identification papers. The proclamation also contained a definition of the concept *Jew*. Thus, the systematic anti-Jewish policy was introduced to Norway. The German security police was behind the policy, but the Norwegian authorities carried it out. They saw to it that stamps were produced and lists of Jews made. Most Jews, although apprehensive, reported to the local police stations and had their identification papers stamped. Now the Norwegian police had the names and addresses of all the Jews who had dutifully come forward.

As if to further humiliate the Jews, the statistics division of the Nasjonal Samling made sure that all Jews filled out a "questionnaire for Jews in Norway," which included questions regarding their economic condition and criminal history. Along with the rest of the Jews in Norway, Moritz Nachtstern reported to the police, had his identification papers stamped, filled in the questionnaire, and so was caught in the net.

Then everything calmed down for a while. It is unclear why; perhaps it was a psychological pause on the part of the aggressors so that the Jews should feel safe before the blow was struck, as had happened in other countries. In any case, the pause ended first in Trondheim. On October 6 and 7, 1942, Jewish men were arrested by Norwegian patrols during a general state of emergency, and the women were gathered in two apartments. All property was confiscated. No laws or ordinances were issued. Hitler's Reichskommissar (government commissary) in Norway, Josef Terboven, was present in Trondheim, as were the leaders of the German security police. Then all was calm again.

But on Thursday, October 22, something happened that was used as a pretext to tighten the grip further. A border guide, who accompanied a group of Jews across the border to Sweden, was discovered by a border policeman. The border guide shot first and the border policeman died. The day after, all the major newspapers reported that the Jews were behind the incident. Now there was a pretext. The very next day Wilhelm Wagner of the German security police, who was responsible for the "Jewish question," began conferring with Karl Alfred Marthinsen, chief of the State Police, and other high-ranking officials in the Norwegian State Police.

At the same time the Quisling regime published a law that permitted the internment of "enemies" of the state without trial. The planning of what would later be called "the Jewish action" had begun.

The State Police spent the weekend of October 24 and 25 making lists of Jews and sending telegrams to the country's police authorities, while at the same time, Quisling and his cabinet ministers wrote a law about the confiscation of Jewish property. The action against all male Jews fifteen years old and over was to take place on Monday, October 26, 1942. Many Jews, including Moritz Nachtstern, knew that some action was imminent. No one understood how serious it was, but neither Moritz nor his friend Leo Løgård slept at home on the night of October 25. Shortly after Moritz came home the next morning there was a knock on the door. He thought it was his talkative neighbor, but it was a State Police patrol. Moritz Nachtstern was arrested and brought to the police barracks on Majorstua.

During a strange incident there, the Jews were lined up against the wall, and policemen, or perhaps members of the Norwegian SS, cocked their guns and pointed them at the Jews. Had the frontline soldiers who now volunteered to participate in the arrest of the Jews in Oslo taken part in similar operations before, perhaps in Russia? One of the prisoners had a framed picture of his daughter under his arm. Nachtstern did not know who he was, but it has since been possible to identify him. His name was Jakob Meiran, and he was thirty-six years old. His daughter's name was Ellinor, and she was only five years old. He had lost his wife earlier that year. He and his daughter were both deported and killed.

A month in the Berg concentration camp followed. Today this is not a well-known camp and is used as a prison. Then, it was called "Quisling's chicken run." It was originally intended as a prison for opponents of Quisling and "the new times"; however, the Jewish men were the first prisoners in the camp. It consisted of only two barracks, with no toilets, no real kitchen facilities, and no proper washing facilities. It was a foretaste of what would happen later. At Berg an incident took place that is difficult to understand without an explanation. During a roll-call on the night of November 26, 1942, the men were split into two groups; brothers were separated from each other, as were fathers and sons. The strange selection was due to an order issued by Adolf Eichmann's office in Berlin the day before. The question of who should be killed and who should be spared now was a dilemma for the SS. Because Jews married to non-Jewish women had ties to the community at large, they would remain in the camp while the others would be deported.

Those who were to be deported were brought by guards down to a freight train waiting on the tracks below the camp. I myself have walked there. The tracks are almost overgrown now. The train had been ordered from the Norwegian National Railways only the day before. According to the telegrams sent by the National Railways to the different district chiefs, the loading of the Jews would commence at 5:00 a.m. and end at 5:30 a.m. The train was to arrive at the Vestbane Station in Oslo at 10:05 a.m. The tracks would then be switched to Pier 1 before noon. In 1942 the railway tracks crossed the Tordenskjold Square and went around the *Akershus festning* (fortress). It was morning in Oslo. People were on their way to work as though nothing special was about to happen. Through cracks in the freight cars Moritz Nachtstern and the others would have been able to look out. Nachtstern saw three of his friends stroll across the square. He realized now that this journey would take him and the others out of the country.

At the same time that Moritz Nachtstern and the other Jewish prisoners selected to leave Berg were being forced onto the freight cars in nearby Tønsberg, the arrest of Jewish women and children began in Oslo. The State Police had about 300 men at their disposal for this action, consisting of about sixty men from the Oslo criminal police force, 100 men from the auxiliary police force, sixty men from Quisling's storm troops, and thirty men from the Norwegian SS. The rest, about fifty men, were from the State Police. In addition, the State Police ordered 100 taxis and numerous buses and trucks from different companies.

The women and children were instructed to pack a limited number of essential items and were then sent straight to Pier 1 of the Oslo port. Their apartments were sealed. The previous day police authorities outside Oslo had also been instructed to arrest immediately all persons whose identification papers were stamped with a "J." The Final Solution had started.

The German ship SS *Donau aus Bremen* was waiting in the Oslo port at Pier 1 (also called America Line), where the State Police had opened a reception center, complete with telephones, in one of the sheds. The action was coordinated from the pier in the presence of the chief of the Oslo and Aker division of the State Police, Knut Rød, as well as Wilhelm Wagner of the German security police and his two colleagues, Harry Böhm and Klaus Grossmann. Grossmann would accompany the prisoners as transport leader because he had leave back home in Germany to look forward to, as did fifty men from the German riot squad, who had been selected to act as guards on the wharf and on board the ship.

This dual use of the ship reduced the costs of the transport.

The SS *Donau* was a freighter that had been partially converted into a troop transport ship and usually ran a regular service between Oslo and the German port of Stettin (now Szczecin, Poland). The ship brought troops and supplies to Norway and also brought Russian prisoners of war to work at German defense installations. From Norway to Germany the cargo consisted of soldiers on leave, Norwegian export goods, and political prisoners. That day, however, the cargo was Jews. With a simple sentence, an employee at the Oslo port authority expressed the fact that something extraordinary was happening that day. In the records of foreign ships in port, he did not only write the usual "loading" or "unloading," but qualified it, writing "loading Jews." That day, 532 Jews were forced on board.

The voyage to Stettin was in itself traumatic. The women and children were kept in the hold of the ship, separate from the men. Nachtstern met and spoke to some of them. They told him they were keeping up their spirits. None of them would come back. The weather was stormy during the crossing, which delayed the arrival in Stettin. At the German security police headquarters in Stettin, the planning for the continuation of the journey to Auschwitz was in full swing. Guards had been earmarked. Eichmann's office in Berlin had ordered the freight transport.

Because the number of Jews exceeded 500, Eichmann received a discount from the German railway. A memorandum says that the ship arrived at 10:11 a.m. on November 30, 1942. The train with the freight cars was directed to the port, the Danzig wharf in the free port of Stettin. The report from the security police in Stettin states that everything went according to plan. The train left Stettin at 5:12 p.m. The train ride was indescribable. There was no water provided in the cars, which, to say the least, were not designed for the transport of human beings, and the occupants were very apprehensive about what the future would bring. When they arrived they were dehydrated and hungry. This was intentional, as they were easier to handle this way. A series of photographs the SS took of a transport of Hungarian Jews on their arrival in Auschwitz in the spring of 1944 clearly shows the victims' exhaustion. This series was later published as the *Auschwitz Album*.

Many visualize Auschwitz with train tracks leading into Auschwitz-Birkenau's heart, where the gas chambers waited. This was not how it was in the autumn of 1942. The train tracks were only laid in 1944, when plans were made for the murder of 400,000 Hungarian Jews. In 1942 the end station was still some distance away from the gas chambers, and the victims were transported there by truck. But first they had to go through a selection process, in which women and children were separated from the men, and old people from the young. More often than not one of the camp doctors was responsible for separating those who were fit to work from those who would die. But the result of the selection also depended on the number of prisoners in the camp. Perhaps the women's camp was full on December 1, 1942. At any rate, no women were chosen to work, not even young women without children.

Moritz Nachtstern's description of the arrival is brief and sober, but very accurate. The luggage was collected in a heap, he says. The prisoners were probably told that it would be forwarded. The women and children were ordered to get into waiting trucks. He mentions his friend Bernard Gordon, who chose to go with his family. He was thirty-seven years old; his wife Edith was thirty-one, and the three children Arne, Leo, and Doris were fourteen, ten, and eight years old, respectively. Nachtstern would never see any of them again. The trucks drove straight to the gas chambers.

What then was Auschwitz? Many have called the camp a separate, almost inexplicable, world. When the Final Solution was accelerated in the autumn of 1941, the decision was made to establish several killing centers in eastern Poland. The three camps Belzec, Sobibor, and Treblinka were under the authority of the German security police in Lublin, their first and main objective being to annihilate the Jews in Poland. Their common characteristic was that they were not classic concentration camps. There were prisoners in these camps, too, but they were few, and their main purpose was to "process" what the dead Jews left behind that could be utilized—mainly clothes, money, and the victims' hair and gold teeth.

The origin of Auschwitz was different. The camp was established in May 1940 as a classic German concentration camp, where mainly Polish political prisoners would be incarcerated. The commandant of Auschwitz was Rudolf Höss. At the time it was not an important camp in the German camp system, but this did not mean anything to the unfortunate prisoners sent there. The conditions were terrible. The following summer, in 1941, Auschwitz's role began to change. Höss was summoned by SS chief Heinrich Himmler in Berlin and told that Hitler had decided that the Jews were to be annihilated. It was Himmler's decision that Auschwitz would have a vital role in this process. The camp was located near central railway junctions, while at the same time it was relatively isolated.

The first gas chamber in Auschwitz was built in the main camp itself (Auschwitz I) early in 1942. The difference between this and other killing centers was that in Auschwitz, the insecticide Zyklon B was used as a killing agent. The construction of Auschwitz-Birkenau (Auschwitz II) began in the late autumn of 1941. In the spring of 1942, two temporary gas chambers were built in two old Polish farmhouses in anticipation of the construction of more "modern" installations. It was in one of these temporary gas chambers that the Jews from the SS *Donau* who had been selected to die were killed in December 1942.

Moritz Nachtstern and the other men declared fit for work were brought to Auschwitz-Birkenau. In the reception barracks they were met with blows and kicks. Early on an older prisoner told them the truth about the women and the children. "They have gone on the *Himmelkommando*," he said. *Himmelkommando* (heaven unit) was one of the euphemisms the prisoners used for the gas chambers, as were the terms "on transport" or "on recreation." The latter expression was often used by the prison guards in the camp.

For the men who had been selected for work, life in Auschwitz began with a depersonalization process. Moritz Nachtstern saw prisoners "stagger around" while they worked. The prisoners were not supposed to have any willpower or comprehension of what was happening. The writer and critic Tzvetan Todorov has called the camps an absurd reflection of the totalitarian society that Nazi Germany wished to build. But in the camps the people were reduced to one function only. Their right to exist depended on whether they were able to carry out the work they had been set to do. The supply of manpower was relatively constant, and individual lives meant nothing, either to the camp leadership or the prison guards. It was *Vernichtung durch Arbeit* (extermination through work). The prisoners had been reduced to prison numbers.

The prisoners had not been prepared for the "life" they now had to live. They either adjusted or died. One of Moritz Nachtstern's friends,

David Jelo, said in the beginning that he could not go on. He died while most of the SS *Donau* prisoners were marched from Auschwitz I to Auschwitz III (Monowitz) a few days after their arrival. When the prisoners came to the quarantine block in Monowitz, the foreman told them that those who were married would be reunited with their families within three months. Everyone probably understood what this meant. To be selected for work was only a temporary reprieve for a Jewish prisoner. They would all die.

In the first month 25 percent of the group of Norwegian Jews who had come to the camp died. Moritz Nachtstern himself was extremely weak and near death. He was brought to the *Revier,* the prisoners' term for "sick barracks." He had reached rock bottom and was about to become a Musselman, the prisoners' expression for a living skeleton with only a short time left to live. "We always said good-bye to each other in the morning," he notes. No one knew if they would pull through that day. Moritz Nachtstern would undoubtedly have been one of those who did not come back, if fate had not intervened. He was called up because he was a typographer.

"We were selected according to our numbers," he writes. The fact that he believed he was picked out because another Norwegian prisoner, Henry Nachemsohn, stepped behind him in line is a detail that later absorbed and troubled Nachtstern. Nevertheless, this is not how it was. Nachemsohn's number was 79193 and Nachtstern's was 79194. As always, the Germans were meticulous. It did not matter where in the line the prisoners stood; their numbers were assigned according to the alphabetical order of their names. Perhaps Nachemsohn had already died when Nachtstern was chosen. According to Kristian Ottosen's survey of the deported Norwegian Jews, Nachemsohn had already been killed on December 1, 1942, which is unlikely. Since he was given a prison number, he was probably sent into the camp, but exactly when he died is not clear. However, because of this incident, which he believed saved his life,

Nachtstern had terrible feelings of guilt in the postwar years. This is an extra burden all Holocaust survivors have had to struggle with.

After a long wait, Nachtstern and several others were sent to Sachsenhausen, under close watch. The transport arrived in Berlin on March 8, 1943, only one week after a new transport of 158 Norwegian Jews, deported on the freighter *Gotenland*, had been brought through the city on their way to Auschwitz. Moritz Nachtstern was marched through Berlin. The windows were loaded with food, people looked well fed, and children stared at them contemptuously. They were sent on the S-Bahn (suburban railway) to Oranienburg, the same S-Bahn one takes today to visit the Sachsenhausen monument. It seemed like a model camp to Nachtstern and the other prisoners from Auschwitz.

From guard Marok's welcome speech, Nachtstern concluded that he had come to a new death kommando (work detail). Laconically, he noted that it was hardly different from the death kommandos in Auschwitz.

Block 19 was a part of Operation Bernhard, the counterfeit operation run by the SS and Himmler. Its aim was to produce perfectly forged English pound notes. For this to work, the notes had to be dated back to the period between 1930 and 1939 and look as though they were well used. SS Sturmbannführer Bernhard Krüger, the leader of Referat (a German term for office) VI F 4a of the SS-Reichssicherheitshauptamt (main security administration) in Berlin, was in charge of the operation.

Nachtstern and the other prisoners knew that their participation in Operation Bernhard was a death kommando because the operation could not be exposed. Therefore, it was important for the prisoners not to work too fast, but to do their job so well that the SS leadership would not be suspicious. It was a balancing act. When the front lines approached Berlin, Krüger managed to have his counterfeiters evacuated toward the south—first to Mauthausen, and later to Ebensee—so that they could continue their work. There were 142 prisoners from fifteen different countries.

At that time the situation in Germany was becoming chaotic, especially in the concentration camps, which were overcrowded with evacuated prisoners on death marches from the east and from the west. There was no room to continue the work in Mauthausen, or in any other place either. Moritz Nachtstern and the other prisoners were preparing to die. That this did not happen must be attributed to the German collapse at the end of the war, rather than to Krüger's protection. At the time no one with complete knowledge of the situation could have doubted the eventual outcome of the war, and Krüger probably understood that "saving" his prisoners might be useful for his own survival later. When he was on trial in the 1950s, several of the prisoners testified as part of his defense.

In a postwar interview Nachtstern told how he saw a French prisoner beat an SS guard senseless after the camp had been liberated. He turned away in disgust. To think of revenge was impossible for him after the liberation. The transition to a "normal" life was difficult, as it was for other survivors too. He got married, had two children, and began to work again. But his nerves had been affected. During his time as a prisoner he had grown used to the thought that death was his closest neighbor, and many of his statements after the war show that he struggled with feelings of guilt, not least because he was allowed to survive while so many had died.

After the war, even in good times, it was difficult to suppress the certainty of death. In an interview in July 1967 with Helene Høverstad of the Norwegian Broadcasting Corporation, Moritz Nachtstern spoke about his disabilities. Bæreia, the convalescent home for disabled veterans, became his constant support system. Nachtstern died on December 11, 1969, at the age of sixty-seven. His book was the first among the Norwegian Jews' prison stories to be published. In itself, this is reason enough to read the book. In his own scrapbook, which his daughter loaned to me, I found an undated review in the *Moss Arbeiderblad* following the first publication in 1949. Per Wollebæk wrote that it was essential to read this book—not because it contains "sensational disclosures" about the Nazis' counterfeit workshop in Block 19, but because it is a naked and human document about a horrific era that many of us tend to forget.

This consideration is even more appropriate today than it was in 1949.

Block 19 and Operation Bernhard

By Lawrence Malkin, author of *Krueger's Men:*
The Secret Nazi Counterfeit Plot and the Prisoners of Block 19

OF THE HALF-DOZEN MEMOIRS WRITTEN BY THE PRISONERS WHO WERE conscripted into the greatest counterfeiting operation in history, Moritz Nachtstern's is the most reliable and psychologically acute version of the drama as seen from inside Sachsenhausen's Block 19. Shortly after he returned home in 1945, when his extraordinary experiences were still fresh in his memory, he dictated his reminiscences to his new wife, Rachel. Her typed notes (still in possession of their daughter, Sidsel) were later turned over to a Norwegian journalist, Ragnar Arntzen. He wove them into a story of deceit and survival by the counterfeiting crew of about 145 prisoners and their master, SS Major Bernhard Krüger. The book was first published in Norway in 1949, and republished in 2006 in conjunction with the opening of the Oslo Centre for Holocaust and Genocide Studies. This is its first appearance in English.

At first, Nachtstern's memoir attracted little attention outside Norway because the enormity of Operation Bernhard was not fully recognized.

The prisoners kept a secret count of their production: counterfeit notes with a face value of 132 million pounds sterling—in today's money, more than 3 billion pounds, or 6 to 7 billion dollars. They knew that the Nazis planned to use the notes to undermine Britain's currency, and they also prepared sealed envelopes of fake notes to be dispatched by diplomatic pouch to German embassies in neutral capitals. During the last months of the war, they switched to dollars, unsuccessfully. As Allied troops closed in, the prisoners crated the remainder to be dumped into the Toplitzsee, a deep lake in the Austrian Alps.

Caged behind the barbed wire woven around their barracks, the prisoners knew little more than this about the fate of their almost-perfect product. They knew nothing about how the operation began, or whether any notes were actually air-dropped on England. About 15 or 20 million pounds in false notes found their way into circulation, but this sum was more than enough to leave a trail of financial deception and official embarrassment for many years. Although the Bank of England did its best to cover it up, the details gradually slipped out—not always accurately—and the picture was not complete until long-secret documents of the postwar investigation were finally declassified more than half a century later.

The plot was hatched in Berlin by Hitler's espionage and economic chiefs in the Finance Ministry at Wilhelmstrasse 61 on September 18, 1939, only a fortnight after the start of World War II. Josef Goebbels, Hitler's propaganda minister, described it in his diary as *einen grotesken Plan*—a grotesque plan. But all he could do was watch, because no one outside the SS-Reichssicherheitshauptamt—the Reich main security administration—was allowed to talk about it under Hitler's Basic Order No. 1, which mandated secrecy for all war plans on a need-to-know basis. So no one ever inquired whether the Luftwaffe could muster enough planes to scatter tons of fake notes across the British Isles. In fact, it was not able to resupply German forces in the decisive battle of Stalingrad, so there certainly were not enough planes to spare for harebrained schemes like this.

Nevertheless, the SS forged ahead. Their first attempts were at their own print shop in Berlin under a technical chief who had been trained as a code-breaker, not a printer. He was regularly overruled by Nazi ideologues, and by 1941 the first attempt was over. The next year Walter

Schellenberg, SS chief of foreign intelligence, was ordered to start again by the Reich security chief Heinrich Himmler, whose diary entry for July 16, 1942, cryptically records: "Pound notes authorized for use for the time being." Two months earlier, Schellenberg had called in his chief passport forger, Bernhard Krüger, a thirty-eight-year-old major who had managed textile factories in civilian life. Krüger was ordered to use Jewish prisoners trained in the graphic arts.

As a stereotypographer, Nachtstern was in the second batch of prisoners in this elite group. Like Nachtstern, many others were plucked from Auschwitz by Krüger himself, who courteously addressed them with the formal German *Sie*. This was an example of his management strategy of encouraging them to work by treating them as if they were not Jews, although they knew that when they finished their jobs, they were to be buried with their secret. They began arriving in December of 1942 and faced an unprecedented prisoner's dilemma: Should they stretch out their work and risk execution for sabotage? Or should they perform efficiently and thus hasten their own deaths? How they maintained this excruciating balance—even cooperating with Krüger to the end on trying to produce counterfeit dollars—is the dramatic core of the story.

The Bank of England had learned about the German counterfeit plan from a spy as early as October 1939. Led by Sir Kenneth Peppiatt, the chief cashier whose facsimile signature was on every note, the Bank's officials concluded that their complex system of serial numbers, batch codes, and secret markings on every note would foil any counterfeiter. Nevertheless, the British government issued a rare wartime ban against the import of pound notes, publicly warned the British people against counterfeit notes, and stopped printing the large old-style "fivers" (£5 notes). In fact, the few fakes that actually reached the Bank in London were detected by its sharp-eyed tellers. But the British overlooked the fact that the pound sterling was an international currency. Forgers abroad simply had to duplicate a note, copy the batch and serial numbers, and present it to a foreign bank, which would then cable London for verification. As long as the counterfeit notes did not actually reach the Bank of England for inspection, they could be blithely passed from hand to hand, and on the continent, millions were.

This should give a clue about what happened to the pound notes. The Nazis spread the notes across occupied Europe in a money-laundering operation run by Friedrich Schwend, a businessman who built a financial empire on his commission: one-third of the face value of the counterfeits, plus whatever he could steal. The pounds that passed through his network were used to purchase raw materials from neutral countries, small arms from Yugoslav partisans, and paintings by lesser Dutch masters. The Nazis' best spy, codenamed Cicero, and later played by James Mason in the movie *Five Fingers*, was paid £300,000 in false notes by the SS for documents purloined while serving as valet to the British ambassador in Ankara. They showed that Turkey would remain neutral, but Hitler mistrusted his feuding intelligence services. By the time he realized that the information was genuine, it was too late to move German divisions from the Balkans to the Western front to bolster German defenses against the Allied invasion. After the war, Ciccro—whose real name was Elyesa Bazna, and who had served as the British ambassador's valet in Ankara—sued the West German government, which refused him any compensation for the false notes, and he died penniless in Berlin.

It also should come as no surprise that the most tenacious guardians of all these wartime financial secrets were their most embarrassed victims, the grandees of the Bank of England. They refused to tell even the Swiss how to spot the secret markings, so eventually the Swiss banks stopped accepting pound notes.

In Budapest in 1944, a young black-market runner later known as George Soros exchanged £2,000 for a bracelet and was personally relieved when the pounds were accepted as genuine. But someone down the line must have gotten a very rude shock when the notes were presented to a bank after the war. (Half a century later, George Soros became known as "the man who broke the Bank of England" after making almost 1 billion dollars by speculating against the pound.)

When the U.S. Secret Service officers arrived in 1945 to hunt for counterfeit dollars, the British told them as little as possible, not even a word about Krüger, whom they interned for two years and then handed over to the French. One Bank of England official on occupation duty in Germany received a letter from London instructing him to keep mum. Across the bottom of the letter he wrote in a neat hand, *Let sleeping dogs lie.*

Some of the pounds are now on display in the Bank's museum. Others fell into Jewish hands at the Museum of Tolerance in Los Angeles, memorializing the great Nazi hunter, Simon Wiesenthal, which leads to the story's crowning irony. One of Schwend's money launderers was a Jewish con man posing as an officer of the International Red Cross under the name of Jaac van Harten, doing business in Budapest. His real name was Yaakov Levy, and when the men of the Jewish underground arrived after the war to help Jewish survivors run the British blockade of Palestine, they accused him of working with the Nazis. To get in their good graces, van Harten handed over bundles of counterfeit pounds. The fake notes paid for ships that were chartered to smuggle refugees, with equipment lashed to the decks for the underground Jewish army. Van Harten was relieved of a suitcase of jewels and shipped to Palestine too.

When the British came after him in Tel Aviv for his role in the counterfeit operation, he was protected by the chief of foreign affairs of the Jewish Agency, a young woman named Goldie Myerson, later prime minister of Israel as Golda Meir. As for Schwend, he escaped to South America on a forged passport, ran the Volkswagen agency in Peru, and received regular remittances from Switzerland, where he had banked his wartime profits. Today, espionage experts would call this part of the caper "blowback."

This was why the Allies passed up the opportunity to try the same trick on the Germans. Without any knowledge of the Nazi plot, Winston Churchill himself wrote to the Chancellor of the Exchequer at the start of the war, suggesting that the British drop counterfeit reichsmarks on Germany. The British Treasury politely overruled him. They realized that any German found trying to pass counterfeit currency would probably be shot, while no democratic government in London could impose such penalties on its own citizens, even in wartime. And since anything of value in Germany was rationed, there would be little to buy with the fake reichsmarks anyway. Some of them would probably have slipped into German bank accounts, but that would have only expanded the banks' monetary base for the loans Hitler forced from them to finance his war machine. The British realized that if they tried the scheme, it would only backfire.

In America, novelist John Steinbeck, a New Deal activist, escorted a German-trained professor into Franklin D. Roosevelt's office in 1940 with what he also considered a foolproof secret weapon—fake reichsmarks! The president shrewdly sent them to his secretary of the Treasury, Henry Morgenthau Jr., who glared through his pince-nez and harrumphed that Americans didn't do that sort of thing. After America went to war in 1941, Washington's spymasters ran the idea past the Treasury's Bureau of Printing and Engraving. The experts there reckoned that printing enough fake reichsmarks would cost as much as the price of a small warship, and that as soon as the Germans figured out what was happening, they would change the design of the notes. And for the Allies, that was the end of that.

After the war, Krüger faced a denazification hearing and was exonerated with the help of affidavits from several former prisoners attesting to his character. He lived quietly as a salesman for the paper company that had supplied his wartime counterfeit operation. German magazines and American television both sponsored diving expeditions to the bed of the Toplitzsee in search of buried treasure and secret documents; they found little more than the counterfeit pounds, preserved in crates sunk below the oxygen level. Krüger went on one of the dives, protesting to the last that he had been treated like a scoundrel for simply doing his duty.

He died in 1989.

The tale of Operation Bernhard was used by the propagandists of East Germany in a 1965 book, *Der Banditenschatz* (*The Bandit Treasure*), to attack the West German government for harboring Krüger as an arch criminal. Otherwise, the prisoners mainly went their separate ways, and during the last two decades of the twentieth century, several wrote memoirs. The principal authors were Avraham Krakowski, who settled in New York City and attributed his survival to divine intervention; Peter Edel, a young artist in Block 19 who became a celebrated intellectual in East Germany; Max Groen, the Dutch boulevardier; and Adolf Burger, a Slovak printer who compiled his memoir with some official help after retiring as a communist functionary in Prague.

Burger's book followed the communist party line against Krüger, and in 2007 formed the basis for a German-Austrian coproduction, *Die Fälscher* (*The Counterfeiters*). The film's Austrian director advanced the preposterous thesis that the prisoners had a choice between serving the Nazis or refusing and being martyred. This was too much even for Burger, who told an Israeli journalist: "Bullshit. The important thing was to survive." Like Burger, many did, and to a comfortable old age.

I visited Max Groen at his apartment by a quiet Amsterdam canal in 2002, two years before he died there peacefully. Still animated by his wartime experiences, he remembered Nachtstern fondly as a member of "our kommando." When I told him of the memoir, Groen exclaimed: "Moishe Nachtstern wrote a book? Wonderful!" Indeed it is.

COUNTERFEITER

Chapter 1

Leo Løgård stopped suddenly and grasped my arm. I followed his glance. A huge poster in the window of *Fritt Folk* (*Free People*), the Norwegian Nazi newspaper, announced: two jews on their way to sweden shoot norwegian policeman. (Only when I came home in 1945 did I find out that it was their guide who had shot the policeman.) We continued in silence through the arcade of Folketeatret (the People's Theatre).

"Let's stop by my office," Leo said. He was a dental technician and had his office on Brugata.

"What do you think of this?" I asked when we had taken off our coats.

"Well . . ." Leo went over to the window and adjusted the blackout curtain.

"If they retaliate it will be us Jews who will suffer for it."

Leo gestured with his arms impatiently. "Now, don't start being the devil's advocate because of this poster, Moritz. They have been here for almost three years without persecuting us any more than other Norwegians."

"Okay, but nothing like this has ever happened before. Now they have a welcome opportunity to come after us. I wonder if it's not high time to beat it across to Sweden."

"Oh, just take it easy," Leo said, and put a bottle of beer on the table. "Don't look as if the Gestapo is already on the stairs."

"Don't brag, Leo—you're just as upset as I am. Do you intend to sleep at home tonight?"

Leo quickly looked at me. "Do you? Otherwise, this sofa is big enough for the two of us."

We slept in Leo's office that night, but there was not really a lot of sleep. We discussed the situation and talked most of the time. Leo did not believe that anything would happen. At any rate, nothing serious. "Good God," he said, "they arrested about a hundred Jews last year and imprisoned them in Grini [a Norwegian prison camp] and then released them. Surely, nothing worse will happen this time either, and that we can definitely handle."

I myself was not quite as optimistic. I decided to stay away from my studio apartment for the next few days.

Before we went our separate ways in the morning, Leo mentioned that, to be on the safe side, he would speak to an acquaintance who worked for the police department, to find out if there was any trouble brewing.

I went to work and the day went by without anything happening. In town I spoke to several of my fellow Jews. All of them were nervous, but most of them thought that there would be no retaliation in the wake of this incident.

I spent Sunday night at my old friend Asbjørn Steen's house.

On Sunday I spoke to Leo by phone. Now he wanted to listen to my suggestion to leave for Sweden even less than before. He had spoken to his acquaintance in the police force, who had said that the Germans would not avenge themselves on the Jews for this murder. Leo was so sure and confident that I too decided to go to work on Monday.

"Don't," advised Asbjørn. "Stay here a few days to wait and see what happens."

I did not follow his advice. On Monday morning I got up and stopped by my apartment to pick up a few things to take to work.

At 7:30 a.m. I was ready to leave my studio apartment on No. 15 Brugata. The doorbell rang. I was so sure that it was the cleaning woman as usual, wanting to have a chat with me, that I opened the door without the slightest suspicion. Two men stood outside. The one closest to me pushed me into the room. The other one closed the door behind him.

"You are Moritz Nachtstern, correct?"

"Yes."

"You are under arrest." He produced a document and put it on the table. "Please sign that you are voluntarily turning over all your possessions to the state."

I looked from the document to the two men. Both were keeping their right hands in their coat pockets. I knew what that meant.

The apartment was on the fourth floor, so it was no use thinking of the window.

"Get on with it, Nachtstern."

I signed my name.

"You can bring some clothes in a suitcase."

I took what I could find at that moment.

"Where am I going?"

"To the barracks on Kirkeveien. At least for now."

While we waited for the streetcar near the gasworks, one of my Nazi guards said, "I can tell you some very sad news."

"What?" I asked, and looked at him in surprise.

"Minister Gulbrand Lunde [a Nazi] and his wife have been killed in a car accident."

"Oh, thank God," I blurted out.

"What?"

Of course I did not repeat what I had said.

The streetcar arrived and we stepped onto the platform. I said goodbye to the ugly gasworks as if it were a beautiful and beloved building.

Don't get upset, I said to myself while the streetcar rolled through the city. Surely I could get through a month or two in Grini with my health intact.

A long row of Jews stood in the yard of the barracks. The noise grew after I arrived. A young Nazi in uniform went around shouting that we should stand still. The man in front of me showed me the large photograph of a sweet little girl around four or five years old, which he held under his arm.

"My daughter," he confided in me with a touching smile on his frightened face. "She is the only one I have left," he added.

Just then the young Nazi came running.

"Give that to me," he shouted, pointing at the picture. The owner hung on to the photo for dear life and did not want to hand it over.

The soldier became wild with fury and grabbed the picture. The next moment it was stamped to pieces under his iron-heeled boots. Then he started in on the man and forced him to stand facing the wall. A while later the rest of us were also ordered to assume this position. We were entertained with screams and shouts on the part of the "frontline soldiers," who entertained themselves by loading their guns behind us.

We stood this way for about an hour. Then we were ordered into buses that had arrived in the yard in the meantime. A Norwegian Nazi in German uniform got into the bus that I had been assigned to.

"The slightest movement or attempt at talking will be considered sabotage. The individual in question will be shot on the spot."

He emphasized the threat by hooking his finger around the trigger of his gun. There were two mentally handicapped boys among us who made faces and gesticulated with their arms. It was only at the last moment that we were able to make the Nazis understand that they could not be held responsible for their actions.

None of us had any idea where we were heading. When the bus drove up Kirkeveien, everyone looked anxiously out of the window. At the corner of Suhmsgate I caught sight of Nils Behak, a Jewish acquaintance. He carefully glanced at us before he turned the corner and continued along the street with long steps, his coat collar turned up. I did not envy him his freedom, but I cursed myself for not having followed Asbjørn's advice. *Why had I stayed here instead of running away to Sweden?* Ever since I had seen the poster in the window of the *Fritt Folk* I had had a feeling that something would happen to us Jews. True, I was a bachelor and unattached, my parents had passed away, and my sisters and brothers were all in England and America. What on earth had kept me back? My friends? Work and duty? No. I gave up trying to get to the bottom of this puzzle.

The bus drove through Kirkeveien, past Ullevål Hospital, across Sagene to Trondheimsveien, past Akers Hospital and Bjerkebanen.

This, my life's first journey toward the unknown, ended at Bredtveit Prison. Many of my fellow Jews had come there before me and many followed. One by one we were called in to be interrogated. Two men sat at a table and made notes, and a third man—somewhat older, but a dangerous, gruff, and zealous representative of the "new times" in Norway—looked at me with eyes filled with Quisling fervor, and ordered "Hands up."

I obeyed and was robbed of all my possessions in true gangster fashion. But my wristwatch slid up my jacket sleeve when I put up my hands, so he did not find it. After we had been interrogated and deprived of our belongings, we were lined up in the hallway for several hours, facing the wall. White-haired seventy-year-old men stood next to thin fifteen-year-old boys.

Only when everybody had been interrogated and robbed were we assigned to the different rooms in the barracks. Many were ready to collapse from fatigue and hunger. Most of us had had nothing to eat or drink since the day before. Late that night we were finally given some food, consisting of a little soup, a bite of bread, and two small herrings each. Everybody ate the ration all at once, except the youngest of the mentally handicapped boys. He did not have the heart to finish the herrings; he wanted to take them home to his mother.

* * *

"Get ready to leave!" shouted one of the high-ranking gentlemen at Bredtveit two days after our arrival.

"Where do you think we're heading now?" I asked Georg, who stood next to me.

"I don't care where we're going, as long as it's not to Grini." He was one of the men the Germans had arrested and imprisoned in Grini for a month, in celebration of the attack on Russia the preceding year, 1941.

"Was it so terrible there?"

"Don't even mention it. A real hell, my friend."

"Line up!" The order was given a while later.

It was a grotesque army that took to the road at a fast march and under strict surveillance; weakened oldsters marched side by side with men in their prime and young adolescent boys. After marching for about twenty minutes we stopped at Nyland, where we were stowed into a freight train that waited for us. Two armed Quislings in each car were our tour leaders.

Where will this journey end? I asked myself once the train had started to move. If I had had any idea of what the answer was, I believe that I would have risked trying to escape.

In Drammen more prisoners joined the transport, but all of them were assigned to passenger cars.

Many people waved to us as the train rolled across the railway bridge in Drammen. I was probably not the only one to whom this sight gave a strange, painful feeling of gratitude. It stayed with me and helped me in the hardest of the hard days facing me.

Chapter 2

The train stopped near Tønsberg.

"Everybody off. Hurry!"

The rest of the trip to Berg took place on foot. There were about 200 of us who trudged across the slushy marshes. Wet and tired, we arrived at the camp that the Germans had allowed their Norwegian counterparts to establish.

The head of the camp, Lindseth, received us. Strutting importantly, with his hand on his revolver holster, he spoke to us. His speech was full of important prohibitions and dangerous threats, and ended approximately like this: "Those who try to escape must be aware that ten other prisoners will be shot. Furthermore, the fugitive's entire family will be killed. That he himself will be shot the moment he is caught, I obviously do not have to mention. Now you will be given some food, very good food, gentlemen. But before you go to your barracks you must get your visits to the toilet over with, because once you are inside you will not be allowed out again until tomorrow morning. At ease."

After this uplifting speech we were ordered to urinate. We were, however, not allowed to go to the latrine.

There were only two barracks at Berg at the time. And what barracks! Dirty, drafty, and cold—we shuddered at the sight. The rooms we were stowed into, twenty-four men in each, were as naked and empty as any room could be. Four walls, ceiling, and floor—that was all. The windows were not nailed down properly. They were also protected by barbed wire—just in case.

The meal consisted of a sour soup. When the doors were closed we stood in the dark.

"Can you tell me how we can sleep here?" said Georg, who was in the same room as me.

I was mean enough to remind him of what he had said about Grini.

"Stop it, man," he grumbled angrily. "Grini was a sanatorium compared to this hole."

Little by little fatigue forced us all down to the dirty, ice-cold floor. But we could not sleep. Those who had eaten the sour soup suffered violent stomach pains and lay moaning on the floor. Some for whom the cramps became unbearable started to knock on the door to be let out to the latrine. It was a tormentor named Kristiansen, an insolent eighteen-year-old, who was on guard duty. He opened the door and shone his torch into the room.

"If you don't stop knocking I will fill this whole barracks with lead!" he shouted before he slammed the door shut again.

For quite a while no one dared to knock. Many fainted where they lay, squirming on the floor. Undoubtedly the man who had recently undergone surgery for an ulcer suffered the most. I did not believe he could survive the night. In desperation some of the men eventually ignored the camp commandant's warnings and Kristiansen's threats. Fortunately there had been a change of guards in the meantime. It was a man from the State Police who opened the door when the knocking resumed again.

"What is the matter?" he asked, and did not even sound irritated. "To the latrines? Of course you may go outside. Come with me, five at a time."

This pleasant and helpful man, who was only at Berg that one night and whose name I never found out, had a busy night, because, when the prisoners in the other rooms realized that they could go outside to the latrine, they too started to knock on the doors. In fact, our unexpected benefactor risked both his position and his freedom to help us. When we told him that we were hungry, he took two men and went looking for turnips. He stole a lot of the blessed vegetables for us. True, the turnips were covered with sand and earth, but good God, were they ever delicious. The darkness was filled with the sounds of crunching and happy swallowing until the last turnip was consumed.

When the feast was over we lay down again on the drafty floorboards. But no one was able to get much sleep. Like me, everyone else probably lay there thinking of everything that had happened and what the outcome would be. They regretted that they had not taken themselves and their loved ones to a safe haven while there was still time. Now it was obviously too late. Escape was out of the question because of everyone's concern for relatives and friends. I heard deep sighs and suppressed moans all around me before I finally went to sleep. It felt as though I had only been asleep for a few minutes when Kristiansen wished us good morning in what we soon learned was his characteristic way: "It's seven a.m. Time to get up and make yourselves useful. Line up outside the barracks."

After we had lined up, each man received a drop of milk and a piece of bread, and when breakfast was over, we were made to dig ditches. The earth was frozen, so it was not an easy job for people unaccustomed to this sort of work. The ditches were supposed to be approximately six and a half feet deep. The digging taxed our strength. As we dug through and reached the swampy earth, the icy water began to rise up our legs. At noon we got our lunch, which consisted of more of the disgusting sour soup that had been brought from Tønsberg.

It began to rain and sleet, and the entire camp soon resembled a dirty mud pond. The hard work—Kristiansen and his sidekicks made sure that we did not have too many breaks—and the mud were tough on our clothes and shoes.

"If they do not want to work, just shoot them," said Olausen, a soldier who had recently returned from the front and who was on a tour of inspection in the camp.

During the two weeks before we finally received beds, the mornings were a trial in themselves. When it was still pitch dark, all of us crawled around on the floor on all fours, trying to find our boots, while Kristiansen stood outside and threatened us with blows and kicks because we were not quick enough.

But we also made fun of Kristiansen. One day he came into the barracks to teach us how to behave. Among other things our room elder, Bernhard Bodd, was to call out *Attention!* and the rest of us were to get up when one of the camp personnel entered. Kristiansen was far from satisfied with the way we carried out his order. Finally he devised a clever scheme, according to which he and Bodd would change roles, and that would teach us how to behave. Bodd more than willingly agreed to the plan.

It was obvious that Kristiansen was very proud of his pedagogic wisdom. "Well, men," he said, in high spirits while we waited for Bodd to come in. "You know what this is all about."

Yes, we completely understood the gravity of the moment. "Attention!" Kristiansen shouted when Bodd showed up in the doorway.

Everyone quickly got up and stood at attention. Kristiansen himself stood ramrod straight like a robot Hitler Youth boy. Bodd was quite a sight as he stood and copied Kristiansen.

"Good morning, boys. Yes, this is good." Obviously he intended to continue, but now Kristiansen thought it was enough.

"Stop," he said. "I am the one who has to speak."

"What are you saying? I am Kristiansen. You are Bernhard Bodd."

"For heaven's sake!" exploded Kristiansen, his fuzzy face becoming red with anger.

Bodd pulled himself together. "I apologize, *Chazer* Kristiansen."

Instinctively Kristiansen saluted. He thought that the word *chazer* meant one or another important title. We almost died laughing. The word is Yiddish and means, quite simply, "pig." Although Bodd addressed

Kristiansen with this word several times a day for quite a while, Kristiansen never realized that we were making fun of him.

Ten minutes after this episode with Kristiansen, I, like all the other prisoners, was on my way to our workplace, digging ditches.

"Hello, Moritz!"

I turned around quickly. There stood Leo Løgård, as dirty and sooty as I was.

"Why on earth did you not get away?" I blurted out.

"And why didn't you?"

"Get the hell to work!" said slave-driver Johansen, another guard who came running.

All we could do was to continue in our ditch. It was like jumping down into an ice-cold mud bath.

"How long do you think they will torment us this way?" asked Gordon, who worked with me in the ditch.

"They probably don't know that themselves."

"It looks like they want to try to kill us, but I'll bear up; I have a wife and three children at home. If only I knew that they were okay." (Gordon was later allowed to spend half an hour with his wife and children, on board the SS *Donau*. He was subsequently allowed to board the truck with his family. None of them, however, came back from Germany.)

"Take off your caps, damned Jewish rabble!"

Standing at attention, caps in hand, we were contemptuously looked over by his highness, camp commandant Wallestad.

～

The days went by as we dug ditch after ditch, with inspections in true German form. One day we were introduced to a new guard dog, quite literally speaking. When we were ordered to line up in one of the hallways, Johansen was there with a German shepherd at his side.

"It is strictly forbidden to pet or talk to this dog," he said in a thundering voice. And that was all. But the dog must have grown up in an anti-Nazi home, because he wagged his tail as soon as he saw us. I never saw him behave this way with the Norwegian offshoots of the "master race."

Chazer Kristiansen had, among his many outstanding characteristics, a strange sense of humor. One of his favorite forms of entertainment was to make prisoners chop and saw wood without the wood or the tools. We felt as though we were in a madhouse when we saw the men chopping and sawing the air with their empty hands.

When we had been at Berg for three weeks, something happened that rekindled our hope. First of all, we were allowed to shave—that is to say that the barbers among us were put to use, as our own shaving kits had been confiscated. Second, and far more important, all prisoners sixty years of age and over were released. Each of them received ten kroner and their identification cards before they left us, their eyes filled with happiness and gratitude. There was much joy in the camp, and expectations ran high. Now it seemed like only a question of time before we too would regain our freedom.

But that was not to be.

⌐∾⌐

On Wednesday, November 25, we were summoned for a roll-call.

We were told to appear in the square with the few belongings we still owned. Lindseth walked around spot-checking our luggage. He found some extra underwear here and a bar of soap or an item of rainwear there. "Back to the barracks!" he hissed. "Everybody. Those who have forbidden items in their luggage at the next roll-call will be shot without pardon."

The camp head's zealous henchmen chased us into the barracks with kicks and shouts. While we sat in the barracks waiting for the next roll-call, our mood, which was like a barometer before a typhoon, swung from the wildest optimism about being released to the darkest misgivings.

At 4:00 a.m. the doors were yanked open.

"Roll-call!"

Armed soldiers and Nazis in uniform stood in the square. One by one we were called to a table which had been placed outside. Lindseth sat at the head of the table.

"Married?"

"Yes."

"To a Norwegian woman?"

"No."

"Go to the right. Next. Married?"

"Yes."

"To a Norwegian woman?"

"Yes."

"Go to the left. Next. Married?"

"Single."

"Go to the right."

This is how the "men were separated from the boys." Those who were married to Gentile women were permitted to remain in the camp. All others were going on "transport." Where to, no one knew. We guessed that we might be sent to a work camp in northern Norway, among many other alternatives.

When this selection was over, those of us who were leaving were ordered to get the sick prisoners. In the dark we all marched down to the waiting train. Several of the prisoners were suffering from a severe bout of influenza, and two had just had operations for appendicitis. Two more were so ill that we had to carry them, one suffering from an intestinal obstruction, the other from a cerebral hemorrhage. They had to come along on the transport just the same, as they did not seem to be married— at least, not to Aryan women.

We were stowed into cattle cars and driven away. We were still guessing at where we were headed, although the optimists were now clearly in the minority. In vain we tried to find an explanation for the strange sorting of the prisoners that we had witnessed. Dangerously ill people had been forced to go on this transport, while healthy men were excused only because they were married to so-called Aryan women. Ordinary Norwegians were being sent all the way to Germany. It was impossible to understand. The discussions continued all the way to Oslo. The sick men moaned with pain and were, for the most part, out of it.

I stood looking through a crack in the door as we approached Oslo, when I noticed, to my surprise, that the train did not go all the way to the West End train station; instead, it followed the track which bypassed the station itself and continued across Tordenskjoldsplass. What did this mean? Why were they taking us in this way? Would my worst misgivings become reality?

When the train rolled slowly across Tordenskjoldsplass I caught sight of three of my friends. I would have liked to call out to them, but it was too risky. All I could do was say a silent good-bye to them and the city, because now I was sure we were on our way out of the country.

The train stopped at a fenced-in area near the old shed of the America Line. Crowds of people stood outside the fence.

Chapter 3

WE WERE LINED UP ON THE WHARF. JUST IN FRONT OF US LOOMED THE huge hull of the camouflaged SS *Donau*, the slave ship that would later become notorious when it was sunk by the Oslo Gang (an anti-Nazi organization) at the end of the war.

Prisoners from Bredtveit, who had already been registered, struggled up the steep gangway carrying sacks of potatoes and cabbage. Even those who had been picked up from different hospitals had to participate in the heavy work, while the German guards hovered over them, abusing and taunting them. It was upsetting to watch this scene, but even worse was the sight of pregnant women, mothers with infants in their arms, and old people being forced to climb the steep gangway. A man named Gittelsen, in his seventies, stumbled at the top and almost fell down to the stone wharf. Two German officers who stood at the railing could have helped him simply by reaching out to him. They looked at him indifferently and continued chatting. Some Norwegian Nazis stood close to me. They were very impressed with the Germans' equanimity.

Then it was the Berg prisoners' turn. First we were all called up and then we climbed the gangway in goose step.

On the second deck and all the way to the bottom of the ship, hundreds of temporary cots had been set up. Women and children were separated from the men. When the last person had boarded, we numbered between 500 and 600 prisoners, stowed together on the "death ship." Those of us who found ourselves on the very bottom of the ship adjusted as best we could.

German soldiers continually ran up and down the narrow staircase. Heaven help those who stood nearby and did not call *Achtung!* when the boots of one of the members of the "master race" appeared. The German soldiers were on the prowl. What little luggage the prisoners had been allowed to keep was carefully scrutinized. Anything of value that the soldiers found, they put into their pockets. They risked nothing, because of course they knew that none of the prisoners would dare to report them to the officers. I myself used every trick in the book to keep my watch, because not only the luggage was searched. I managed to save my watch throughout all the body checks.

All around me prisoners lay or sat in their bunks hour after hour without uttering a single word. Others tried desperately to find out if their wives and children were on board or if they had managed to get to Sweden. But a few young fellows on the second deck played bridge as though they were on an ordinary Sunday excursion. Either they had not yet realized how serious these circumstances were, or they felt that they might as well make the best of a desperate situation. Later in the day I talked to one of the older men who had been released from Berg and sent home with ten kroner and his identification card. He shrugged his shoulders when we touched upon this incident.

"The release was only a trick," the man said. "By freeing us they caused the women and those who had not yet been arrested to remain calmly where they were, without trying to escape to Sweden. Then they could strike much more effectively once this ship was ready to receive us. Those of us who had been let go were foolish enough to trust the Germans' promises. I only know of one person who escaped to safety after his release."

"Where do you think they are sending us?" I asked.

The man only shook his head and lay back in his bunk, his hands under his head.

Just then Leo Løgård came over to me. We sat down and talked.

He told me that there were still many who thought we would be sent to northern Norway to work for the Germans. Others guessed that we would be gathered in ghettos somewhere in Europe. While we sat there and chatted, I pressed him to tell me what had actually happened when he was arrested; he had been evasive each time we had touched upon this subject before. Now he gesticulated helplessly with his hands and looked almost embarrassed.

"To tell you the truth, Moritz, it was a tragicomic event. The night after you slept in my office, there was a burglary there. Among other things, all my boxing trophies were stolen. As you know, I kept them in the office. I was insured for theft and got in touch with the insurance company. On Monday morning two men came to see me. I was so sure that they were from the insurance company that I began to talk about the burglary as soon as they had closed the door behind them. I must admit that my face fell when the fellows produced their police badges and said they had come to arrest me."

Sometime later we were allowed up on deck to get some fresh air. Both in front of us and behind us ships were headed in the same direction as we were. Escort planes circled above us. It was obviously not the SS *Donau*'s cargo they were afraid to lose.

Leo glanced at the railing with a desperate look in his eyes.

"Don't even think about it, Leo," I said. "The two guards with the machine guns would riddle you with bullets long before you could jump over the railing."

He realized himself that chances of surviving such an attempt would be minimal, and banished the idea. Had he known what awaited him in the Buna camp, he would surely have risked it—and I would not have advised him against it. Of the 500 to 600 prisoners on this voyage, only seven men came back.

For the first days on board we had to get along with the spoiled provisions we had brought from Berg, and each evening when the light was turned off, a long and tortuous night began. As my thoughts drift back to that first night, it seemed to me then that an eternity had passed since I had been arrested. Was it really only a month ago that I was a free man among colleagues and good friends? Would I ever see them again? One scene after another from Wolfgang Langhoff's book, *The Peat Bog Soldiers: 13 Months in a Concentration Camp,* passed before my eyes as I lay staring into the unpleasant darkness, which was filled with black hopelessness and the fear of an uncertain fate. If it was terrible for me, how much worse was it for those who had wives and children and other relatives to worry about?

At seven o'clock the next morning, I heard for the first time the words I would later come to hate more than anything else. A hoarse, vulgar voice called, "Get up!"

Some of the prisoners were ordered to do kitchen duty in a field kitchen set up on deck. Bernhard Bodd, Rubin Steinsapir (who was engaged to Bernhard's youngest sister), and I were made to carry potatoes and cabbage down to the women. They would peel the potatoes and cut up the cabbage before we carried it all back to the field kitchen.

The women had no cots. Old and young, pregnant women and mothers with infants, slept on dirty straw mattresses on the deck. Here and there toddlers crawled around and played. The women took care of themselves and the children as best they could under the dismal conditions. It was both touching and admirable to see how courageously they struggled to keep up their own morale and that of the little ones.

"Look," whispered Rubin suddenly. "There's Tulla."

It was not only Rubin's fiancée who sat nearby, but also her mother and her two sisters, Anna and Edith. Edith, who was married to my old friend Gordon, was surrounded by her three children.

Both Bernhard and Rubin completely forgot that a guard stood behind us. They dropped their sacks and ran over to the women. But their joy at seeing each other again was short-lived and their tremulous caresses few before the guard swooped down on them.

"No lovers' scenes here!" he thundered, pushing the two men brutally away with the butt of his gun. From then on he made sure that the army's sense of decency would not be perverted.

As for me, he did not watch me too closely; I had, after all, learned something in Berg. While I gathered the peeled potatoes in the large tub, I was able to talk to Anna at length, which the guard did not notice. She told me, among other things, that Tulla had tried to call Edith to warn her when the Nazis had come to their home. One of the policemen had seen what she was doing and had struck her down before he pulled out the telephone cord with a furious tug. None of the women were searched before they boarded; their valuables were a great catch for the German soldiers. Anna also told me that most of the women had displayed great courage, as did the children. What troubled the married women most was that they were unable to speak to their husbands. Other than that, they were determined to bear up, no matter what.

None, absolutely none, of the women or children came back.

On my way up to the field kitchen with the filled tub, I met Gordon and Edith's eight-year-old daughter on a landing. She recognized me and curtseyed.

"So, Doris," I said, searching in vain for the right words, "how do you like it here?"

"I think it's lots of fun," she said, and cocked her head. "Mummy says that we'll soon be with Daddy, and I'm really happy about that."

I did not dare talk to her further. It was not the German guards I was afraid of, but questions I would not be able to answer honestly.

The potato-cabbage soup was distributed in ordinary tin washbasins. Two or three, sometimes four men had to eat from the same basin.

The majority had to eat with their fingers because camp chief Lindseth had forbidden us to take eating utensils with us from Berg. I shared the washbasin with Gordon. Clearly moved, he thanked me when I brought him regards from his wife and children. It was obvious that he wished with all his heart they had escaped to Sweden. He himself had reported to the Gestapo in order to give them a chance to flee.

Later that day the married women were permitted to speak to their husbands for half an hour. The most harrowing scenes took place. When the women saw how thin and dirty their husbands had become during their stay at Berg, their suppressed fear and despair became apparent. Sobbing and fearful children clung to their parents. At the end of the half-hour, the women and children were driven back to their section of the ship like cattle.

Those who had hoped that a Swedish warship would seize the SS *Donau* when it passed the narrow Øresund (the sound separating Denmark and Sweden) were of course disappointed.

The ship lay anchored outside Copenhagen for twenty-four hours. There, several women, desperate with illness and despair, tried to jump overboard. As this occurred during our daily airing, we could observe from our side of the deck how the more level-headed women had to restrain them by force.

On the way from Copenhagen to Stettin the weather turned miserable, and many passengers got seasick. Four days after its departure from Oslo, when the ship arrived in Stettin, it was completely iced over. During disembarkation only the women and the older people were allowed to use the gangway; the rest of the prisoners had to slide down something that resembled an icy chute. The Germans standing on the wharf laughed and enjoyed themselves as we tried in vain to keep our balance. When everybody had come ashore, more or less battered, we were chased into the cattle cars of a train that would transport us to our next destination.

"Faster, faster, damned swine!" Insults and blows rained down on us. When the loading was finished, the person in charge shouted, "Close the stable!" Then the train started to move. None of us had any idea where the journey would take us.

The cattle cars were not only indescribably filthy, but they were also full of cracks which let in the ice-cold air. It was impossible to get any sleep during the two-day trip. Neither did we get anything to eat or drink. We froze miserably as we sat there hungry and thirsty, and we had to relieve ourselves through the cracks in the walls of the cars. One time, when the train stopped at a station, we asked a man who stood there for some water.

"Shut up, you dog!" He shouted through the cracks in the cattle-car door.

The landscape changed as we rolled through it. Suddenly I realized that we were passing some signs with Polish names. It made little impression on me in the condition I was in. We huddled close together on the hard benches and stared apathetically in front of us. One is not inclined to talk—or think—under such conditions.

Gittelsen and Mankowitz, the oldest men in my car, sat silently and without moving as long as the train trip lasted. After almost two days in the cattle cars the train stopped and the doors were pushed open. It was the middle of the night. We fell more than walked out of the rolling torture chamber.

The women and children were ordered straight into waiting trucks. Gordon ran over to the truck where his wife and three children were. To my surprise I saw that the man to whom he spoke allowed him to get into the truck. *Perhaps they are not so inhuman here,* I thought as the trucks left.

We had to gather the women's suitcases and our own wool blankets into a pile. We were told they would be sent to us later. We never saw any of the items again.

We who were left were divided into two groups. My group marched off first, heading toward the blinking lights of the Birkenau camp a few miles away. During the march we were accosted by German soldiers several times.

"If you have anything of value, let me have it," one of them said to me coaxingly. "Everything will be taken away from you anyhow. Give me what you have, and I'll be your good friend when you need it." I still had my watch, but nothing would convince me to hand it over to these crooks. Instead, without being noticed, I threw it into a puddle of water as we went by.

When we had passed two electric barbed-wire fences we arrived at the camp. Here we were ordered into a barracks that resembled a large barn. Once again we were searched. One of the men was foolish enough to ask the barracks head if he could have something to eat. The answer was a blow to his face. Another prisoner tried to ease his hunger with a cigarette butt that he had somehow managed to hide. This almost cost him his life. The barracks head beat him until he lay motionless on the floor. It was then that we realized that worse things were ahead of us than the terrible train ride.

Three-tiered concrete bunks were arranged against the wall. Seven of us would sleep in each bunk. We lay on the bare concrete without anything with which to cover ourselves. While we were in the process of lying down, one of the older prisoners came over to see us. We saw that he was a fellow Jew, and asked him if he knew what had happened to our women.

"They have left with the *Himmelkommando* [heaven unit]," he said, shrugging his shoulders.

We looked at him, bewildered.

"*Himmelkommando?*"

"Yes. They have gone to God," he said, and pointed in the air. "At any rate, they are better off now than you will be here. You can count yourselves lucky that you landed in this barracks. Here you will have a chance to survive for two days. Had you ended up in one of the other barracks, you would not have survived the night. I have been here two years and know what I am talking about."

We stood there as if paralyzed. "It's not true," someone called out.

"Yes, it is. The men in the other barracks were each handed a towel and told they would be taking a shower. It was not a shower room they were taken to, but a gas chamber. This happens here every day."

There are no words that can describe how we felt while we stood there and stared at the man. When my head had finally cleared, he was on his way toward the other end of the barracks. I followed him.

"Are you sure that it was our women and children who were sent to the gas chambers?"

He stopped and looked at me with his totally expressionless eyes.

"Yes. They created a stir because they were so well dressed. Also their clothes were not marked with a 'J.' Anyhow, the women who are trucked here are always sent directly to the gas chambers."

It was extremely cold and hard to lie on the horrible cement bunks, but I believe that few of us noticed it. Had we not been so weak and apathetic, there would have been a mutiny in Birkenau that night.

Early the next morning we were ordered to line up for breakfast, which consisted of lukewarm brown water they called coffee. Two men received less than a pint of this "breakfast" to divide between them, not many drops for each. Only a few minutes later we were marching toward an unknown destination.

Until now we had not seen much of the other prisoners in the camp. Now we saw them at work. Were those human beings staggering around the workplace? I shuddered at the sight of the emaciated, ragged human wreckage. How much could a person really endure before he collapsed for good? Now and then I saw how the unfortunate prisoners bent down to pocket rusty bits of barbed wire or pieces of paper. They looked around, frightened, as if they had stolen items of value. I wondered what on earth they would do with this rubbish. It would not be long before I did the same.

We marched for about half an hour and arrived at the large and notorious Auschwitz camp.

Chapter 4

ARBEIT MACHT FREI (WORK WILL SET YOU FREE) PROMISED THE SIGN above the gate of the camp. Dante's "Abandon every hope, ye who enter here" would have been closer to the truth.

Auschwitz did not consist of the usual wooden barracks. Streets and pavements led to three-story brick houses. The entire area was fenced in with barbed wire and electric fences. In this, Himmler's hellhole, between 20,000 and 30,000 people languished at any given time. The numbers can be counted, but there is no way of measuring the suffering of the individuals.

We had to line up on the pavement outside the bathroom. While we waited to be let into the showers, we saw other newcomers, prisoners from Holland and Belgium, line up on the opposite pavement. All of them had the Star of David and a "J" sewn onto the poor clothing they wore.

Some of the Norwegians owned mittens, knitted in a black-and-white pattern, which they had managed to keep. Old prisoners circled greedily around the lucky owners of these mittens. When they were sure that the guards could not see them, they came over to us.

"Norwegian, give me your mittens," one of the prisoners begged the man next to me. "They will be taken away from you anyhow."

"How do you know that I'm a Norwegian?"

"I know because of your mittens. When I was a little boy, a Norwegian friend sent me a pair just like this."

"But why do you think you'll be able to keep them any more than I can?"

"Because I know how to hide things. You newcomers are bound to be robbed of everything."

Just then the butt of a gun struck the prisoner's back so that he almost flew through the air. No one had noticed the guard sneaking up behind us.

Eventually we were ordered into the bathroom in groups of twenty men.

"Hurry up, damned swine!"

We began to recognize the tune and the words. In the bathroom they used thick leather straps. One of our men lost his composure for a minute and fought back. We had to carry him with us when they were finished with him.

"Hurry, hurry!"

From the changing room we were driven into a room where our body hair and the hair on our heads was torn off more than cut with the blunt instruments they used. When this was done, we were sprayed to prevent lice. And then we were let into the bath itself, which consisted of showers of alternately icy cold and boiling hot water.

"*Raus* [Get out]!"

We had to run outside into the cold, stark naked. They had "taken care" of our clothes. We stood outside a long time until it was convenient for the bullies to bring us to another building, where we were handed "new" clothes—dirty rags, which only fit a few of us. I was about to put on my socks when I noticed that I had one long silk stocking in one hand and a small child's sock in the other. This did not happen only to me. Worn wooden shoes completed our outfits.

It was a grotesque group that marched to the block where the tattooing took place. After I had been handed the silk stocking and the child's sock—it was not difficult to imagine what had happened to their owners—I believed that nothing would make an impression on me anymore. On the way to being tattooed, something happened that made me change my mind. In the miserable December weather, between a dozen and fifteen completely naked living skeletons staggered toward us. All of them were covered with boils and wounds full of pus. They clung together in an entangled mass to stop each other from falling.

The old prisoner showing us the way motioned with his hand when he saw how upset we were.

"They are headed for the crematorium; they can't work any longer."

Do not think, do not think, I said to myself over and over again. I knew that I would become mad if I did not banish all thoughts. "Work will set you free." The words above the camp gate expressed a macabre truth.

<hr />

During the tattooing we stood in alphabetical order. Here in this line occurred the first of many coincidences that enabled me to get home alive when the war was over. Henry Nachemsohn stood in front of me. When he saw how the men squirmed when a needle was stuck into their arms, he instinctively took a step back and let me go first. This minor and seemingly insignificant incident later became a matter of crucial importance for me.

Tired and hungry as we were, we hoped that we would now be let into one of the barracks to get some food. But there was no room for us in any of the blocks, so we ended up in the old camp bathroom. We waited and waited for food, but nothing came. There was water in the bathroom, but the signs on the wall said that those who drank this water better be prepared to contract typhus. We circled around the taps and became more and more thirsty. In the end we could not resist the temptation.

"Do you intend to croak immediately?" called a guard who saw us drink.

A few of the men thought they had stomach cramps, but they only imagined it. Not one of us got sick from the water. In the evening we had no choice but to lie down on the concrete floor, with nothing to cover us and nothing to lie on.

The following day we were given some food. I do not think I ever ate anything that tasted as good as the pint of potato and cabbage soup I was handed then. While I stood there enjoying every drop, I promised myself that should I ever return to Norway, I would eat this kind of soup often.

New prisoners arrived constantly. The following morning they chased us out because of lack of space. We were ordered to pass the time by marching around the block. Hour after hour we walked and jogged around in a circle to keep warm. Several times old prisoners came over to us to find out where we had come from. Many of them had no idea where Norway was.

"Norway? Why didn't you escape to Switzerland then?"

"Did you come by ship to Germany?" asked somebody who was better informed.

"Yes, we did."

Then he motioned with his hands in resignation. "And you didn't jump into the sea?"

Such reactions told us a great deal about what awaited us here.

Late that afternoon we received our second meal since we had left the train in Birkenau. This time it consisted of a piece of bread in addition to the pint of soup. Just a few minutes later, more than 200 of us marched out of the camp. We were headed for Monowitz, also called Buna, located three-quarters of a mile away. Just before we left through the ARBEIT MACHT FREI gate, we were surprised to catch sight of the other group of men from the train. A German soldier was harassing them, ordering, "Take off your caps! Put on your caps!" over and over again.

Outside the camp we constantly encountered work units staggering home, carrying their dead fellow prisoners between them. They had to sing on command, but we did not understand the words. The sight of these columns of death filled me with black hopelessness.

About two miles from the camp we walked through the city of Auschwitz. It had been destroyed, and the stench from the ruins was terrible. The few people we met were ragged and seemed totally apathetic. They did not bother to look at us. The German guard, who walked next to me, became suddenly talkative.

"Do you know what this city is called, Jew?"

"No."

"It is called Auschwitz. One hundred thousand Jews lived here before. Now there is not a soul left. This is what will happen to you too."

For an insane second I thought of choking him.

Just then the man next to me, my old friend David Jelo, collapsed.

"I can't go on," he moaned.

He was finished when we lifted him up. His weak heart was no longer able to tolerate the stress. We carried him between us the rest of the way. He was the first among us who succumbed to the Germans' inhumane treatment.

The camp head in Monowitz, a German criminal who was clearly proud of the green triangle on his prison garb, welcomed us in what we would discover to be his characteristic way: "I imagine you are hungry. Coffee and sandwiches will be served soon. While I remember it, does anyone here know how to ride a bicycle? So many? Then it's a pity that bicycling is forbidden. But those of you who are married will join your wives and children in about three months—that I can promise you."

It was not long before we understood what he meant by this promise. None of the prisoners were supposed to live longer than three months in this camp, and he did his utmost to ensure that this time frame was not exceeded.

In Monowitz it was the quarantine blocks that we became acquainted with first. Most of us ended up in Block 2. There we immediately witnessed an intense interrogation. The barracks head, a criminal, suspected two newcomers of having hidden away some money. They denied it.

"Well," sneered the devil that the Germans had picked up straight from jail, "I know how I can make you talk." He produced two long ropes and bound the hands of the two prisoners behind their backs. Then he threw the ropes across a beam and lifted up the poor souls by their tied wrists until they barely reached the floor with their toes. Both screamed loudly with pain.

The barracks head stood in front of them, his feet wide apart.

"I know it hurts like hell, because I have tried it myself. Now you will hang until you talk or die. In this block it is I who make the decisions; don't you forget it, Jew pack." He hit them so that they swung back and forth. Both fainted from the pain. Then the brute fetched a pail of water and threw its contents into the faces of his victims. When they regained consciousness they gave up. Wally—that was the name of the monster—sneered with satisfaction when he lowered the poor souls down again.

It became appallingly obvious to us that human lives were worth nothing in this camp.

———

At 3:30 a.m. the hated words *Get up!* pierced body and soul. The prisoners in the quarantine block lined up separately. Those who got out first were chosen to peel potatoes. This was not a desirable job, as the foreman was a true copy of the barracks head, but digging ditches in the cold was considerably worse. In the kitchen one not only had a roof over one's head, but also the chance to steal a potato or two. Soon we, like the other prisoners, took part in the ruthless fight to get far enough to the front of the line in order to be allowed into the kitchen. We also soon learned to steal potatoes. It was extremely dangerous, but hunger defeated fear when the opportunity presented itself. No lucky gold digger has ever taken better care of his gold nuggets than we did of the potatoes we stole. We put them on the heating pipe in the barracks and enjoyed looking at them as long as we managed to restrain ourselves. The theft of potatoes was an art, and like all other art forms it had its masters along with its less-gifted craftsmen.

Wally marched around as a brutal reminder that life could be short. One evening he decided to open all the windows just before we went to sleep. A few hours later those who lay closest to the windows woke up and found themselves partially snowed under. They closed the windows and went to sleep again. Wally had clearly counted on this, because it was not long before he arrived to inspect the barracks. In a perverse fit of fury he began to beat the unlucky prisoners who lay closest to the windows. He was so preoccupied with what he was doing that he did not notice when I crept over to the heating pipe and managed to salvage the potatoes some of us had stolen. I did not dare think about what would have happened to me if he had caught me red-handed. I shook like a leaf when I lay beneath the dirty, thin blanket again.

A few nights later, Wally beat Leo Løgård almost to death. He had forbidden us to sleep on our straw pillows at night; they were only supposed to serve as decorations during the day. Leo, who did not know more than a few words of German, had not understood Wally, and had lain down on his pillow in the evening. When the barracks head arrived and saw what had happened, he beat Leo, who was asleep, relentlessly. It was horrible to hear him scream with pain, and call out "I don't understand!" in his poor German.

I never thought that he would be able to get up the next morning, but he did, his face blue and swollen. He tried to smile when he saw how scared I was.

"Hello, Moritz. I have endured many hard blows in the ring, but damn it, that swine really hit me hard last night."

That day I was made part of the ditch-digging unit. It was bitter cold outside with a dense fog. We were terribly cold in our thin rags. And we were starved, because all we had had for breakfast was a pint of "coffee." We worked near the kitchen and the rubbish heap. If only we could get there without being shot by the guard. Thanks to the fog, there was a possibility that we could—in theory.

We got excited, dreaming about the potato peels and the cabbage leaves that were in the rubbish heap. I knew just as well as the others that it was a dangerous undertaking, but I was almost fainting from hunger. It was sheer desperation that drove me to risk it.

I waited for a moment when the guard disappeared in the fog, and then I ran. I succeeded! Like a maniac I rooted in the rubbish heap and filled my pockets with sticky potato peels and yellow cabbage leaves. Now I had to get back without being noticed.

I could hardly believe it when I stood safely among my fellow prisoners again; they surrounded me and almost tore off my rags to get their share of the haul. By that time we were already so hardened that we had become completely inconsiderate. Our only thought was to get something to eat, something that it was possible to swallow. The concept of "right of ownership" had entirely vanished from our consciences. We did anything to get some food. No job was too hard as long as it was rewarded with an extra ration, however scant that ration was.

One day young Herman Sachnowitz, one of the few who was able to return to Norway, was lucky enough to get a cleaning job in the barracks. In the evening he could barely stand on his feet. The Stubendienst (room supervisor, another prisoner) had harassed him all day by beating and kicking him, claiming that his work was not good enough. That was the extra ration Sachnowitz got.

<hr />

On December 24, the quarantine ended. Camp head Wally, the brute who bragged that he had been sentenced to fifteen years in prison, gave us the following comforting words at the last moment: "Here you have been well off—much too well off. Now things will be different. Outside in the big camp you will find out what real heavy work is like. You won't live long—you can be dead sure about that, Jew pack."

Those of us who were sent to Block 8 did not have to go to work that day, but many of the others were sent out on an extra work detail in the evening. At 3:30 a.m. on the first day of Christmas, the really dark times began for us.

With the same merciless shout of *Get up!*, the day's misery began. We had to dress in our rags and put our naked, frostbitten feet into the ice-cold wooden shoes. Then we went out into the snow and cold, to wait for hours until it was convenient for the local representatives of the "master race" to approve the results of the count and order us to march to the workplaces. We watched people collapse all around us on the roll-call square and freeze to death, while no one lifted a finger.

If you did not want to be left lying in the snow when the others marched out of the camp, you had to stand at attention all the time. The snow clung to the bottom of the wooden shoes during the march to the workplaces, but you could not fall or lag behind; this could cost you your life. The young German soldiers did not want to have sloppy people in their companies, and they knew the simplest way to get rid of them. Their shots were as accurate as their kicks. Maybe the leather straps of your wooden shoes tore during the march so that you had to drag your leg in order not to lose the shoe. If you were as lucky as me, you might be saved because the soldiers had to stop to relieve themselves. The delay was brief, but you managed to fasten the wooden shoe to your naked leg with a piece of rusty barbed wire that you had found outside your barracks the other day.

At the workplace you only had your naked, swollen fists with which to dig out the coal briquettes from the snow. But you could not pay attention to the pus that ran from under your nails, or to your skin that was cracked and bleeding. Tempo, tempo. If you did not work fast enough, you were struck with a club or the butt of a gun. Then you had to resist the temptation to cover yourself with your arms. If you did, you would never be able to use them again. Maybe you were allowed to squat down to relieve yourself, but it was not certain that you would ever get up again. This was because sometimes one of the courageous guards thought, just then, that he should check his marksmanship, for which he had once received a medal.

Why did you not do the same as some of the others—take a step, just one step was needed—beyond the line of guards and allow yourself to be shot because of an "escape attempt"? Was it because you did not want to miss the pint of cabbage soup which would soon be ladled into your tin bowl, covered with coal dust, the only meal of the day? But you could have had half a loaf of bread for breakfast today. True, you received it last night, but why would you eat it during the night? Why did you allow your damned intestines to rule over what little sense you had left?

To hell with it; having any sense just drove you mad.

Chapter 5

Of the 200 Norwegian Jews who came to Monowitz with me, about 25 percent died during the first month. The most frequent causes of death were hunger, dysentery, and the cold.

One morning a friend, Isak Shotland, had to help me outside to roll-call. He even managed to get me into the infirmary. He himself died only a few weeks later. He was kicked to death.

Three of us Norwegians were let into the infirmary that day; it could only accommodate sixteen prisoners. I suppose that the Germans' weakness for Norwegians probably played into it, even in a place like this. We lay completely naked in the dirty beds, and the treatment consisted of not eating anything but coal tablets for three days, which was supposed to settle the stomach.

The three days were like a wonderful dream. I did not have to hear the dreaded *Get up!* in the morning; I was spared roll-call and the march to the workplace, the terrible toil and the cold. No kapo (foreman, a prisoner appointed by the SS) shouted at me or beat me; no barracks head or Stubendienst turned my free time into a nightmare. To be able to pull the dirty wool blanket over my head and close my eyes was a pleasure beyond comprehension. The only thing that bothered me was that time passed much too quickly.

When the three days were up, an SS doctor came to see us. He did not come to help us, but to see if we were fit to work. He scrutinized us while we paraded naked in front of him. Those who he felt could be sufficiently useful in the workplace were told to go into another room; the others were sent naked into the hallway.

"Where are they going?" I asked the orderly.

"To the oven," he replied indifferently.

I had to pull myself together with all my might to remain on my feet.

"Come with me," said the orderly.

The bed I was shown to in the new room made me shudder, as weak as I was. Everything was covered with dried blood and pus: the dirty mattress, the thin blanket, and the ragged pillow.

Just as I was going to lie down I heard someone call my name, barely audibly. I went to the bed where the voice came from. I had seen many half-dead people in this camp, but never had I seen anyone as horribly emaciated and shrunken as this person. Who was it?

"Don't you recognize me, Moritz?" It came haltingly. "It's Bernhard."

It was my old friend Bernhard Krupp who lay there. A skeleton with parchment-like skin was all that was left of the strong young man who had been almost six feet tall. He was suffering from dysentery and pneumonia for the second time. His ration had been put down beside him. I tried to help him with it, but he was unable to swallow. He had been completely helpless for several days; his bed was full of excrement. He asked me to get him to the toilet, a square box in the corner of the room. I helped him as best I could in my weakened condition, but the four times he fainted I had to lay him down on the floor.

Immediately after I had gotten him into bed again, it looked as though his eyes were about to burst, but he came to again. He groped for my hand and whispered: "I know I'm going to die now, Moritz. Give my love to my fiancée when you get home. Yes, Moritz, I know you are going to get home."

And then he lost consciousness again.

That night I cried myself to sleep for the first and last time in the concentration camps.

In the morning I woke up when the orderly came into the room.

Did he come to see how we were? He stopped for a moment near one of the beds. I froze when I saw him pull a blanket off the patient and stick a syringe into the bony body. A little weak whimpering and then everything was quiet. In my overwrought imagination the orderly turned into a black-striped huge insect with a gleaming stinger ready to strike. There it struck again, and there, and there.

I curled up and tensed what few muscles I had left. I would not let the devil strike me. *Just you try and I'll smash your damned stinger, and as for you, I'll cut your throat,* I said to myself.

"Get up, Norwegian. You are leaving here today."

I turned cold and clammy all over my body. There were five of us who were sent out and pronounced "recovered."

Outside in the hallway stood a group of Musselmänner (living corpses), waiting to be sent on their last transport. A boy of seventeen or eighteen was on his knees, clutching the doctor for dear life. He cried and begged to be allowed out into the camp again. He kissed and caressed the doctor's boots. The scene was so heartrending that the five of us stopped instinctively, but the orderly pounced on us right away.

It was icy outside, and all five of us were so weak that we had to support each other on the way to the office. The soles of our wooden shoes were slippery, and time after time we fell and landed in a heap. But eventually we reached the office where we would be told where to go next. Coming from the infirmary it was out of the question to go back to one's old barracks.

"If only we don't end up in Block 2," said Simon when we stood on the steps, "because Satan himself is the barracks head there." But it was Block 2.

When we reached the barracks I went in first. As soon as I opened the door, my face was struck so hard that I fell down. When I got back on my feet the barracks head was gone. The Stubendienst, the next in command to the barracks head, approached us with a sneer.

"Okay, men, you have already found out where you have ended up. Here you must be careful—careful, I said—if you want to stay alive." He nodded at Simon. "You have been here before, so you know how it is."

"I know," said Simon in a low voice.

But even in a hellhole such as Block 2, something good could happen. That same day a new barracks head appeared. Although he was a criminal prisoner, too, he was not as sadistic as his predecessor. No one ever saw the old barracks head again. Rumors circulated that he had been hanged. Like so many other barracks heads, he was supposed to have beaten prisoners to death in order to get to the gold fillings in their mouths. The camp commandant never complained about these crimes; quite the reverse. But when he received a report that the teeth of many of the victims of certain barracks heads were suspiciously missing, he changed his tune. It was one thing to kill a prisoner, but quite another to steal the property of the German state. More than one barracks head ended his career with a rope around his neck.

It was minus-4 degrees Fahrenheit when, the day after my hospital stay, I marched out of the camp in work detail No. 7. We were set to do heavy leveling work. Between fifty and sixty men in this work detail were carried back to the camp as frozen bodies. I myself managed to survive, but I spent most of the night trying to save my frostbitten feet. I rubbed and massaged them until they eventually began to tingle. I seemed to have just fallen asleep when the barracks head's infernal *Get up!* ripped away sleep's merciful veil and announced a new day full of pain and humiliation; a day that no one knew if he would survive. We always said good-bye to each other when we separated in the morning.

I was glad when I succeeded in getting into a new work detail after roll-call, but relief turned to despair when we reached our workplace and found out that we would have to carry cement. It was to be my absolutely worst day so far. Thousands of 110-pound cement sacks had to be carried into a huge shack and piled under the roof. The foremen and kapos in this work unit were simply a gang of sex murderers who competed to release their bestial tendencies. When the sack pile reached the height of a man, narrow boardwalks were set up from both sides.

At each end stood a kapo or a foreman who used his thick club as soon as one or another poor soul was unable to run fast enough to keep up his speed. Those who keeled over beneath the sack or fell down from the boards were finished. There were enough slaves, and all of them would be annihilated soon anyhow.

I did not think I would survive that day. *You were wrong, Bernhard,* I said to myself, time and time again. *I'll never make it home.* But somehow the words of my dead friend drove me on each time I was about to collapse under the cement sacks. *You must not give up, Moritz. You promised Bernhard that you would go and see his fiancée. You must go home and tell her and all the others about this hell, where Bernhard and tens of thousands with him perished.*

I got through that day, but I knew I would not survive another one like it.

Fortunately, I did not have to. That same evening six other typographers and I were told that we were leaving for a print shop in Auschwitz. We were chosen according to our numbers, and I was the last of the seven. I could not stop thinking of Nachemsohn. If he had not stepped behind me in the tattooing line, he would have had this opportunity instead of me. The first order said that we were to leave within an hour, but then a different order came from the office. The transport was postponed until the following day.

After I got this message I went around in the camp to say good-bye to my friends. I was just exchanging a few words of farewell with eighteen-year-old Lillegutt Steinmann when another coincidence occurred. A Czech prisoner was standing close to us as I spoke (in Norwegian) about my unexpected luck.

Suddenly the Czech approached me. "Are you a printer?" he asked, in German.

"Yes."

"Then you have to hurry up. The car parked near the office is ready to leave."

I have no idea how it happened that this Czech understood what I said in Norwegian, and at the time, I was in too much of a hurry to find out. I limped off as quickly as I could on my frozen feet and reached the office at the last moment.

During the brief trip to Auschwitz the others said that the Germans had been looking for me in Block 2. When I was not there, the guards were ordered to leave without me. It went without saying that a German car would not wait for a lowly prisoner. By chance the other men had been in their respective barracks when the third and final order was issued by the office.

There we were—three Poles, two Germans, one Frenchman, and I—happy that we had escaped Monowitz, "the carousel of death." It was the first time we had met, but now we chatted together as though we were old friends. We all wondered about the print shop we were going to, but it was mostly to pass the time. What was important was that we would be working indoors and not in the snow and the cold.

As for me, I was quite nervous. I was a stereotypographer by profession, and not a printer. True, my index card said "printer," but that was strictly due to the fact that the clerk in Monowitz had had a natural aversion to words that were difficult to spell. Imagine if they had no use for stereotypographers in the print shop we were headed for! I would fail helplessly if I were made to work a typesetting or printing machine, and then what would happen to me? I would be back to carrying cement, or worse.

The trip to Auschwitz took only fifteen minutes. From the car we were sent straight to the bathroom, where we were given the regimented treatment of the clippers, the lice spray, and the alternately icy-cold and boiling-hot showers. The next step was Block 26. We only spent twenty-four hours in this block, but something happened there that none of us had experienced before. The Stubendienst insisted that we had stolen a piece of bread that lay on a shelf. When none of us admitted to the crime, the Stubendienst chose a victim that he dragged away with him. The fateful choice fell on the Pole, Josel. None of us thought we would ever see him again. In our experience, those who were suspected of having stolen anything from a Stubendienst, with or without reason, were doomed.

We could hardly believe our eyes when Josel returned half an hour later. True, his face was swollen and bruised, but the mere fact that he came back alive was a miracle. Was it really possible that a "green-striped" Stubendienst had been so merciful that he had spared a life in a situation like this? No, there had to be some other reason . . . but what could it be? We could not find a plausible explanation.

And when on the following morning we became acquainted with Block 11, we had something else to think about.

Block 11 was a quarantine barracks for prisoners who were to be sent on to other places. Apparently, we were not going to stay in Auschwitz after all. We were happy about that, because in this camp the gas chambers and crematoria worked incessantly. From a few prisoners I met briefly, I found out that practically all the Norwegians were dead. They knew of only one who was still alive. They had no idea what his name was, but he was known as Narvik among the prisoners.

The seven of us from Monowitz were the first Jews who had come to this quarantine barracks. We were stowed in a room where sixty to seventy Polish and Ukrainian prisoners lived, a mix of political prisoners and criminals. It was obvious that both categories considered it beneath their dignity to live under the same roof as Jews, something they pointed out to us at every opportunity.

But despite all the trouble these men gave us, this quarantine block was far better than the one I had been in last. In Monowitz the quarantine prisoners had to work like slaves outside in the cold, just like the other prisoners. Here the work consisted of mending socks. We were even allowed to sit in our bunks while we worked.

As mentioned, we were the only Jews who had been allowed to come to such a quarantine block here in Auschwitz. We often wondered about the reason for this gross violation of "Himmler etiquette." One day, somebody hinted at the word *Sonderkommando* (a special unit working in gas chambers and crematoria). When we thought how Josel, despite all experiences to the contrary, had survived the incident with the stolen bread, and how we had been allowed to live in this barracks, the word did not seem quite so implausible. But what kind of special unit could it be?

During the course of about three days, our little group had been augmented by three new printers and thirty watchmakers, all Jews. Surprised, they climbed into their bunks with the regulation five pairs of socks for the day. *Socks* was actually a flattering term for the rags we sewed together.

To look around the room when every man was busy with his pile of rags, two or three men to a bunk, was a sight to behold. The crouched positions and the plucking hand movements made one feel as if one had been transported to a monkey cage flooded with fleas.

Most of us now suffered from painful boils all over our bodies. I myself had a boil on my thigh that was extremely painful. When, on top of it, my left arm became paralyzed and dysentery began to ravage me, I almost gave up. To ask to get into the infirmary was the same as suicide for us Jews. Of the eight men who had gone there with the orderly, not one had come back.

One morning while we stood waiting for the barracks head and the German soldier to come to check attendance, I fainted. When I came to, I was lying in my bunk. Fear and defiance gave me the strength to get down on the floor and out to the long hall where roll-call took place. "Let me have his number," I heard the barracks head call out.

"Here I am," I said as loudly and steadily as I was able. "There is nothing really wrong with me."

It worked. I cured the dysentery by not eating for three days. The paralysis of my arm was a worse problem. When the Poles and the Ukrainians discovered how sick I was, they offered to mend my socks in exchange for my food ration. I declined their generous offer and struggled on. I succeeded in making my paralyzed fingers work by using a complicated string system, which was fastened to my elbow. The work was slow, but I managed to finish within the stipulated time every day.

But I was unable to conquer the damned boil on my thigh. It grew and grew and became more and more painful. The night before I was sent to the infirmary was a nightmare of pain.

"The Norwegian will die tonight," I heard one of my fellow prisoners say during a clear moment.

In the morning I was so exhausted that I staggered after the orderly to the infirmary without protest. I knew what I was facing, but I could no longer bear the infernal pain. It was better to end this miserable life in a gas chamber. Besides, it would have been no use to object. Those whom the orderly chose to take with him had no choice but to go.

The two watchmakers who came with me to the infirmary had no choice either. They were also so ill that they were unable to work. I left the day's five pairs of socks with a young Dutchman, as I had been ordered to. He was anything but enthusiastic, but of course he could not refuse to take them.

In the first room we came to in the infirmary, a man ordered us to take off all our clothes. When we stood there completely naked, he wrote our numbers on our chests with a huge indelible pencil that he first dipped in a bowl of water.

"What's this for?" asked one of the watchmakers.

"You will find out soon enough in the crematorium. Next."

This is the end, I said to myself as we limped into another room to pick up our index cards for the doctor. Printed on the cards were name . . . age . . . nationality . . . death . . .

It was only the last column that had not been filled out. It was like reading one's own epitaph.

Twelve of us stood waiting for our turn, only we three Jews with the numbers painted on our chests. The doctor was a Pole and a political prisoner. An ordinary barracks table stood in the middle of the floor. The first man ordered to get up on the table had a huge boil on his back. He was tied down with solid straps; a mask was placed over his face, which was probably not very effective, because the man squirmed like a worm when the doctor cut into the boil. Sticking plaster. Finished. Next.

I staggered over to the table when it was my turn. The doctor had not exchanged a single word with any of the patients before. Now he suddenly turned to me and asked, "Where are you from?"

I told him and rolled onto the table. The doctor's helper stood ready with the mask.

"Ah, Norway. A beautiful country and splendid people," he chatted in a friendly voice. What he said while he cut into me I did not comprehend—for obvious reasons. But when I crawled down from the table more dead than alive, he said something that I understood with all my heart. He said: "You can take your clothes, Norwegian, and go back to your barracks."

Outside in the dressing room I was in agony while I struggled like mad to get into my rags. It took so desperately long, and every minute I expected one or another German tormentor to come, who would not care about what the doctor had said. The paper sticking plaster that had been put around my thigh fell off and the blood oozed down my leg. I had to lie down on the floor and use all my strength to pull my trousers over the swollen thigh. Somehow I had a new life to take care of, and the fear of losing it made me forget the physical pain. Fortunately it was not a tormentor but a kind prisoner who came. The doctor had sent him to help me back to the quarantine block.

In the hallway of the barracks I met the orderly. He considered my return a personal insult and boxed my ear so hard that I fell to the ground.

My fellow prisoners in the barracks could hardly believe their eyes when they saw me. No wonder, because of the eleven Jews who had been sent to the doctor, I was the only one who came back.

I had only been back in the barracks for a few minutes when the Stubendienst arrived to check the sock repairs. When it was my turn I stood there without a single sock. Each time I tried to explain, he struck me so hard that I fell down on the floor. When I got up for the third time he threw five pairs of sock rags at me and shouted, "Take these. If you do not deliver ten pairs of mended socks tomorrow, I will skin you alive, damned Jew devil!"

When I went over to the young Dutchman who had my socks, he had only three pairs left. The other two pairs had been stolen from him. What now? I had to have ten pairs of socks for the Stubendienst; I was simply not strong enough now to tolerate his club. I knew that the Poles had lots of socks, but I also knew that none of them would give anything to a Jew without being paid blood money. Meanwhile, I got hold of three socks in return for my lunch. One was a long ladies' stocking that I cut in half. I held my breath with fear and tension when I delivered the ten pairs to the Stubendienst the following evening. He spot-checked the socks to see if they were mended, fortunately not looking too closely at the pair of socks that I had made from the long stocking. It was not pleasant to cross this man, but he was still much better than the Stubendienst we got a few days later.

The new Stubendienst began his career in the barracks by creating a ghetto. All Jews were moved to the end of the room where the smelly toilet was. When he distributed food for the first time, he ordered us Jews to line up separately. We had to stand there and watch how the other prisoners were handed the biggest pieces of bread in the morning and the best portions of soup for dinner. Only clear water was left in the soup pot when we were allowed to come forward with our tin bowls. At times the Stubendienst knocked the bowl out of someone's hands. The poor wretch first got a cuff on the ears because he had not held onto the bowl properly, and then he was forced to lick up the soup from the floor. The man among us whom this criminal enjoyed mistreating the most was an almost sixty-year-old watchmaker from Vienna. When the victim moaned loudly during the blows, the sadistic tormentor would call out ecstatically: "He has the most beautiful scream on earth!"

This watchmaker owned one of the largest stores of his trade in Vienna. One day while the soup was being distributed, the Stubendienst said, "You are not going to get any dinner today if you do not sign over your business to me. Will you do it?"

"No."

"Well, then, you will have to go without dinner."

The old man died in the quarantine block. Some Ukrainian prisoners simply beat him to death. He had a weak heart, and the water, called soup, gave him constant trouble. One night when he lay moaning in his bunk, the Ukrainians attacked him with sticks. In the morning he was dead.

———

The Poles and Ukrainians did with us whatever they pleased. They were well fed and in the majority, and both the Stubendienst and the barracks head were on their side. The Germans were also partial to them, because once their time in quarantine was over they would all be released to enlist in the German army. It was just as dangerous to try to get even with these thugs as with a Stubendienst or a barracks head. I thought about these men when I heard that the Jews in Poland were persecuted even after the war was over.

Our exercise yard was surrounded by a tall board fence, which was generally used for a far more sinister purpose. At one end of the fence a black, square wall had been put up. All prisoners who had been condemned to death were made to stand against this wall. The number of executions varied from 50 to 200 a day. On several occasions, during punishment drills, we had to crawl and roll in the blood of the executed prisoners. These drills were the order of the day.

Once, in the middle of the night, we were awakened to a cry of "All Jews get out!"

"What's going to happen now?" we asked ourselves as we got dressed. Actually, we did not take it too seriously, because we were used to the most ridiculous ideas on the part of the Stubendienst and the barracks head.

But when we were outside in the hall and were instructed to get undressed, we got scared. When a prisoner had to hand over his clothes, nothing but the worst was likely to happen to him. However, we had no choice; we had to start getting undressed.

When we had taken off our caps and coats, we were sent back into the barracks. The whole uproar was due to the fact that new prisoners had arrived, for whom there were not sufficient clothes. And who else should suffer the consequences but we Jews in the quarantine block? To be without a cap and a coat was only a matter of minor importance for us. It was worse when, for two days, we had nothing to wear at all. The barracks head had decided that our clothes needed to be gassed because they were vermin-infested, so they took us to the bathroom. From there we had to walk through the snow back to our barracks, completely naked. To make things really pleasant for us, the Stubendienst left all the windows open day and night during those two days. The bedding had also been taken from us, so that we did not have so much as a thread to warm us at night either.

One week after another went by, and still we had not heard one word about being transported to another place. Eventually, we no longer believed in the print shop we had heard about in Monowitz.

But—after five weeks' stay in the block—the order about another transport finally came. We were going to Sachsenhausen in Germany, where the print shop in which we were to work was located. We were even going to have the great honor of carrying out work that was considered important for the war effort of the Greater German Reich.

Our group had been reduced by 25 percent during those weeks.

Prior to departure an SS man acted as our host by giving us as much soup as we could eat. The lavish farewell meal was even consumed in the kitchen itself. And when we were handed our travel provisions we found to our great surprise that they consisted of bread, margarine, and sausage. We looked at each other to make sure this was not just a dream.

The group that marched off to the railway station in Auschwitz that morning was almost in high spirits.

"You'll see that we'll be allowed to travel in a passenger train," joked Perez while we waited for the train. He was not in the least surprised when the guards ordered us into an ordinary passenger train.

It seemed as though we had come to another planet. But what did this actually mean? Why were these monsters beginning to treat us almost as though we were human? We discussed this mystery among ourselves without finding an answer. But never mind; we would surely find out the reason in time. Now we would simply enjoy the wonderful experience of traveling like human beings. Perhaps this would be the last time.

Three hours later the train stopped in Katowice. When we heard that we could use the toilet in the station, everyone left the train in a hurry. True, we were closely watched all the time, but we were as happy as kids in the toy department of a store. The highlight occurred when a kind civilian distributed small change so that we could even use the flush toilet.

But when I was suddenly faced with my own mirror image in a window, all joy vanished. I thought I had never before seen anything so emaciated, ragged, and horrible. Instinctively I looked around to see if anyone I knew was nearby. It was a bitter and terrible experience to be nauseous at my own misery. A brief crazy impulse almost caused me to commit suicide by running a few steps across the platform.

Chapter 6

WE ARRIVED IN BERLIN ON MARCH 8, 1943, AROUND 8:00 A.M. ONE OF the watchmakers, Blaustein, who hailed from Berlin, cried when we rolled into the railway station. The man next to him, a printer called Schnapper, pushed him irritably with his elbow.

"Don't be ridiculous, you old sow. You'll soon be able to walk in the streets and look around as much as you want."

Actually, there was some truth to the harsh words. Two soldiers came into the car. When they had greeted our guards with *Heil Hitler*, the more unpleasant of the two gave us some brief instructions. We would march through the city to another railway station. In this city no money would be spent on a car for Jewish riffraff. Needless to say, we would march on the road. If any one of us so much as glanced at the nobility on the pavement, he would be gunned down like the insolent dog he was.

"*Raus!*"

Our loose-fitting wooden shoes clattered against the cobblestones when we began to march. People in Berlin still lived well, off stolen goods. The windows of the bakeries and butcher shops were bulging with wonderful things. Women carried baskets and packages of all sizes. The sight of all this wonderful food, which was so close but still so out of reach, made our stomachs growl. Little by little the pavements became more and more populated—women and more women, well-nourished and well-dressed, on their way to factories and offices. There was looted food and stolen clothes everywhere.

We did not see many men, and those we saw were in uniform. A few of them carried well-filled backpacks. We also saw round-cheeked kids, nicely dressed, playing in a small park.

"This is how their kids live," said Blaustein bitterly. "Ours are sent to the gas chambers."

When the children saw us, they stopped playing and stared. Their eyes were filled with disgust.

"I don't blame them," said Glantzer, a Hungarian, walking behind me. "After all, we look more like sewer rats than human beings, the way we hobble along. Their fathers did their work well."

"Stop!" called the brute who was in charge.

We had come upon a beer cellar, and the representative of the "master race" was thirsty. Three of the soldiers took turns watching us while the others left with a *Heil Hitler* to drink light and dark beer in the beer cellar.

"You better stay away from the Jewish swine if you don't want to have lice," said one of the soldiers, warning the curious Berliners who had stopped to glare at us.

The march to the railway station took an hour. This time, too, we traveled in an ordinary passenger carriage. It was an S-train, and the trip to Oranienburg took only half an hour. From here we marched roughly two miles to the big concentration camp of Sachsenhausen. We were very tense when the large iron gate was opened.

Was this a concentration camp? Compared with the other camps we had come from, the place seemed like a model colony. The well-kept barracks lay in a semicircle around a beautiful square. For now, that was all we glimpsed of the camp. As soon as we had gone through the gate we were told to stop and stand still, facing it. We were given strict orders to look straight ahead and nowhere else.

When we first noticed the big clock on the gate, we were amazed. It was like a fairy tale to see a clock with hands that actually moved. This was how I felt, even though I had only been without a watch for a few months.

For those of my fellow prisoners who had spent several years in captivity, the fine clock must have been a miracle to look at.

I could hear one of the watchmakers giving the printer Shurak a long and detailed lesson on the secrets of the movement of a watch, and on many other fine points in general. Even though it was strictly forbidden, little by little we took a chance and turned our heads, but there was not much of the camp we could see this way. Schnapper, the oldest and perhaps the most daring among the printers, was able to tell us that a group of men in civilian clothes stood on the right-hand side of the exit gate.

"They are probably prisoners who have been released, because they have been handed packages and suitcases."

Prisoners freed? It sounded almost unnatural.

We stood like this for three hours. Suddenly we were ordered "about face."

A young officer scrutinized us. He was so well built and polished and handsomely dressed in a tailor-made uniform that he could easily have been part of an operetta scene. On one of his sleeves stood the letters SD (Sicherheitsdienst—Security Service of the SS). He produced a sheet of paper and called out the names of the eight who were going to the print shop.

"All printers come with me. The others will remain here, standing."

"The Adonis is an Oberscharführer [senior squad leader]," whispered Schnapper, the know-it-all, when we marched across the square. "I wonder if we're finally going to see the confounded print shop."

No one answered. We were too nervous to play guessing games now.

The officer took us to the notorious Block 19. At the time we actually had no idea about the block at all, but we realized that there had to be something special about it when we saw that it was completely isolated from the other barracks. Not even a cat could have managed to get safely through the barbed-wire netting. There were iron bars on the windows, and the windowpanes were dull. If this was the print shop, whatever was produced here was surely mysterious. I had a strange feeling of being lost when we walked through the gate in the rough board fence.

A man in his forties, dressed in civilian clothes, stood in the long, narrow exercise yard. We realized that he was an important person because the officer saluted him and stood at strict attention before him. The man came over to us.

"Hello, gentlemen!" The warm deer eyes looked at us almost in a friendly manner. "I think you're going to like it here. What is your profession?"

"Printer," answered Schnapper. He was not easily at a loss for words, but this man, who was so formal and polite, confused him so much that it showed.

"Excellent, sir," said the man, and continued with the next prisoner.

"Oh, stereotypographer," he exclaimed when I had answered him. "Great, sir—we will make good use of you," he added, touching my shoulder. When he had, so to speak, greeted us all personally, he left with a friendly nod.

"This way," called the officer, who had kept a respectful distance all the time.

We followed him to a room where five or six fellows sat around a table, eating. It was the first time we had seen prisoners sit at a table and eat, and it was also the first time we had seen prisoners whose hair had not been clipped off.

"Are you hungry?" asked a stocky man when the officer had gone into another room.

We were.

"So, sit down at the table."

I was actually reluctant to sit down at the white scoured table.

The clothes these prisoners were wearing were party outfits compared to the filthy rags we had on. None of us had had anything to eat all day, so we threw ourselves on the soup dishes with greedy hands. The men let us eat in peace, but then they began to inquire about relatives and friends. They told us their names and prison numbers and wanted to know if we had met any of them.

Schnapper was able to give the little Stubendienst Herman Güting some information about a mutual friend they had. The rest of us did not know any of the prisoners who were mentioned. Our hosts—it was their food ration we had eaten from—continued to ask about everything under the sun. But when we tried to make them tell us about their work, they only shook their heads. The only thing we found out was that the German officer was Oberscharführer Marok. The name of the man who had offered us something to eat was Krebs, and he was the barracks head. He was Jewish and a political prisoner, like everyone in this block. Immediately afterwards he came to speak to us again.

"Would you like to smoke?"

Surprised, we accepted the cigarettes he offered us. We were just about to put them into our mouths when Marok appeared in the doorway. Quickly we hid the cigarettes.

"No, please, just go ahead and smoke."

I simply refused to believe my eyes when I saw the officer go over to Schnapper and light his cigarette.

The cigarette was anything but first-class, but I have neither before nor since enjoyed a smoke as much as I enjoyed this one. I could hardly believe that it was me who sat with my elbows on a clean tabletop, holding a lit cigarette between my fingers.

When we had finished smoking, we were sent back to the wall.

The watchmakers were no longer there. While we discussed where they could have gone, Marok came to fetch us for the second time.

"Okay, men, now you will first go to the bathroom and then you will have to spend a week in quarantine. I thought that I would get you into Block 19 right away, but the camp commandant did not agree."

The bathroom was complete luxury compared to the torture chambers in Monowitz and Auschwitz, and each man was handed a towel and a bar of B-soap.

Later, we sat in a circle around a stove and baked some watery bread while we talked. The smell of the blobs of bread on the stove was terrible, but by baking it, it became reasonably edible. We had been strictly ordered not to leave the barracks, but other than that, we had been left to our own devices. Once in a while an SS man came to check on us—that was all. Had he known that we had used the bottom boards of the empty bunks to light the fire in the stove, he would have given us a hard time. In the camps we had come from, it would have been deliberate suicide to touch so much as a splinter of the barracks, but everything was different here. We did not work, and the food was brought to us by other prisoners from the camp.

"No, this Marok is not hard to figure out," said Schnapper, putting a piece of bread on the stove. "He looks like a film star, which he knows very well himself. I bet it takes him a whole hour to get groomed and dressed in the morning. Didn't you notice how great he smells? Lots of pomade and salves. Why do you think such a big, strong fellow does not serve at the front? You can call me a spittoon if he does not carry on with the daughter of a general or some such thing."

"He's wearing a wedding band," protested Josel.

Schnapper scoffed. "Listen to the naive Pole. You don't really think that a wedding ring makes a difference in times of war? Not even in times of peace, for that matter. The German women are completely horny when it comes to a blond Adonis like Marok; trust me, they don't worry about a wedding band."

"Who do you think the pleasant civilian was, Schnapper?" asked Shurak. "Outside I would definitely have thought he was Jewish."

Schnapper looked up quickly. "Yes, here you have something to think about, Shurak. When a German uses the formal *Sie* [you] and *meine Herren* [gentlemen] when he speaks to Jewish prisoners, something smells funny. Anyway, it's probably not hard to understand that he's the chief of this mysterious print shop."

"*Achtung!*" called Perez, who stood closest to the door.

We quickly snatched the pieces of bread from the oven, jumped up, and stood at attention.

It was the camp commandant himself who had come to check on us. He remained standing in the doorway.

"Do all Jews smell?"

No one answered.

"Do all Jews smell?" he shouted at Perez.

"Yes," answered Perez. He could not very well tell him about baking the bread.

The camp commandant turned on his heel and left.

The pieces of bread reappeared and we continued the discussion. What kind of mysterious things took place in this secretive print shop? The twenty-five watchmakers who were also in the quarantine block were more relaxed. They knew that they would work in the camp's large watch-repair shop. The oldest among them was fifty-seven years old, and the youngest, seventeen. The former was Russian. His wife and three children had been killed by the Germans when they occupied the city where he lived. He himself had been sent to Birkenau.

The Russian told them how the prisoners at Birkenau had been exterminated by the most horrific methods possible. On their way to work they had had to pass a river. Kapos had forced the prisoners to jump across an icy board bridge, and one after the other, the unfortunate, exhausted men had slid and fallen into the river. They were all beaten to death without exception when they tried to crawl up the embankment. The kapos had been ordered in advance to bring back a certain number of bodies when the kommando returned to the camp after the day's work.

"I'll never leave this camp alive," said the Russian when he had finished his story. "I prefer to be shot here rather than beaten to death in another camp."

The first days we were in the quarantine camp, we received ample amounts of both soup and potatoes. But as the days went by, the soup became thinner and thinner.

"I bet that the prisoners who carry the food steal some of the contents of the keg," said Schnapper.

The food-bearers denied the accusation vigorously. They had never touched our food. But the following day, we kept an eye on them after they had come through the gate in the quarantine block. We saw how they removed the lid of the bucket and helped themselves to potatoes. When they had no room left in their pockets, they put some potatoes alongside the barracks wall. They probably suspected that we had seen something because they were in an awful hurry to leave once they had left the bucket inside the door. But they did not get out before we had helped ourselves to the potatoes that were in their pockets, and we treated the men far from gently. Everyone in the block was so starved that we badly needed the rations we got.

Three new men came with the food the following day. They told us that their predecessors had been caught with their pockets full of potatoes outside in the camp. I really felt sorry for the poor wretches when I heard that their punishment had been twenty-five lashes on the backside. Generally such punishment caused the victims to become invalids.

But we did have some fun too. The Hungarian, Glantzer, used his hands more than his mouth when he spoke. One day when we sat around the oven, chatting, Schnapper said, "Listen, Glantzer, I'll bet half my bread ration that you cannot talk to us for five minutes without gesticulating with your hands."

Glantzer accepted the bet. He crossed his arms and squeezed his fists firmly into his armpits. Blaustein began counting the seconds because no one had a watch.

To watch Glantzer talk to Schnapper was quite a sight. His shoulders jerked and pulled each time he opened his mouth. In the end his entire upper body shook as though he was suffering from a nervous disorder. The effort of keeping his hands in his armpits caused his thin and anemic face to become red, and his tongue struggled for dear life when he had to answer the series of bold questions and insinuations that the merciless Schnapper put to him.

The unbelievable outcome was that Glantzer won the bet. But the joints of his fingers creaked badly when, moaning with relief, he managed to free his hands again.

"You have gained my respect, Glantzer," said Schnapper, genuinely impressed when the five minutes were over. "And you'll get the bread."

Glantzer waved with his hands magnanimously.

"Keep your piece of bread; you need that little bite of bread yourself. But instead, you can tell me how you managed to get so bald."

Schnapper let his hand glide across his completely hair-free head.

"I lost it in prison. I spent three years in solitary confinement because I had been engaged to an Aryan girl. From there I came straight to Monowitz."

Marok had given us false hope that we would spend only one week in quarantine. Two weeks went by before we were moved to Block 19. It was Stubendienst Güting who came to fetch us.

Three men stood in the exercise yard awaiting our arrival. We recognized Krebs and Marok immediately, but we had to take a closer look at the third man. He was none other than the kind civilian with the deer eyes, but today he was in uniform.

"The man is a Sturmbannführer [major in the SS]," whispered Schnapper without moving his lips. Of course he was right.

"I am Sturmbannführer Krüger, and I hope you will get along well here, gentlemen," said the man, when Krebs and Marok had closely checked that the names and numbers tallied with their short list. Krüger was just as charming and polite in uniform as he had been as a civilian. One would have thought that we were a delegation of esteemed guests and not eight ragged prisoners.

Suddenly he asked: "Is anyone half-Jewish here?"

Leib Epstein from Paris stepped forward and clicked his heels together with a bang of his wooden shoes.

"I am, Herr Sturmbannführer," he lied boldly. It was the thought of gaining some advantage that made him take this highly doubtful chance.

Krüger walked around Epstein and looked at him with a sly smile at the corner of his mouth.

"So, you are half-Jewish. You must forgive me, but I actually think that you look like a real double-Jew," he said, and left the exercise yard with two friendly fingers on the visor of his cap.

And that was the end of the joviality. Now Marok began to speak, and what he had to say to us was anything but encouraging.

"From now on you belong to Block 19. This barracks is a world unto itself and has nothing to do with the rest of the camp. We have a print shop here. What you see there, you don't see. What you hear, you don't hear." He took a poster that Krebs handed him and read threateningly: "It is forbidden to make any attempt at getting in touch with the other prisoners in the camp. Violation thereof is punishable by death. Any attempt to sabotage the work is punishable by death. It is strictly forbidden to talk about the work, except during work hours."

Marok lowered the poster.

"Those are the most important paragraphs. The others you can study on the notices in the print shop. The barracks head will now take over."

When we followed Krebs into the block, none of us had any doubts that it was a death kommando we had ended up in.

"Take off your filthy zebra rags," said Krebs when we got into the barracks. "No, you are not headed for the ovens," he added sneeringly. "On the contrary, you are supposed to be smartened up. But first each one of you must take his turn on the scale over there, so that we can weigh your skeletons."

Emaciated and scarred from boils and beatings, we gathered near the scale. It was not necessary to use the heaviest weights for any of us. I for my part weighed 106 pounds. (The last time I had weighed myself—in a bathroom in Oslo—my weight was 156 pounds, and I was not troubled by any superfluous flab.) Now my arm was so thin that I could fit my hand around it and my knees were thicker than my thighs. The skin on my body was gray and disgusting. I avoided looking at myself.

The clothes we were handed were as nice as parade uniforms compared to those we had worn until now. The suits were shiny from wear, but not torn. Wide red stripes were painted on both trouser legs, and the jacket was decorated with crosses of the same color. We each got a cupboard, a food dish, a towel, and a bar of soap. Still, the bread knives and soup spoons were the most welcome. I had not owned anything of this sort since I had been at home in Norway.

Güting, the dwarf-like Stubendienst, stood and looked at us. I did not like his crooked smile, nor did I like the dirty hands with which he distributed our food.

When the other prisoners returned from the print shop, which was situated at the other end of the block, we made a renewed attempt at persuading them to tell us about their work. They shrugged their shoulders without answering.

Just an hour later we stood with Marok inside the mysterious print shop. With the iron bars and the dull windows, the ninety-eight-foot-long room resembled a kind of strange cage. The sharp electrical light glimmered on the complicated and well-kept machinery.

Marok picked up a piece of paper from the table.

"Does anyone know what this is?" he asked.

"It is a British note," said Max Blaustein.

"Correct. Can anyone see if it is genuine or false?"

No one could.

"We have beaten England militarily," Marok continued. "Now we are going to break the country's economy with these notes. They have dropped false bread-ration cards down to Germany from their planes; we will answer with these notes until inflation hits them like a tornado."

So it is a death kommando you have ended up in, I said to myself when I was lying in my bed that evening. *But were the work units in Monowitz any different? You are still alive, which you might not have been had you remained there. And the prisoners here appear to lead an existence reasonably fit for human beings—compared to the conditions in the Polish camps, at any rate.*

But the fact that I would ever become a "counterfeiter apprentice" was something I had never dreamt about.

Chapter 7

WE WERE WOKEN UP AT 6:00 THE NEXT MORNING. THAT DAY BREAKFAST consisted of a coffee-brown liquid. Roll-call for us thirty-three counterfeiters took place in the hall indoors, where there was ample room for us. No German appeared; only the barracks head checked to be sure that everyone was present. After the brief roll-call the foremen made sure that we were at work by 7:00 a.m. Nine different countries were represented in this work unit: Czechoslovakia, Poland, Germany, Serbia, Austria, Hungary, Russia, France, and Norway. All were Jews, and I was the only one from Scandinavia.

All newcomers were shown their apprentice work stations. I myself began my more than two-year-long career as an international counterfeiter at the table where paper was torn up. For several days I sat hour after hour and tore up paper with the help of a ruler. This work was important, as the British pound notes had three serrated sides at the time. During our apprenticeship we of course practiced on less-valuable paper.

The really precious paper came from a factory in western Germany. The sheets came in boxes that weighed between 220 and 330 pounds, and eight five- or ten-pound notes were made from each sheet. The large sheets were first cut up according to fixed watermarks. Then the paper was scrutinized by an expert in the field. The sheets that were not approved by his sensitive fingertips or his critical eye landed inevitably in the return box. The half-sheets that were accepted continued on to the printing machines, from where they went to the drying racks and then to the tearing and trimming process. When the notes had gone through these procedures, they seemed as new and perfect as if they had come straight from the Bank of England.

But that was exactly how they were *not* supposed to look. The notes had to have the appearance of being used, because none of them were dated later than 1939. Therefore, the print shop had experts to take care of this too. Not even the pinholes that all English money notes incur during their circulation were forgotten. The employees of English banks use pins instead of rubber bands when they bundle the notes together. The Bank of England in Block 19 had millions of pounds available at all times, despite the ever-growing demand in Berlin.

It was a Czech engineer in his late twenties who helped me take my first wobbling steps in my career as a criminal. He was from Prague and his name was Richard Luka.

"Why did they arrest you?" he asked during a "lesson."

"Why? Because of the persecution of the Jews, of course."

"The persecution of the Jews? You're not telling me that they arrested you even though you did nothing wrong? Nobody does that."

Only then did I understand that the question was meant to be ironic.

"They are the same wherever they are," he continued in a somewhat different tone of voice. "They came to get me just like that, four years ago. It wouldn't be for long, they assured me and my family. Four years have gone by since then. They almost killed me in Buchenwald. To be honest, I wasn't worth a penny when they began to look for printers in the camp."

"I thought you were an engineer," I said.

"Yes, I am, but had they wanted to get ahold of sword swallowers, I would have signed up as an accomplished showman. Anything was better than the inferno in Buchenwald. It all turned out all right, and now I'm sitting here preparing England's economic catastrophe. What are you looking at?"

"Oh, I was just sitting here wondering how you've managed to keep your nice horn-rimmed glasses."

"I had to; without them I would have been as helpless as a child."

"How long have you been doing this?" I asked carefully.

"Oh, about three months. The whole undertaking almost fell apart because we were unsuccessful in achieving a really first-class result. It was a nerve-wracking time. If they had discontinued the print shop, it wouldn't have been long before all of us would have ended up in the crematorium."

Neither Luka nor I noticed that the foreman Kurzweil had approached us.

"What did Luka tell you, Nachtstern? Speak up!"

I pointed at the paper I was working on. "I only asked him what would be the best way to hold the ruler."

Kurzweil grumbled and continued across the floor.

"You're getting the hang of it," whispered Luka. "Kurzweil is actually not that bad; he mostly makes a fuss to keep his job. But you must watch out for Marok and Weber. They can pester you to death with punishment drills for less than nothing."

"Who is Weber?" I whispered without looking up from my paper.

"An Oberscharführer who takes turns with Marok to guard us. You'll probably see him soon."

No sooner had Luka finished his sentence than a German fellow in his thirties, who bore the insignia SD, entered the print shop. He sauntered around the room and stared at the newcomers before he sat down at a table farthest away, near the end wall. Now and then he peeked up from the papers he was thumbing through and looked across the room with a watchful eye. He did not exactly look like a thug, but there was something about his eyes that suggested all sorts of things.

Luka did not say a word as long as Weber sat at the table. Only when Weber got up and went into a room at the opposite end of the print shop did he whisper: "Be careful; Weber is in a foul mood today. He will soon be back. He only went into the guardroom to fetch some cigarettes."

While I continued to tear up paper strips, I fantasized about lunch. I was so hungry that my stomach was screaming. Since everything else was so much better here than in the Polish camps, I assumed that the food had to be better too. Of course, we could not go by the little we had tasted here in the block, because it had only been tiny bits taken from the old prisoners' portions. Now that we were on the barracks' regular ration list, things would surely be different.

Lunch was a bitter disappointment. The soup consisted quite simply of stalks and grass, and some potato and tomato leaves. The mess had a terrible odor. I held my nose and swallowed the whole ration to ease the eternal ache below my chest.

"Did you hear what the Stubendienst-dwarf called this?" asked Schnapper from across the table. "Spinach, my foot. Had he said poached tar paper I might have believed him. But look—there's someone who does not spit into the trough. Did you ever see such an appetite?"

At the end of the table where the old prisoners sat, one of them, a heavy, bloated man, had a whole battery of soup dishes in front of him. He emptied one after the other with a voracious appetite. Not that he gulped the mess down; no, he used the spoon like a genuine count. I noticed that Luka was among those who had given him his dish.

When we sat again at the worktable in the print shop, I asked Luka who this man with the incredible appetite was. Marok was on guard duty now, and he was engrossed in a magazine that lay on the table.

"Oh, him," said Luka, shaking his head. "He is a strange character from Vienna. He insists that he's a journalist and an unqualified monarchist. He is half-Jewish and half-Christian, so he gets very insulted if you so much as insinuate that he is incarcerated here for the same reason as the rest of us. I actually believe he is convinced that the Germans arrested him because of his monarchist scribbling. Nonsense, of course. The only remarkable thing about this fellow is his grotesque appetite. We five Czechs here receive food parcels from relatives and friends now and then, and as long as they last, none of us touch the mess that Güting serves with his filthy hands. The monarchist idolizes us during that time, because he gets to eat our soup. He calls it a vegetable dish. The rest of us call it shit."

Josel sat directly in front of me and struggled with the paper and the ruler. Starved and weak as we were, all of us tended to nod off from time to time. Josel was the worst. If he was left alone, he could sleep standing up. Now I saw that his head was nodding. *This won't end well,* I said to myself. And it did not. Just as Josel's chin fell down toward his chest, the barracks head came ambling through the print shop. He stopped and looked at Josel for a while. Then he struck the table with the flat of his hand with a bang. Josel jumped up and began to tear up paper like mad.

"Are you tired?" asked Krebs.

Of course Josel let himself be fooled by the barracks chief's sympathetic voice and answered, "Yes."

"We're going to remedy that. Come with me, and I will make sure that you wake up."

Marok looked up from the dirty magazine he was reading as Krebs went out to the exercise yard with Josel.

"This will be half an hour of punishment drills," said Luka without looking up from the work.

"But has Krebs any authority here in the print shop?"

"Krebs does as he pleases in the entire barracks. Neither Marok nor Weber dare criticize him. They too have skeletons in their closets, and Krebs knows it. Wait until you have been here a while and you will soon understand."

Josel was dirty and totally exhausted when he came staggering back.

"Now I believe you'll stay awake," grumbled Krebs before he left the table. He lit a cigarette right in front of Marok's nose and went into another room.

There was no doubt that Krebs could take all kinds of liberties.

Marok got up and came strolling across the floor. It was obvious that he enjoyed the perfection of his own shapely and well-dressed body as it was reflected in the wan and hollow-cheeked faces at the machines and tables. Here and there Marok stopped to check our work. When he came to my table he remained standing. I did not look up, but I knew that he was staring at me. His knee-high boots shone like lacquered glass columns. I tore strip after strip from the paper sheet.

"You are too slow," he said, bending down over the table and pushing me away from the paper and the ruler. "This is how it should be done," he said, and tore a strip from the sheet. It tore in the middle.

"Yes, Herr Oberscharführer."

He looked at me stubbornly. He was the big boy in the class looking for a pretext to demonstrate the right of the strong, without finding a reason to do so. After all, I had learned something from the bitter experiences I had had in the other camps.

"Okay, continue." He removed a package of cigarettes from his pocket. "Here is a smoke for tonight," he said, and threw a cigarette on the table.

Luka peeked over his glasses after Marok, as he sauntered across the floor.

"You'll have to pay for that cigarette with a cuff on your ears at the first opportunity. His cigarettes never come cheap."

The subdued noise from the printing and numbering machines emphasized the somber atmosphere in this hidden print shop. I was happy when the workday was over.

Dinner that night consisted of a piece of bread and more of the soup from lunch.

The bread was supposed to be for breakfast the following day, but I bolted down both the soup and the bread. I was just as hungry as before when I had finished everything. Suddenly I caught sight of a small piece of bread that lay on the floor. It had to be Krebs who had lost it, because he was standing close to it and munching on a huge slice. I already knew that both he and Güting boldly helped themselves from the Czechs' packages when they arrived. I could not tear my eyes away from the piece of bread on the floor. It attracted my gaze like a magnet. *If only he wouldn't discover it,* I thought while my hands became clammy with tension. Krebs chewed and munched with an absent look on his face.

I could not sit still any longer; I had to move. It had not occurred to me to go over to Krebs, but the piece of bread drew me. I was only two steps away from Krebs when Güting called him. I pretended that I had lost something and bent down for the piece of bread. It burnt like fire in my hand before I reached my bunk. It was a piece of Czech bread. It was sheer bliss to have it in my mouth. My eyes filled with tears at the marvelous taste. It filled me with a pleasant buzz when I closed my eyes. I could not afford to swallow the bread, so I sucked it up through my palate. It took me home to my cozy studio apartment in Oslo, to friends and colleagues, to warmth and to parties and to women I had known well. It was not just a piece of bread that I enjoyed beyond all comprehension; it was a piece of the wonderful life I had once enjoyed, in a past as far away as eternity.

"Hey, look at the Norwegian. By God, I believe he's lying there, dreaming that he's at home in his snowy country."

It was Güting who stood at my bunk, grinning. I had an almost violent need to plant my fist into his slimy face.

"Just don't think that you'll get out of here alive, Your Honor," the fellow continued maliciously.

"But of course you will," I said.

"Yes, that's exactly what I aim to do," said Güting. "First of all, I'm half-Jewish, and secondly, I have a permanent promise from the highest authority."

Since I could not be bothered to make any further comments, he strolled over to the table where some prisoners were playing chess with chessmen they had managed to make themselves. Some of the fellows had even made card games from cardboard. It all looked so homey that I could hardly believe it was a group of doomed counterfeiters sitting there. And the most incredible thing was that I myself belonged to this group, and that I too was a small wheel in this amazing counterfeit machinery.

Would any of us survive this? It was unlikely. Why were only Jews chosen for this work?

Because the Germans intended to exterminate all of us, of course.

Chapter 8

THE FIRST SUNDAY WE EIGHT NEWCOMERS SPENT IN BLOCK 19, WE DID not see Marok or Weber until late in the morning. When they came rushing into the print shop they were in a boisterous mood, their faces flushed, their caps on the backs of their heads.

"Last night they must have whored and messed around something fierce with the generals' wives in Berlin," whispered Luka. "There is an abundance of wanton women in the city and few fit men, so they can probably pick and choose as much as they want. They do not have to worry about us; here, no one can get either in or out at night. But one day they are bound to talk too much when they are drunk, and that will be the end of them."

Marok sat down at one of the inspection tables, whistling. Weber continued into the guardroom.

"Soon you'll get to hear the block's world champion play the accordion. You are going to jump up from your chair when you hear what he plays—or rather, what he tries to play."

Just then Weber came out from the guardroom with a magnificent accordion in his hands. He opened the musical session with a false bellow that totally drowned out all other sounds in the print shop. Because of what Luka had said, I was prepared for almost anything with regard to the repertoire. But when I realized that it was the "Internationale" (communist anthem) the fellow was playing so intensely, I actually jumped up from the chair. True enough, his "recital" was so shrill that it would have caused any red flag to tear out of disgrace, but just to see and hear an

SS officer struggling with this melody with such determination made no sense at all.

Weber's face had turned completely red with the effort. He finally put down the accordion and flung himself into a chair at the table where his colleague Marok sat.

"How are you, Herbert?" he shouted. "I think the little admiral's wife did a good job of pumping you empty, right? Was she good, you dog?"

Marok leaned back in the chair with a blissful grunt. "Oh, yes. She was absolutely the most luscious woman I've ever bedded. I almost passed out when she started in earnest. But it's no use for you to go and see her; you can save yourself the trouble, Heinz."

"Take it easy, Herbert," slurred Weber, getting up. "I know that you are number one on the women's wish list," he added enviously before he staggered into the guardroom.

Marok walked through the print shop. He stopped for a moment at the closest printing machine.

"Now you probably overheard something that made you itch, fellows? You would have liked to take part in the fun last night, I think. But don't stand there and drool, or else your work will be sloppy. Can I have a look at those notes? Well, they will probably pass."

"He does not know any more about it than a cow," said Luka.

Marok strutted restlessly back and forth on the floor. Suddenly he turned on his heels.

"Pack up!" he called. "Everybody to the bathroom. Kurzweil will make sure that all notes and all paper are put away in the cupboard. Krebs will go through every man's pockets. No one must have even a trace of paper on him when we leave here. Those who make the slightest attempt at getting in touch with other prisoners will be shot in the head. Get started."

Under Marok's supervision Krebs carried out a thorough search of our pockets. But no one thought of the caps or the towels. Everything was so true to form in this circus.

When, led by Krebs, we walked out through the gate in the board fence, Marok had already ensured that the other prisoners in the camp were at least a hundred feet away from us. In the bathroom there was of course no one but us from Block 19, as long as we were there. It was pleasant to get washed under the showers, until Marok began to display his special form of humor. We newcomers thought all was well till he began aiming at us with an ice-cold water hose. He shouted and laughed when he saw us turn and twist. It was the worst for those who tried to wriggle away from the damned water stream. He practically impaled them on the ice-cold spear.

"Stand still—it's not so bad," he gasped happily when he had hit his man.

There was no choice but to let him continue with his game until he got tired of it. But when he had thrown the water hose aside, he caught sight of a bandage that lay on the floor.

"Who threw away this filth?"

No one answered.

"Is that so? The one who did it will have one minute to think it over."

The minute went by without anyone coming forward.

"Well, then, everybody will have to take the consequences. Get dressed on the double. Krebs will bring you over to the block. Get going."

"Now you have something to look forward to," sneered Krebs, hassling us while we got dressed.

When we arrived in our exercise yard, Marok was squirting water all over the narrow place.

"I thought you should be allowed to exercise a bit after your showers, gentlemen," he chuckled boisterously. "Nothing is as healthy as some quick exercise after a refreshing shower. But I do not want you to breathe in any dust, and that is the reason why I've sprayed the place with a little water. Now I think it is enough."

And it was enough, that's for sure.

When he had driven us for fifteen minutes with "Run! Lie down! Get up! Lie down! Hop! Bend your knees!" we looked anything but freshly showered. Once he saw that we had become thoroughly dirty, he waved nonchalantly with his white gloves.

"I assume that you have learned to take care of your bandages now. But since I have started to teach you good manners anyhow, I might as well extend the program a bit. All newcomers are to stand eighty feet away from me and ask to be allowed to go to the toilet. Of course, in German—perfect German. I am tired of hearing you ruin the German language."

One after another we newcomers had to stand far away from him and call out: "Herr Oberscharführer, may I be excused?"

After many corrections, everyone except Josel managed to get through the carefully chosen language test. Poor Josel twitched and stuttered until he had no voice left. But Marok's inventive head was not empty yet. Now he asked that all foreigners repeat this request in their respective mother tongues.

"But do not try to fool me, gentlemen. I have a good command of practically all European languages."

During the "examination," Marok carried on and pretended that he understood what each of the approximately thirty men said in nine different languages.

When it was Luka's turn, he said: "We're five Czechs here. If you like, I can speak Italian, so you won't have to hear so many repeat the request—in Czech, I mean."

Marok gesticulated generously with his gloves.

"Go ahead, sir; I understand Italian just as well as Czech."

Luka said something or other in Italian.

"Well, well," praised Marok condescendingly, "that wasn't bad at all."

"He should only know what I really said," whispered Luka.

"Let me hear you, Norwegian. I know your Viking language better than you think."

"Is that so?" I said. When I realized that he did not understand a single word, I exploded with a violent need to abuse this stupid lout, and said in a loud voice: "Herr Oberscharführer, you are a damned shithead. I thank you for the word." Fear almost strangled me the minute I had said it, but when he swallowed my remark, I was filled with pleasure. I knew that thinking of the "damned shithead" would make life easier to bear for a long time to come.

After harassing us Marok was in a great mood.

"Okay, men, I am not unreasonable if you'd only behave properly. Now you can go inside and take it easy. You will not have to work anymore today."

His benevolence did not limit itself to giving us the rest of the day off. While we tried as best we could to scrub the dirt off our bodies, he came into our room with a fistful of cigarettes.

"Here, have something for a smoke," he said in a friendly manner. He put the cigarettes on the table and went on his way with a nod à la Krüger.

"I wish I'd met this fellow when I was a free man and still had my strength," said Schnapper bitterly behind me. I was startled because these were my own thoughts put into words. "He wouldn't have been such a success with women after such an encounter," Schnapper added, grumbling.

We shared the cigarettes as best we could when we sat down to wait for our Sunday dinner, which as usual consisted of potatoes and sour cabbage soup. The potatoes were far better than those we were given in the other camps, but the soup was worse, if possible.

Later in the day we played cards or chess or talked together as usual. Luka told us about his love affairs in many countries. The stories were perhaps not the healthiest for a group of incarcerated men, but no one moved away from the inspired storyteller for this reason. He was in the middle of a more than piquant story from Turkey when Krebs came in with a confused expression on his face.

"You can be dead sure that something is about to happen to Marok and Weber. By the way, I have regards for you from a woman in Berlin, Bober."

The typographer Bober looked questioningly at the barracks head. "This is wild talk, Krebs; what the devil do you mean with this nonsense?" Bober was the only one who allowed himself to speak his mind to the barracks chief.

"So help me God, it's not nonsense. The phone rang in the guardroom ten minutes ago. I picked it up as I usually do when both Marok and Weber are away. Of course it was a woman. When I told her that neither Marok nor Weber was here, she asked me if it was Krebs she was talking to. I almost hit the ceiling, as you can imagine. I did not say yes or no. Oh yes, she knew about me, she slurred. But when she said 'Give my regards to Bober,' I thought it advisable to hang up."

Then it suddenly dawned on Bober. "It's that damned picture, Krebs," he blurted out.

"What picture?" Güting asked curiously.

"The one Marok took of Krebs and me in uniform jackets and steel helmets. He gave each of us a package of cigarettes for letting him photograph us in SS uniform. Now, of course, he's shown the picture to this woman and told her our names. The man can't be all there."

"I think their drinking and these stories about women will put them against the wall before they have any inkling," said Krebs. "Just to take that kind of a picture is probably quite enough—not to mention the folly of giving these women the phone number of this place. You can be damned sure that the Gestapo listens to every single phone conversation. I hope you won't get into hot water because of this idiotic picture, Bober."

"Don't be silly," said Bober coldly. "I am a prisoner here, the same as you, even if you are a barracks head. The prisoner who refuses to obey orders from a German officer is shot as an agitator. Just take it easy, Krebs; they are not going to kill us because of this photograph. The fact that they will do it sooner or later anyhow is another matter."

Bober's last remark touched upon something the prisoners rarely mentioned but brooded over every day.

We played cards haphazardly, and even a magician at the chessboard like the mathematician Tubler made huge blunders with the chess pieces. Then the words began, and questions were asked among the men; dangerous and pent-up thoughts came to the surface.

Luka was playing against Tubler.

"What do you think about this?" he asked in a low voice as he fiddled nervously with a chess piece.

Tubler suddenly became completely calm. He spoke loudly enough for everyone to hear him when he answered Luka. "It doesn't do any of us any good to discuss this, Luka. Do you remember the inferno in the stone quarries and all those who were beaten to death, or who worked themselves to death there? Neither you nor I would be alive today if we hadn't been brought to this place. Here we live under a roof and we don't have to watch people freeze to death or collapse from exhaustion all around us. We must put up with beatings and punishment drills, but how can this be compared to the mass murders by the kapos and foremen in the other camps?

"True, we're facing an uncertain fate, but so are millions and millions of other people. Luka, let's make the best of the situation we're in. It serves no purpose to discuss a future that none of us knows anything about. When all is said and done, we're all tiny pieces on life's large chessboard. But watch out now, Luka, or else I'll checkmate you on the little board that is between us."

All around these two, cards were gathered together and chess pieces set up again. And the talk went on like before—or at least, it seemed to.

⁓

But when we had gone to bed that night I could hear twenty-two-year-old Perez Zimmermann sobbing under his blanket. The words *gas chamber* could constantly be heard in his otherwise-unintelligible stream of words. I leaned toward his bunk.

"Don't think of it, Perez. Try to sleep."

"I can't, Moritz," he moaned, and drew himself up on his elbow. "I have lived too long on the threshold of the gas chamber. Would you listen to me?"

"I'll listen, Perez."

"While I was in Birkenau, the camp was so overcrowded for a while that they sent masses of prisoners to the gas chambers whether they were Musselmänner or not. During the morning roll-call everybody shook with fear that their numbers would be called up. I escaped for a long time, but then one terrible morning I heard my number called up. I realized what it meant and had only one thought in my head—to hide so that the barracks head would not catch me.

"I knew there was a pile of corpses somewhere in the camp—prisoners who had died from the cold or had been beaten to death. I crept over there and lay down in the pile. While I lay there I heard the barracks chief run around in the camp, calling out my number. I was deathly afraid that it would occur to him to look for me in the pile of corpses, but I was just as afraid that the trucks would come to bring the bodies to the crematorium. Fortunately none came that day for one or another reason. Perhaps the ovens could not absorb any more corpses just then.

"At night I slipped half-frozen into another block; of course, I didn't dare go to mine. I was discovered and the barracks head threatened me, so I had to tell him everything. 'Which block do you belong to?' he asked afterwards. When I told him, he hit his thighs and laughed. 'You can stay here,' he said. 'I've wanted to play a trick on that damned louse for a long time.'

"When I realized that the man really meant what he said, I embraced his knees and cried hysterically with gratitude. I did well in that block, but I had a constant fear of being discovered. And one day I was. The old barracks head came into the block and by sheer chance caught sight of me. I'll never forget how his brutal face lit up with wicked pleasure when he recognized me. Just when he was about to drag me away with him, my new barracks chief came into the block. He was furious. He was taller and much bigger and stronger than the other one. 'Where do you think you are, you louse?' he shouted. 'If you don't leave here in a second, I will make mincemeat out of you. Since Perez has managed to fool you, by God I will make sure that he is safe in this block. In a few days he will become Stubendienst, just so you know it. Hurry up and get out, you snail!'"

Perez was silent for a while before he continued: "I became Stubendienst in the block. I did well and felt protected from the gas chambers, for the first time in several years—until they sent me to this eternally damned print shop."

I put my hands on his shoulders.

"Do not look at the dark side of the situation, Perez. Let us make the best of it, as Tubler says. You'll see that one day we'll all be free again."

I myself heard that my words sounded less than convincing.

Chapter 9

Josel was quite a sight as he strutted through the print shop in his white jacket and white paper hat. He barely looked at those of us who worked at the tables and machines. He had been appointed Stubendienstassistent (room supervisor's assistant) and Marok's private orderly. The reason for these appointments was not that he had excelled at the work in the print shop. In truth, the contrary was probably the case. The connection he had had with a print shop before he came to Block 19 had most likely consisted of wielding a broom. But Josel was a kind and pleasant boy who deserved to survive the deathtrap of Block 19 just as much as anybody else.

"Look at Josel," said Luka. "God help me, now he's sleeping with his nose down inside a boot."

Josel was sitting on a stool near the guardroom, polishing Marok's boots. At least, that is what he was supposed to be doing, but he had been overcome by his constant need to nod off. He was sitting with both arms around the tall leg of the boot, his face supported by the boot opening. It looked so funny that I had to pull myself together not to laugh out loud.

Of course Marok had to arrive at exactly that moment. Others could commit a blunder ten times in a row without being discovered. If Josel, who was always unlucky, made the same stupid mistake as them just once, he was caught red-handed.

Marok looked at the poor sinner for a while. Then he hit Josel across the neck with his gloves. Josel's round face flew like a bullet out of the mouth of the black-boot cannon, and his hand with the polishing cloth moved like a twirling drumstick.

"Are you sleeping again, Josel? You had better come with me outside to the exercise yard. Nothing is as stimulating as a quick run outside in the fresh air."

Ten minutes later Josel came back, breathing heavily. The boot was polished in no time.

We did not see anything of Marok again until he came into the print shop together with Krüger, "the old man," as the two Oberscharführers called him when he was not around.

Krüger said hello and nodded to everybody as usual when he passed them. At Kahn's table—Kahn screened the notes—he remained standing for quite a while, talking to him. For one reason or another he had developed a soft spot for him. Now he took a pound note from the sorting table and held it up.

"Gentlemen," he said in a loud voice, brandishing the note. "Through you, we will cause England to become bankrupt. These notes are one of the most important weapons we have. When the war is over you'll all receive your well-deserved reward."

"When you hear and see the man talk like this, you would think he was serious," I whispered to Luka.

"Yes, he is an unusually talented actor. Anyway, he seems serious enough with his 'well-deserved reward' talk."

"Take it easy, Luka; they won't win this war any more than they won the last one."

"How does this help us here? Damn it, don't talk about it anymore."

I regretted bitterly what I had said, not only because of Luka's fear, but because I had the same fear myself, which came over me at the slightest carelessness on my part or that of others. I looked up from my work and found something else to think about. I started to sweat. Krüger and Marok were watching me while they talked together. They could not possibly have heard what Luka and I had said to each other, but it was dangerous enough if they saw that we talked together at all.

"My best wishes for continued good work, gentlemen," called Krüger like a kindly school superintendent after finishing his inspection.

Now Marok will appear at this table any minute, I thought when the old man had left. And indeed, he was already on his way. I was on tenterhooks.

"Come with me, Nachtstern. You will start working in the engraving workshop."

Relieved and surprised, I followed him.

Besides the engraver, Cytrin, typesetter Bober also worked in the large engraving workshop. Krebs was there when we came in.

"Here's somebody who will help you," said Marok.

Cytrin looked at me sullenly. "What can you do?" he asked. It was easy to see that he could not have cared less about getting any help. "Show me your tricks." He threw me a sheet of zinc and an engraving tool.

I did the best I could, but after all, I was not an engraver.

"Hmmph," grunted Cytrin when he saw my output. He looked at Marok. "The man cannot do anything."

"I'm not an engraver, and I've never passed myself off to be one either," I said. "Give me a cliché [a printing plate cast from movable type, also known as a stereotype]. That is my field."

"A cliché? You can have heaps of clichés, man. Cut this one then, if you can."

Marok and Krebs bent over me curiously while I worked with a magnifying glass and an engraving tool. Krebs took the cliché out of my hand when I was finished.

"Look at this, old man," he said to Cytrin. "This is how it's done. This is different from the mincemeat you serve."

Krebs bore a grudge against Cytrin, and now he undoubtedly thought this was an opportunity to let him have it. For me, who would be working with the engraver, this scene was anything but comfortable. I knew all too well how an old prisoner could make the life of a newcomer he did not like unpleasant. I also knew that Marok and Weber had taken a liking to Cytrin.

When Marok and Krebs had left, Cytrin lit a cigarette to mark the difference between the two of us.

"Continue with your cliché," he grumbled, without looking up from what he was doing.

"Hello, Norwegian," called Bober. "Come here and give me a hand."

"You have to speak to the master," I replied. It was important to be diplomatic if I did not want to get into serious trouble with Cytrin.

"Just go ahead," said Cytrin gruffly, but obviously flattered.

"Look at this," Bober said, handing me a piece of paper when I got to the typesetter case. "Is this right?"

To my surprise I saw that he was printing Norwegian songs—*"Kjerringa med staven"* ("The Woman with the Stick") and several other well-known Norwegian folk songs.

"Who is this for?"

"For the Norwegian prisoners outside in the camp. They are the really prominent prisoners, you see. But what kind of strange letters do you use up there in your polar bear country?" He pointed at an "å" in the hand-written manuscript. "I don't have such an odd letter."

I explained to him that it was quite acceptable to use a double "a" instead.

I looked at his table. "You seem to be printing all sorts of things here."

"Oh yes. Would you like some tickets for the whorehouse outside in the camp? I print those too. Anyhow, I print all kinds of notices and post-ers. The canteen is my best business connection—they pay with tobacco. As you must have seen, I smoke when and where it suits me. But then, I have been incarcerated since 1937."

Cytrin was actually talkative when I came back to him. Among other things we touched upon the subject of Güting, the Stubendienst.

"He's a dirty sewer rat," he said angrily. "He only thinks of devilry all day long. Watch out for him, Norwegian."

"I have already been exposed to his big mouth. The first day I was here, he told me that no one but him would get out of here alive." It was the first time I had mentioned this to anyone.

"What?" Cytrin looked at me, frightened.

I bit my tongue. *Why the hell had I said that?* To cover my words, I added: "That's just his way of being funny."

"The miserable snake," snarled Cytrin. "I hope that a tough piece of rope will stop his poisonous big mouth one day." The day would come when his wish was fulfilled.

Cytrin was no longer talkative. He smoked incessantly as he bent over his work. Marok and Weber gave him the cigarettes for all the fine metalwork he did for them. Suddenly I heard him mumble, "No, none of us will get out of here alive."

I promised myself that from that point on, I would watch my big mouth.

We sat for more than two hours without saying anything.

Then he asked me to pick up something in the print shop. As soon as I got there I noticed that something had happened. It was somehow in the air, but I did not find out what it was until I passed one of the numbering machines. Marok was standing there and staring at Shurak, who was pale as a ghost. The arm of the machine was broken.

I did not dare to stop. I picked up what I had come to collect and went back to the engraving workshop.

"What the hell is wrong with you?" Bober asked, looking at me searchingly. "You look as if you had met your own cremated ghost."

"Shurak broke the arm of the numbering machine."

"So what? Maybe you think that he will be shot for sabotage? Take it easy. An accident can happen here just like in any other print shop. No one would suspect Shurak of anything as reckless as destroying a machine.

And even if someone did, nothing would happen—not the first time, anyhow. What would be the consequence if one of us were shot because of an accident? Mutiny, man. They would not risk that. Of course they could exterminate every one of us, but what would happen to the print shop then? What about the millions with which they plan to destroy the British economy? Do you believe that Krüger would run the risk of causing so much as one small feather of his beloved golden goose to be bent? Neither would Marok or Weber. Because the day this print shop is discontinued, it is off to the front for them."

"But one day the powers that be in Berlin will think they have enough pound notes," said Cytrin gloomily.

Bober shrugged his shoulders.

"That's a different story. The question won't arise soon, so don't lose any sleep over it. 'It's a long way to Tipperary,' as the song from the last war goes. Much can happen before Hitler gets there."

I thought of what Bober had said while I cut the pound cliché. There was a lot of truth in his words. What if mutiny broke out in the block? Of course they could get new people and train them. But it would take a long time, and time was probably of the essence for them. Who else could teach the newcomers if they liquidated the old experts who were here? Bober knew what he was talking about. He knew what to expect from people. He knew them so well that he played one against the other when it suited him. Our guards meted out cuffs on the ears in abundance when they were in the mood, but they never touched Bober. He worked and smoked and answered them as he pleased. The only time they got the better of him was when they ordered everybody outside for punishment drills according to the principle of "all for one and one for all."

Cytrin looked up.

"Yes, Bober is right; it *is* a long way to Tipperary, and much can happen before they get there. If only the riffraff will be defeated quickly enough, maybe we'll have a chance in this block too. In the meantime, we can always endure sitting here. Speaking of sitting, have you ever been in a real *Sitzenkommando* [sitting detail]? I have. Before I got here, I was in a camp where the prisoners occasionally were ordered to sit on the floor for twenty-four hours. It sounds easy enough, but just try it. God help the poor soul who tried to straighten out his crossed legs. He pulled them back quickly, I can tell you that."

I wanted to ask about something, but just as I opened my mouth, it was as if my ear passage and eardrum were blown into my head.

Weber stood right behind me with a smoking pistol in his hand.

He had fired close to my ear. The bullet had hit the wall behind Cytrin. "I think you will stop talking now."

I thought I heard the words more than I actually did.

Cytrin sneered and laughed to please Weber, but there was more fear than joy in his laughter. When Weber was gone he glanced several times at the bullet hole in the wall behind him.

I felt the noise of the gun in my head all day.

Chapter 10

"Good morning, gentlemen!" Krüger smiled and nodded more cheerfully than ever before. He pulled a pound note from his pocket and waved it proudly in the air.

"Look at this, gentlemen: It has been through the English banks and accepted as genuine. Congratulations on your excellent work! I am proud of you. Now we can safely go ahead in earnest. We are going to extend our business. Well, gentlemen, as a small appreciation for work well done, I have ordered that a loudspeaker be installed in the workshops. I mean, from the guardroom's radio, so that you can hear the news and listen to a bit of music. Good-bye, gentlemen."

"One would think he'd been appointed chief of the Bank of England already," said Bober drily.

Weber came in a half-hour later. "Hey, Bober, you can do all sorts of things, right?"

"That's right."

"Excellent. Now you can show us what you know about radios. Come with me. Loudspeakers are to be installed both here and in the print shop. You can start here."

When Bober came back he was carrying cables and other radio paraphernalia.

"Hmmph . . . you won't be able to do this," said Cytrin grumpily.

"Oh yes, old man," sneered Bober. "I can even pump the bile out of you, but that I won't do. It suits you too well."

Just then Weber appeared in the door with an enthusiastic expression on his face. He and Bober whispered together for a while. Then Weber disappeared and Bober began to work feverishly with his paraphernalia. Cytrin and I did not understand anything of what was going on, but the sly smile at the corner of Bober's mouth revealed that something special was afoot.

"He's planning some mischief, you can depend on that," grumbled Cytrin, while he kept an eye on Bober.

"If so, it was Weber's idea," I said.

Bober's hands moved like those of a magician. Suddenly he held a microphone in front of his mouth and spoke in a loud voice: "This is England. It has long been known in informed circles that counterfeit pound notes are circulating in this country and elsewhere, and it has been determined that the counterfeit notes are made in Germany. Everything indicates that the big counterfeit workshop is located in Sachsenhausen. We also know the names of the two most prominent counterfeiters: Leo Krebs and Hans Kurzweil."

The whole scene was so crazy that I was dumbfounded. I looked at Cytrin. He too was speechless. But suddenly he grabbed the gray wisps of his hair with his bent fingers and moaned out loud: "Stop, Bober, for God's sake! You see that the window is open. Someone will hear you outside in the camp." Cytrin was on the brink of hysterics.

"This is England," continued Bober, without interruption.

Then Weber arrived. His face was flushed with laughter.

"Bravo, Bober," he hiccuped. "You did it beau-beautifully. You should have seen Krebs's and Kurzweil's faces when your announcement came over the radio in the guardroom. Both looked as if they could already feel the rope around their necks. And Marok almost fell out of his chair. He threw the inkwell at me when he realized that it was I who was behind this upsetting item on the program. Ho-ho, I haven't had so much fun in years. You were brilliant, Bober."

Bober sneered.

"Yes, by God, it would have been fun to see their faces." And then he continued with the loudspeaker installation.

Cytrin was so upset that he could hardly hold the engraving tool. "Sometimes I wonder if this is not a regular madhouse that we're locked up in," he said. "This note printing is perhaps something they've invented to make us go completely mad."

"Don't be silly," said Bober without stopping his work. "We're all more or less crazy, but you can bet your life that the printing of these notes is serious business."

"More or less crazy, you certainly are," Cytrin interrupted him angrily. "By God, you are the craziest of them all. You stand and shout at the open window that a counterfeit workshop is located in Sachsenhausen. Even if this block is fenced in and wrapped up in barbed wire, there are people only a few feet away. Or do you perhaps think that the iron bars in front of the windows also lock in the sound?"

Bober struck his forehead and pretended to be frantic. "What have I done? Tonight the English bombers will surely come and squirt mud on my beloved friend Cytrin's worktable."

Cytrin thrust the engraving tool into the table so it stood upright.

The door opened. Krebs and the foreman Kurzweil came in. Kurzweil was still pale.

Bober nodded pleasantly to them. "It's so nice to see you gentlemen in these parts. To what do we owe this honor?"

Krebs looked up at the cable that Bober had installed on the ceiling. "Oh, we just followed a small wire—a clue, so to speak."

"That's exciting," said Bober with affected curiosity. "You don't say that a crime has been committed in the palace?"

Krebs nodded seriously.

"Unfortunately, yes. Our friend Kurzweil here has been exposed to a brutal attack. He barely survived it."

"Oh, don't stand there and pretend that you were not terrified yourself," grumbled Kurzweil.

"What do I hear, Kurzweil?" Bober asked sympathetically. "That you, a man suffering so badly from anxiety, have been so mistreated? Swallow three times without breathing and you'll see that you'll feel better."

Now Kurzweil could no longer control himself. "Go to hell, you miserable bucket of filth!" he screamed, and left.

Even old Cytrin had to laugh.

Krebs told how the whole incident had come about. He and Kurzweil had been called by Marok to help him with a report. While they were busy, Weber came into the guardroom. They had seen him fumble with the radio, but no one found this suspicious. Then he went out and was away for a while. When he came back he sat down holding a magazine until the radio suddenly began to talk gibberish. As mentioned, Kurzweil almost suffered a stroke from fear and Marok nearly fell down.

"And you?" teased Bober. "I could swear that you had goose bumps all over your body."

"Nonsense," said Krebs, laughing. But the laughter sounded quite forced. "Maybe I was a bit startled in the beginning, but then I recognized your voice."

"I did wonder about that ...," murmured Bober, and cut a cable.

Cytrin sneered maliciously.

"Why the hell are you grinning, you crooked goat?" Krebs stared hard at Cytrin. "If you don't watch yourself, you'll soon discover that you're not irreplaceable."

A few days later a new man arrived in the block.

Krebs came into the mess hall with him. He was a ragged and exhausted man in his sixties. Under his arm he carried a huge dirty bundle.

"Hello, folks!" Krebs raised his hands like a circus announcer. "May I present the famous factory owner and paper specialist, Arthur Springer, from Belgrade."

The newcomer put his bundle on the floor and greeted us by bowing politely and very seriously. "I am happy to make your acquaintance," he said in flawless German.

Güting began to roar with laughter.

Krebs raised his hands again. "As you can see, the factory owner has brought his party clothes." He pushed the newcomer hard in the side. "Okay, old man, show your finery. Hurry up, damn it."

Scared and confused, Springer began to remove one rag after another from the bundle. Eventually its entire contents lay at Krebs's feet.

"Did you ever see anything like it?" Krebs guffawed and kicked the rag pile. "Now take off the rags you are wearing, old man. I'll give you a new suit, and then you'll be the guest of honor at the dinner table."

Springer handled the "new" clothes lovingly while he got dressed. He bowed politely to the right and to the left before he sat down at the table. He was unable to swallow much of the horrid soup.

"I came straight from the hospital, so I don't have much of an appetite," he said apologetically.

"Hospital?" asked Schnapper, surprised. "How long were you there?"

"More than three weeks. The staff was very capable there."

Schnapper hit the table with the spoon handle. "Did you hear that, folks? Here is a Jew who has been in a real hospital for more than three weeks. He was even treated well there, he says. The man must be a genius."

Springer looked almost fearfully at Schnapper.

"No, for goodness' sake, don't say such a thing. I know a little about paper, that is all. And the barracks head only joked when he called me a factory owner. I have never owned a single share in any factory at all."

"I could swear that the bum is a rag picker by profession," said Güting sarcastically.

"You are referring to the bundle I brought. Yes, I fully understand that this must seem ridiculous in a place like this. But before I was admitted to the excellent hospital, I was in a camp where such rags meant a lot. And I was sure that I'd be sent back there when I was released."

"You obviously think you've come to paradise," sneered Güting.

"Now I think you should shut your mouth, Güting," said Bober.

Güting glowered at Bober, but he left the newcomer alone.

———

Just before we went back to work after the lunch break, Krüger came in to see us.

"Don't get up, gentlemen, and don't extinguish your cigarettes on my account." He went straight to the newcomer and held out his hand. "I am Sturmbannführer Krüger. I want to welcome you, Mr. Springer."

The newcomer's reply was polite but formal.

"I would like to show you the print shop," continued Krüger in the same, almost respectful tone of voice. "This way, my friend." When they got to the door, he let Springer go first.

Luka grabbed me by the arm.

"That man frightens me more than ten Maroks and Webers put together. Did you see how he playacted in front of the newcomer? One would think that it was he who was the prisoner and the other one the chief."

"What do you think of the newcomer?"

"A piece of precious metal that has landed in a scrap-metal pile. Not even our genius of an actor, Krüger, is able to deceive this man."

Kurzweil came running.

"Everybody back to work. Get on your feet." He shoved the men closest to him out through the door. He was always hysterical when Krüger was nearby.

I dreaded going back to the engraving workshop. My eyes hurt and my head throbbed. It is strenuous working ten hours a day with a magnifying glass and an engraving tool. I reenergized myself by thinking of the cement-carrying in Monowitz. This always helped me when I started thinking that life in Block 19 was awful.

—❦—

In the evening the newcomer and I sat next to each other and wrote letters. It was the first letter I was allowed to send while in prison. As I had no relatives to write to in Norway, I wrote to my old friend Asbjørn. If I had followed his advice and stayed with him that fateful Monday morning, I would perhaps be safe now. But it served no purpose to brood over this. Of course we had to write that we were doing well in all respects, and it was strictly forbidden to ask for food. I got around this ban by thanking him for a letter and a food parcel I had never received. If it worked, it worked. Both Marok and Weber knew full well that nothing had ever been sent to me from Norway. The question was only if they decided to let the letter pass.

"*Achtung!*"

Marok came sauntering in, dressed in his best clothes and with a swagger stick in one hand and white gloves in the other. He stopped in front of Springer and me.

"The gentlemen are writing letters, I see. Let me have a look at it."

He pointed nonchalantly with his stick at Springer's letter. Springer handed him the letter. As he read, Marok tapped his stick against his shiny boots.

"You are a bit absentminded, my friend. You're forgetting something very important. Listen up: You say that you have been moved to Sachsenhausen and that you are much better off here than in the other camps. Oh yes, and then you write that you work in a print shop, right?"

"Yes, Herr Oberscharführer."

"Exactly. But don't you realize that you have forgotten to tell the most important part? It isn't right to tease people this way. Imagine how curious they will be when they find out about this print shop. They will ask each other what old Springer could possibly be printing in Sachsenhausen. It isn't enough if you tell your friends that you are in a print shop. You must tell them what we print here—that we produce pound notes en masse." Marok tore up the letter slowly. Then he pointed at my letter.

I felt my skin tingle while he read it. It meant so very much to me to get in touch with someone at home in Norway. He only looked through it quickly.

"It can pass." He handed my letter to Krebs, who stood behind him. "Put it on my desk. The newcomer has to wait until he can control his pen. Anyway, it is good for him to wait just as long as other newcomers for permission to write. So long. Weber and I are off to Berlin tonight."

Springer looked neither disappointed nor bitter. He just shrugged his shoulders and sat down.

Chapter 11

THE PRINTING MACHINES HUMMED AND WORKED. IN THE BLOCK'S "vault," the piles of five- and ten-pound notes grew daily. Our counterfeit group became more precise and efficient in our shady trade. There was less and less waste, and the strict chief inspector in Berlin very rarely found a note that was not absolutely perfect. Krüger, ever friendly, visited us more or less regularly. When he nodded his good-bye, his huge leather briefcase was bursting with bundles of notes, ready to be used.

As usual, Marok and Weber played havoc with us in the camp and with the women in Berlin. They returned from their escapades in Berlin half or completely drunk, and they were never stingy with the details when they described their most intimate experiences with the sex-starved women there. One night, when intoxicated, Marok began to fight with Krebs, which is something he should not have attempted because Krebs was an old wrestler. The result was that the Adonis had one arm in a sling for quite a while. He could not avenge himself on Krebs for obvious reasons. Instead, we prisoners had to bear the brunt with punishment drills and cuffs on the ears at the most unpredictable times of the day. On a different occasion he came weaving into the mess hall with a machine gun in his hands. When he fired, the mechanism got stuck and a whole series of shots hit the wall.

A prisoner from the camp, who was just outside the board fence, was shot in the arm. But Block 19 was a separate world, where Marok and Weber were the absolute rulers when Krüger was in Berlin. Not even the camp commandant in Sachsenhausen could come through the gate without special permission.

Because of our sedentary work we gained weight, despite the awful food. We were in poor shape though, because the weight gain consisted mainly of water. Our legs were thick like logs. At night we slept with our legs elevated so that they should be relatively steady the following day.

The days became longer and spring was in the air. In our free time we were allowed to walk outside in our narrow exercise yard.

I waited for a letter like a kid waited for Christmas Eve. Many weeks had gone by since I had written to Asbjørn. Had he received the letter, or had it gone astray? Maybe the censorship in Norway had stopped it. Asbjørn might have been arrested too. I knew that he was a member of the resistance movement.

I fantasized and dreamt about the letter. Now the postman was dropping it into Asbjørn's postbox on Dælenggata. Now Asbjørn was picking it up. I could see him looking at the envelope and turning it around before he recognized my handwriting. Then he called out to his wife that a letter from me had arrived. They read it together and were happy that I was alive. Maybe they wrote to me the same day.

I reproached myself for being so silly. *Who would believe that you are a forty-year-old man?* But the thoughts came back again and again.

And then the longed-for letter actually arrived one day. When I had it in my hands I was so happy and grateful that my eyes stung. Everything was well at Asbjørn's. Of course, there was not much he dared to write, but I read between the lines that he believed in a favorable outcome to the war. I read the letter over and over again, and each time I fantasized about something else between the lines, especially about the parcel he said that he had sent through the Red Cross. Would I really receive the parcel? I did not dare to believe it.

The letter went from one man to the other, as did all letters that came to our block. But this letter really created a stir. Glantzer was the first who got ahold of it. He jumped up from the stool and waved his arms and the letter like a signalman in distress.

"Fellows," he roared. "Moritz is getting a Red Cross parcel."

If he had said that I would be receiving a live glamour girl by post, it would not have come close to the effect that the news of the Red Cross parcel had. The silence that followed the announcement was almost solemn. Then the men crowded around Glantzer and the letter.

I only sat there open-mouthed.

Luka came over to my bunk and began fooling around.

"Sahib," he said, and bowed like an Oriental.

This just made me angry. "What kind of nonsense is this, Luka? Why do the men carry on like maniacs? Many parcels have come to this block before; you Czechs get parcels quite often."

Luka looked at me as if I were a twelve-year-old Neanderthal.

"Don't tell me that you don't know what a Red Cross parcel is? A Red Cross parcel is paradise itself. From now on you'll be pursued and idolized, just wait and see."

"*Achtung!*" shouted Krebs in the doorway. Next to him stood—who was it? The man wore the SD uniform, but it was neither Marok nor Weber. His cap was far down on his forehead, and he held his gloves in front of his mouth, so not much of his face was visible.

"A new problem," whispered Luka.

"Hands up!" ordered the man. His voice was brutal.

Everybody dropped what they had in their hands and put them up. We looked as if we were standing in front of a camera in a gangster film.

"Bend your knees! Hop!"

We hopped and bumped against each other in the narrow space like wounded hares. Stools and footstools turned over and created a wild confusion in the idiotic dance. Josel fell down and ended up sitting in a cracked stool as if on a chamber pot.

"Lie down!"

We lay tumbled together on the floor, breathing heavily.

Krebs stood bent over with laughter, and the SD officer hit his knees and guffawed. Now he pushed the cap back.

It was Bober.

We stared at him and did not want to believe our own eyes.

"Bravo, boys," hiccuped Bober. "You were terrific. Now you can get up."

Lying on the floor gasping like fish beached on a rock, we just looked at each other. Although we were seething with anger, we had to laugh. We were such a funny sight, lying there open-mouthed.

Schnapper got up and hit his bald head with the palms of his hands. "I'm going completely crazy in this infernal circus!" He moaned and ground his teeth.

"Bober must be completely mad," said Kurzweil. "Imagine if Marok and Weber had come in and discovered that he'd dared to borrow one of the uniforms hanging in the guardroom. That is the same as misappropriating the possessions of *die Wehrmacht*. People get shot and hanged for less than that. And to take such a risk just to create a bit of chaos among us for a little while! No, there has to be something wrong with his brain," ended Kurzweil, shaking his head.

I strolled over to my bunk. Güting followed me.

"It is very dark here. If you like, you can choose another bunk."

I looked at him in surprise. Not just once but many times I had asked him for another bunk. What was going on with the man now? *I'll be damned*, I thought. *The Red Cross parcel, of course*. It couldn't be anything else. What kind of delicacies did these parcels contain, to cause a lout like Güting to fawn over me? While I was thinking this over, Josel came over to me.

"May I sing a nice song for you?" he asked, and cleared his throat. "I know how to sing '*Sållvei's Lied.*'"

"'*Sållvei's Lied*'? What do you mean, Josel?"

"You must know it, Moritz. It was composed by a Norwegian. Listen."

It was "Solveig's Song" by Edvard Grieg that Josel began to sing in his frail voice. I was so touched that I put my hand on his shoulder.

"Thank you so much, Josel. If I get this package, you'll have a taste of the food."

Josel's innocent face lit up. "You're very nice, but that's not why I sang the song," he added hurriedly. "Bye-bye."

Luka drew himself up in his bunk with his elbow. "So, how is the prominent prisoner?"

I shook my head. "I feel as though I have suddenly and quite unexpectedly won the big prize in the lottery. But imagine if I do not receive the parcel? It could get lost, for example."

Luka laughed.

"Well, then, you'll probably have to pay for disappointed expectations, you can be sure of that. But worry about that when the time comes. Now the only thing that's important for you is to take advantage of all the possibilities that this situation offers. People are the same whether they live in freedom or on the steps of the gas chamber. I'll give you my undying soul in exchange for a cigarette when your paradise parcel arrives."

"Damn it, Luka, stop it now."

❧

Krebs came into the engraving workshop several days later.

"Come with me, Nachtstern," he said pleasantly. "A nice parcel has arrived for you," he whispered confidentially on the way out of the workshop. "It's in the mess hall."

Marok sat at the table with the package in front of him. It was the first Red Cross parcel that had come to Block 19. Shivers ran down my spine when I saw the marvel.

"Nachtstern, here you can see your parcel," said Marok. "You're a lucky dog. Take a look inside it. Ai, ai, man. Come closer and you can see all kinds of delicious things."

I was almost dizzy when I looked down into the parcel. There was a box of milk powder, butter, jam, sardines, sugar, rye crisp, cheese, cigarettes, and chocolate. My hands shook. Marok noticed it.

"Wait a minute, my friend. Surely you weren't thinking of not letting me taste these delicacies. Or were you? Let me see now ... To begin with, I will take these two chocolate bars."

"I will take the third one," said Krebs, and helped himself.

In this way they picked out things for themselves until they had emptied the parcel of three-quarters of its contents. Güting joined in too, but Krebs hit him hard over his fingers when he started to get greedy.

I had to stand there quietly and watch these three steal from me. I restrained myself and kept quiet. I knew that the slightest objection on my part would not only result in the loss of the entire package but a beating as well.

Marok got up with the stolen items in his arms.

"You can keep the rest. You're not dissatisfied, are you? I don't like the look on your face."

"Not at all," I said, and looked into his eyes. I knew that he fervently hoped I would give him an opportunity to hit me and take the rest of the parcel with him.

"No, this is best for you too. Take care of your things and go back to work quickly."

I put the little I had been allowed to keep into my cupboard and went back to the workshop.

Cytrin was ready to burst from curiosity.

I started to work with the magnifying glass and the engraving tool without saying anything. Eventually he could not control himself any longer. He threw me a cigarette, which had never happened before.

"Have a smoke."

I shook my head. "Thank you very much, but I can't risk having that devil Marok all over me today."

"They are trouble, both him and the other one," he admitted. "But in the beginning it was even worse here. The first three weeks we sat from morning till evening and only counted pieces of paper. We were supposed to learn how to count notes. We counted and counted until we almost went crazy. It was a Gestapo swine that kept watch over us, and he was ten times worse than Marok and Weber together. He gesticulated with his revolver and raged like a maniac if we so much as looked up for a second from the damned pieces of paper. But from one thing to the other, did anything unusual happen between Marok and you today? Maybe your parcel arrived?"

"I both got it and lost it."

"Congratulations. I mean, he didn't take everything away from you? You were able to keep some of it? You really are a lucky dog."

"Marok said so too."

"Yes, he is a true devil of Satan. There were many good things in the parcel, right? Imagine a Red Cross parcel in this block. I'd be happy if I could just have a look at one. A poor creature like me will of course never get a taste of the goodies. You can smoke the cigarette during the lunch break. I gave it to you; it's yours."

During the lunch break I shared the rest of the package with the others until there was nothing left. I had not intended to do this, but I would not have been able to swallow a bite with all those hungry eyes on me. There was no more than a little bit for each of us, but God, how good it tasted.

Chapter 12

ELEVEN NEW MEN HAD ARRIVED IN OUR BARRACKS. THEY DID NOT COME from ordinary prison camps like the rest of us, but from ghettos in the Polish-Russian cities of Litzmannstadt (Lodz) and Bialystok. Naturally they were bombarded with questions as soon as we had the opportunity. Among them was a small cripple who had the somewhat misleading name of Italiener—Leib Italiener. He was a cheerful and talkative fellow. He told us that the conditions in the ghettos were miserable. What little food there was available was so expensive that no one could afford to buy it.

"How did it happen that you were sent here?" asked Shurak, who was Polish too.

"The Germans were looking for printers. They chose one man here and one man there at random." Italiener pointed to the youngest man in the group. "He is only seventeen years old. His father, who is also a printer, and of course much more experienced, asked to come instead of the son. His request was refused outright. But he should not worry about the boy, they said. He would be sent to a print shop near Berlin and would be okay. Well, here we are, and it looks quite pleasant. I guess this is a fairly livable place."

"Oh yes," Güting suddenly joined in. "As long as it lasts."

"Long or short," said Italiener, shrugging his crooked shoulder. "Time is only a concept. Life is the only real thing."

"You talk like a fool," grumbled Güting contemptuously.

The newcomers inquired as to what we were printing in the block. It had to be something mysterious. Perhaps the print shop was a front for a secret organization? They had heard that powerful forces were at work to overthrow Hitler. Did we really print illegal newspapers here? Of course, we did not give them any information, but we urged them to keep their dangerous thoughts to themselves.

"Do you get beaten?" I was asked by one of the youngest newcomers.

"Sometimes, but more often than not they prefer punishment drills."

He scoffed boldly. "A little exercise isn't so bad."

"*Achtung!*" Marok entered our room as if it were the stage of an operetta. He did not wear a jacket, but what a shirt he had on! It was made of silk and so dazzlingly white that it practically glowed. On his chest were two shiny emblems, and the letters SD were embroidered on one of the sleeves.

"A gift from a lover in Berlin," whispered Luka next to me.

Marok had come to inspect and impress the newcomers.

Little Leib Italiener sat at the table between two of the tallest men. He barely reached up to their armpits when he was standing. Marok stared at him. "Are you sitting?"

"Herr Oberscharführer, I am standing," answered Italiener quickly.

But Marok was not quite convinced. "Get up on the table. What is your name?"

"Italiener," said Leib as he crawled up on the table.

"I asked what your name is. My God, are we going to have an Italian here too now?"

"My name is Italiener, Leib Italiener," said the Pole, and straightened up as best he could on the table.

"Well, thank God for that then. Jump down. I am not satisfied with you newcomers." Marok looked critically from one to the other. "It's obvious that you came from a ghetto where life was much too good. You have no idea what discipline is. But I will teach you, that's for sure. Get out to the exercise yard. Hurry, hurry." He kicked the closest of the newcomers in the buttocks. The next man got a cuff on the ears that sent him staggering out the door. "You will soon discover that you haven't come to a summer camp."

"Get to work!" Kurzweil called out to the rest of us. He stopped me in the door opening. "How are you doing in the engraving workshop, Nachtstern?"

I sensed a chance. "Frankly, I wish I could get another job, Kurzweil. My eyes are popping out of my head. You are a man with influence here, so you could perhaps help me get back to the print shop."

"Well, it's not quite impossible. That is, it's not going to be easy, but perhaps not completely impossible."

Now I knew that I had hooked him. "Do you think it's possible that I'll be receiving more Red Cross parcels, Kurzweil?"

"I am quite sure you will. It's obvious that, once you have received one, others will follow. All right, I'll do what I can for you. But don't forget that one good deed deserves another. You'll think of me when the next parcel arrives?"

"Of course, Kurzweil."

Late that afternoon he came into the engraving workshop with Leib Italiener. "Here's the man who will replace Nachtstern," he said to Cytrin.

Cytrin stared hard at him. "Don't be silly. Replace Nachtstern? No way can he be replaced; he will stay here. Do you think I want to exchange a capable man like him? No, take this fellow back with you; I don't want to see him. I'll explain it to Marok and Weber."

"It's no use, old man. It's an order from Krüger that Nachtstern is to do the sorting. He has worked so long with the clichés that he knows better than anyone what a pound note must look like. Come along, Nachtstern."

"I took care of that quickly and quite well, didn't I?" said Kurzweil when we were in the hall between the engraving workshop and the print shop. "This is a real advancement for you. Now you must not forget me when your parcels arrive."

"I won't forget you, Kurzweil. But is what you said about Krüger true?"

"It's true, but the suggestion came from me. Krüger asked me to place the newcomers as best I could. I suggested then, among other things, that we should move you to the sorting division. I praised you highly and said you were the best we had to instruct the newcomers in the sorting of the notes. Krüger thanked me for my good advice and said that I could move you over at once. It pays to be on good terms with a man in my position," he bragged.

Luka had also ended up in the sorting division. My place was between him and Glantzer. "Imagine having the most prominent prisoner himself next to me," teased Luka good-naturedly.

Glantzer pretended to be scared. "How dare you talk like that to the Great Mogul of Snowlandia, Luka?"

Kurzweil came running, pointing with his forefinger. "What did Glantzer tell you, Luka? Speak up."

Luka looked at him innocently. "He only asked me if there was ordinary water in watermarks."

Kurzweil stuck his forefinger right into Luka's face. "You'd better watch your gossiping big mouth. One day I'm going to lose my patience, and then I wouldn't want to be in your shoes. Nor in yours, Glantzer-man."

Kurzweil turned to me. "Come with me to see the newcomers. They are getting nowhere without your instructions."

Four of the newcomers were to be trained in the sorting of notes. The gruff fellow I had spoken to earlier in the day was one of them. Now he looked at me fearfully.

"That pig Marok nearly killed us in the exercise yard a while ago," he said in a low but savage voice. "Then he read out one threat after another about offenses that are punishable by death. I really had a shock when we came in here. I have yet to believe that counterfeit notes are actually produced here. Is it really true?"

"It's true enough. But be careful so that no one realizes we're talking about something that is forbidden." I held up a note against the light and showed him the watermarks and the secret markings.

"We thought we were lucky to come here, but we have ended up in a deathtrap."

"Don't look on the dark side. As long as there is life, there's hope, you know. Do you see the cleft in the 'f' here, and the three dots there? Those are some of the things you have to be aware of during the sorting. You must also watch out that the watermarks are where they are supposed to be on the notes. This note is perfect; take a good look at it. The notes you find to be flawed should be put in a separate bundle. The bundles that have been screened are then to be delivered to the foreman."

"I'll never be able to do this," he said, sighing dejectedly when I had finished explaining the secrets of the pound notes. "How many notes do I have to screen a day?"

"At least five hundred. You'll manage it once you get going in earnest. Take another note from the bundle and I'll go through it with you. First, try yourself to see if you can find any defects on it."

He took a note and began to scrutinize it.

⌒

The sun-baked roof and walls meant that the print shop was as hot as a steam bath.

Weber came out from the guardroom. He walked around and studied the newcomers. Suddenly I saw him tiptoe to the table where Springer sat. The feeble old man had not managed to stay awake in the heavy warm air. He did not notice anything until Weber fired a shot from his revolver directly behind him.

"It's because of the terrible heat," he stuttered, dazed.

"Hot? So you think it's hot," said Weber, putting his revolver back into its holster. "Just wait, and you will have reason to think so." He signaled to Kurzweil and whispered something to him. Kurzweil went into the guardroom. When he came back he carried two soldiers' capes, a steel helmet, and a gas mask. He put it all on Springer's table.

"Put it on," ordered Weber. "Everything."

For a moment it looked as if Springer would refuse, but then he began to get dressed.

"Help him with the finery, Kurzweil," said Weber impatiently. "Button up the capes, and put the helmet and the gas mask properly on the old man. Yes, like this. So, my dear Springer, now you can continue with your work. But watch out you don't fall asleep again. Get my accordion, Kurzweil."

The old man had to sit and work for two hours in his torture outfit. It was a miracle that he did not faint.

Weber walked around fussing with the "Internationale" on his huge accordion. It had been "given" to him by a Jew, or so he said. Outside in the exercise yard Marok raced back and forth on a motorcycle, raising hell. The noise was earsplitting, and the pebbles popped and banged against the wall of the block. The motorbike was another "gift" from an admiring Jew, and the two cronies used it on their chivalrous trips to Berlin.

Springer was more dead than alive when we helped him take off the two capes, the steel helmet, and the gas mask. We supported him as we walked into the dayroom.

The mood among the new prisoners was worse than depressed. The punishment drill and all they had heard and seen in the course of the day was enough to fill them with hopelessness and despair. After all, they had been in ghettos and not in such terrible camps as Monowitz and Auschwitz. The only one among them who accepted the situation with composure was the little cripple, Italiener. He talked and joked and actually managed to cheer up the others in the group of newcomers. Moreover, the same Leib Italiener turned out to be an expert engraver.

It was a restless night. The newcomers moaned and cried out in their sleep.

Chapter 13

"Take a look at Kahn," said Krebs in a low voice. "Do you see how he is eating Jackie up with his eyes behind his blue-colored glasses? He thinks no one notices it when the glasses are on his nose, the fool. It's been obvious to me for quite a while that he has something bad in mind for the boy. He doesn't fool me, the dog. I think you have noticed it too."

None of us said anything, but we knew that Kahn followed the young man from the ghetto group around, from morning till night.

"Most of you have probably noticed it," repeated Krebs, "but of course you don't want to tell on him. Well, you don't have to, either; I think I can take care of this matter on my own."

We saw Krebs go over to Jackie to tell him something. Both left the print shop.

Kahn looked after them. His nervous hands and tense posture revealed his fear.

"Where the hell did he get those wonderful blue-colored glasses?" asked Glantzer.

"From his benefactor, Krüger," said Luka. "Kahn complained that his eyes hurt from the strong light, and Uncle Krüger got him these glasses right away."

"Yes, he is very nice to Kahn. One would almost think ... hmmm ... But I would rather not be in Kahn's shoes if Krebs finds out something about him. Because, by God, Krebs is not his benefactor, as you call it."

Kahn worked feverishly and glanced toward the door incessantly.

"The very picture of guilt and fear personified," said Luka.

More than an hour passed by without Jackie reappearing.

"Trust me, he is being grilled thoroughly now."

"What was it Glantzer said, Nachtstern? Speak up!"

"He asked if I wanted to see the note he was working on."

Kurzweil grumbled and left again.

Just then Marok came into the print shop. He had some sheets of paper in his hand. "Everybody to the mess hall," he ordered in a voice that did not bode well.

"Now all hell is going to break loose," whispered Glantzer.

Krebs was in the mess hall. Jackie stood next to him, his face pale and his eyes roving. A rope was lying on the floor.

"Close the windows and pull the curtains shut," said Marok in a strange voice. When the order was carried out, he jumped up on the table closest to him. "Something serious has happened in this block," he began. "Something very serious."

The room was deathly quiet. Everyone glanced at Kahn. He was staring at the floor, his face ashen. Sweat glistened on his forehead.

Marok flapped the pages.

"Come and stand here near the table, Kahn."

Kahn barely managed to take the few steps.

"Look at me, you dog. Do you see these papers? Do you know what is in them? They contain Jackie's description of how you forced him to mess with you. For that alone you deserve to be hanged, you swine. But for the way you went about it, you deserve to be chopped up into small pieces. You threatened Jackie that, unless he did what you asked, you would yell out to the camp what we're doing here in Block 19. Did you threaten him with this, or did you not? Answer yes or no."

"Yes. But I did not mean to do it."

Marok smiled scornfully.

"Did you hear that, men? He says he didn't mean it. Of course he says so now. But let's imagine what would have happened if he had carried out the threat on his way to the showers, for example. What do you think would have happened to you? To me? We're in the same boat, you and me. Weber and I would have been made responsible for such an incident. I don't give a damn what happens to you, but I can't allow you to involve me in the misery. And remember one thing: You are welcome to help yourselves as much as you can, but if you involve others, you must be prepared to face the consequences. Krebs, get started, and do not spare the rod."

Krebs went over to Kahn.

"Take off your glasses. Like this, yes. So, you slimy frog, it was not enough that you made Jackie mess with you, but it even had to take place under the stream of the tap in the washroom. You are clever, aren't you?"

Then he struck Kahn's face with his fist as hard as he could. Kahn flew several feet across the floor. He was unconscious when Krebs and Güting pulled him by his legs and threw him into a small, empty cupboard. In his other hand Güting held the rope that had been lying on the floor. He threw it in to Kahn.

"Now you can hang yourself," he shouted, and locked the door. "The sooner the better, you bastard."

"Everybody back to work!" shouted Kurzweil with a trembling voice. He looked as though it was he who had been the object of Marok's anger.

"When I saw the rope on the floor, by God, I thought they intended to hang the fellow in front of our eyes," said Glantzer as he moved the stool closer to the table. "Do you think he's going to hang himself in the cupboard?"

"Far from it," said Luka. "Marok, Weber, and Krebs would definitely be happy if he did, but Kahn is too sly a fox to give them the pleasure. He knows the score very well. All of them, starting with Krüger, are afraid of having some trouble here. After all, they all owe their comfortable lives to this print shop. If there is trouble here, they themselves will also be caught up in it, and could end up shot against a wall. No, as long as we're inside these walls, we can at least be sure to stay alive."

"There is something in that," admitted Glantzer. "But by God, it was eerie in the mess hall with the windows closed and the curtains drawn, Marok on the table with the sheets of paper in his hand and the gloomy faces all around. I had this creepy feeling that we were a gathering of people condemned to death, just waiting to be sent outside to the wall. I had goose bumps all over my body."

Luka hit the table nervously. "*Halt maul* [shut your big mouth now]!"

I looked up carefully. Weber had replaced Marok. Now he came sauntering across the floor with his hands in his pockets. The steps came closer and closer. The squeaking of his boot soles sounded like the flicks of a whip. He stopped directly in front of us.

"Who talked out loud? Look at me. Who was it—who talked out loud, I asked? I'll give you one minute."

No one answered.

Weber looked at his watch. I imagined that I could hear the watch hand tick past every second.

"Well, well, gentlemen, the minute has gone by. Let me see now. I want to be really nice to you today. You may choose between punishment drills and having your hair clipped off. I am humane, right? Humane is the word. We will even have a vote. What do you choose, Luka?"

"Punishment drills," answered Luka without thinking.

"And you, Glantzer?"

"Punishment drills."

"Nachtstern?"

"Punishment drills."

Weber nodded. "This has to be called a unanimous decision, all three of you choosing punishment drills. Okay, then, it must be clipping. Out to the exercise yard—get out!"

Crestfallen and angry, we ran out to the exercise yard.

"That we should be so damned stupid," lamented Glantzer. "If we had voted the other way around, we would not have to go through this."

"That's what you think," said Luka bitterly. "In the stone quarry work unit where I was before I came here, one of the German guards asked us one day if we had ever slept with an Aryan girl. The first prisoner who was asked answered no. He was struck so hard across his mouth that he fell down. Number two answered the same, and he got the same treatment. Then I was asked. I wanted to be very clever and said yes. Not only was I struck across the mouth, but the toe of a boot landed between my ribs too, while I lay on the ground."

Glantzer looked angrily at Luka. "None of your talk or your storytelling will do any good. It's your fault that we're going to look like monkeys. We'll have to swallow sarcasm from morning till night, just because you could not watch your big mouth."

"What?" Luka jumped up. "You say it was because I wasn't watching my big mouth, you chatterbox? First of all, you talked at least as loudly as me, and secondly, you painted such a gloomy picture that one could go crazy listening to it."

Just then Weber and Güting came outside to the exercise yard. Güting had a stool in one hand and a hair clipper in the other. He put the stool down on the ground and waved invitingly with the clipper.

"First customer, please! Come on, Norwegian, I will treat you well."

I sat down. It was just as well to jump into it as to crawl. But I closed my eyes so that Weber would not see how much his infernal idea affected me. I would gladly have endured both beatings and punishment drills as long as I could have kept the hair on my scalp. The many and long days before my hair grew in were a true nightmare. I felt like a ridiculous "missing link" and was in agony each time I washed myself or passed by a window that reflected my "part-monkey" image. It was bad enough in the other camps where all the prisoners' hair had been clipped off, but it became really unbearable when we came to this block. During the first weeks we walked about like fearful gnomes among the fair-haired old prisoners. And now we would have to go through the same thing again. Sitting there, I hated Weber intensely and fervently. I did not blame Luka. It could just as well have been me who told Glantzer to keep his mouth shut. Luka just beat me to it.

Güting clipped a line from my forehead down to my neck.

"Stop a minute," said Weber, who stood with his legs wide apart, watching the procedure. "Maybe we should leave it like that. Oh, no; clip all of it, close to the scalp, Güting, my man."

"Will do, Herr Oberscharführer." Güting clipped into thin air like a professional barber before he began again. He tugged and tore so the roots of my hair stung.

"It seems to me that the customer's eyebrows are twitching, Güting. Probably he would like to get rid of those too."

Güting chuckled maliciously.

"I can take care of them for the same price. Just a minute, Mr. Polar Bear, I just have to change the comb of the machine. So now we will soon get rid of your disfiguring eyebrows, my friends. They have such a distracting effect on the view."

I could have strangled the man with my bare hands.

"Next, please," he said proudly when he was finished with me.

There was giggling and grinning at the machines and the tables when we came back to the print shop.

In the evening we inspired the fellows to outdo each other in making poor jokes. The only ones who abstained from commenting on our bald heads were Schnapper and Springer—the former for obvious reasons, and the latter because he was tactful.

It is ridiculous, I said to myself, *that we who live in the shadow of the gas chambers make such a fuss about a few inches of hair.* But even though I did not want to deal any further with the thought of ending my life in a gas chamber, I knew that it would be easier with hair on my head, as strange as it may sound.

Anyhow, the men soon turned their attention back to the Kahn affair. No one felt sorry for him. His behavior toward us in general—and Jackie in particular—had been too appalling. Not a sound came from the room where Kahn was. Some of us thought that he had hanged himself; others were sure of the opposite. Bets were made and the odds were almost equal. Güting sneaked over to the door of the cupboard and listened. He obviously heard something, because he knocked on the door and shouted: "Haven't you hanged yourself yet, you dirty dog? Make sure to get it done quickly, or else I'll come in and do it for you." He laughed brutally.

"It's indecent to talk like this," said Springer, who sat next to me. "The miserable fellow in there is sick in both mind and in body."

"I don't defend Güting, the animal, but here probably most of us are sick in mind and body."

"That's exactly why we must be tolerant of each other."

"Listen, Springer, do you believe that we'll survive all this?" I had not intended to ask this dangerous question, but the words somehow slipped out by themselves.

Springer looked at me in surprise. "You don't believe, Mr. Nachtstern, that the Germans will let you go home to Norway to tell what you have done in this block? It will take a miracle to save us. Okay, one should not completely disregard that possibility either. Anything can happen in the crazy world we live in. For the sake of you young men, I hope that the miracle will happen. As for me, I expect nothing more of life. I have no money, and I'm too old and unhealthy to start again."

"The doctor that Marok and Weber take you to—what's he like?" I asked this question in order to change the subject.

"He's capable and pleasant enough, a French prisoner who himself must take orders from the two scoundrels. Last time I went to see him, Marok forced him to torment me with much too large a catheter. My most serious problem is urinating. It was terribly painful; I must have fainted for a moment. Besides, it was surely on Marok's initiative that the doctor asked me what we were doing in this block."

"He really asked you while Marok listened? What did you answer?"

"I said we shoveled sand."

All around us the fellows began to play cards and chess. Luka, Glantzer, and Schnapper sat at one of the tables. They waved to me.

"Sit down here," said Luka. "You have been voted into the exclusive 'Bald Heads' card club. Since Schnapper is the oldest among us, I suggest we choose him to become the president."

"We can safely make him a life member too," said Glantzer with a sneer.

"Kiss my arse," grumbled Schnapper irritably. "In any case, I am the only one in Bald Heads who still has his eyebrows."

I was happy that I had sat with them. The conversation with Springer had not been encouraging.

❦

"Today the old man is coming," said Marok to Krebs. They stood close to me.

Krüger came, although he was not as cheerful and smiling as usual. His face was taut and his deer eyes had a hard glimmer.

"Gentlemen," he began. "I have received a very serious report from Oberscharführer Marok. You know what it concerns. It is a very serious matter, far more serious than any of you suspect. After thorough consideration I have decided not to let the matter go any further. But, gentlemen, the guilty prisoner will not be spared the consequences next time. I will not tolerate another violation of the decency and discipline here. Not even my best worker can expect leniency from me if he disappoints me. I assume that this is clear enough to each of you."

Krüger walked back and forth for a while. Then he stopped and looked from one to the other. His face was no longer taut, and the harsh glimmer in his eyes was gone. "I understand, of course, how difficult it is for you gentlemen. Well, I will remedy the situation; you will be provided with women."

We just stood there open-mouthed when he nodded good-bye with the old, friendly smile.

When we came into the mess hall that evening, Kahn was back from his cupboard. Krüger had obviously not quite disowned his favorite prisoner yet. Any other night Kahn would have been in hot water, but something had occurred today that overshadowed Kahn and his escapades. Had Krüger not promised us women? The discussion was louder than ever before. When would the women come? What kind of women had *Onkel* (uncle) Krüger arranged for us? He was not the kind of man who was apt to bluff.

Among the Bald Heads club, it was Glantzer who expected the most from Krüger's promise. He was bursting with more fiery words and illustrative hand movements than ever before.

"You're just boasting," Schnapper interrupted him mercilessly. "I'm willing to bet that you don't even know the difference between the front and the back of a woman. You boasters have nothing to offer women anyhow, when it comes right down to it."

"Take the cards and stop this nonsense," said Luka irritably. "If you'd use what little sense you have, you'd realize that not a single skirt will ever come to this block. Or do you think that Krüger intends to add a harem wing here? This much you must understand: Krüger would never be able to send the women out again to the camp once they had been in this block. The only thing he could do would be to send them straight to the gas chamber, but one must hope that even Krüger is not that inhuman."

"Eh," objected Glantzer. "You must always be the devil's advocate. Two spades, you double pessimist."

That evening the games at all three long tables were badly played.

"What have you done with Kahn?" asked Schnapper when Krebs passed by our table. "I haven't seen him yet."

Krebs pointed with his thumb. "I've moved him to one of the empty bunks over there in the corner. There he can sleep and eat by himself for two weeks. I'll beat him to a pulp if he so much as opens his big mouth during that time. He will not get away with the two days in the cupboard."

"The world is ungrateful," sighed Luka affectedly. "We ought to send a delegation bringing gifts and warm words to the martyr. It's thanks to him that Krüger will supply us with women."

"That delegation will need crutches," said Krebs with a crooked smile.

Chapter 14

OF COURSE WE NEVER HAD ANY FEMALE VISITORS IN BLOCK 19. ON THE other hand, it happened several times that, when Krüger came to inspect us, he was accompanied by a man in civilian dress. The fellow sneaked around, prying and poking high and low around the entire block. The smell of Gestapo was in the air long after he was gone. Neither Marok nor Weber seemed to like this man any more than we prisoners did. Still, they did not give up on their pleasures in Berlin.

For us counterfeiters, by the grace of Himmler, the days went by in the production of notes and the usual incidents. The latter varied in color and depth, but the main theme in Block 19 was and always would be the same.

Josel was fired and the monarchist from Vienna was appointed his successor as Marok's Stubendienstassistent and private orderly. As Güting's assistant, he was finally able to satisfy his enormous appetite for soup to the point of bursting. And when he wore his white *Kalfaktor* (servant) jacket, his monarchist principles thrived until he came to a thunderous downfall because of his weakness for Marok's lurid magazines. The big-bellied man from Vienna sobbed like a dethroned count when the catastrophe hit him—end of soup and *Kalfaktor* privileges.

As for me, I did not do too well either at the time, despite the fact that both my hair and eyebrows began to grow in, and that the other prisoners continued to spoil me, with the possibility of another package in mind. It was Krebs who made life miserable for me. He was after me for the most trivial matters.

In the beginning I thought it was only something I imagined, but then one day it became quite clear that I had fallen out of the barracks chief's favor. When the cigarettes were distributed I was treated most unfairly. While the others received six or seven cigarettes, I only got one when my turn came. I complained. Why did I not get as many cigarettes as the others?

He stared angrily at me.

"If you don't watch your big mouth, I'll take back the one you got. It is I who decide here; for your own sake, don't forget that."

I did not understand a thing. Why did the man treat me this way? Had I stepped on his toes without knowing it? During the lunch break I tried to figure it out while we were outside in the exercise yard. Krebs was there too. Just as we were going back inside to work, I caught sight of a large cigarette butt. I bent down and picked it up; it would be a welcome addition to my meager tobacco ration. Suddenly Krebs was all over me.

"What the hell are you doing?" He raised his hand to hit me.

I was about to cover my face with my arms, but then I saw something in his eyes that stopped me. I did not move a finger. I knew that if I did, he would have me where he wanted me.

He put down his hand.

"Throw away the cigarette butt and get inside fast," he sneered.

I did as he said without making a sound. Now I knew the score.

Krebs tried systematically to get me to lose my self-control. He had not intended to hit me when he raised his hand; he only wanted to provoke me to get even with him, and thereby make me an outcast. I had seen it in his eyes when he had threatened me with his fist. And it was Krebs and no one else who had thrown away the big cigarette butt. None of the prisoners would have wasted valuable tobacco this way. Krebs had almost succeeded with the experiment. But why did he have it in for me? I realized that there had to be a special reason for his harassment, but that was as far as I got. I confided in Luka to hear what he thought about all this.

Luka began to play fortune-teller with a bundle of notes. He spread them out like a deck of cards, moved the notes around, and tapped them mysteriously with a long emaciated forefinger.

"Spare me your nonsense," I whispered angrily. I was disappointed at his foolish reaction to what I had told him in confidence.

Luka pretended not to hear me and rolled his eyes like a magician. Then he put his bony forefinger on one of the notes. "I see a parcel in the cards," he whispered in a ghostlike voice.

"A parcel?" I began to suspect something.

He nodded like a fortune-teller. "A parcel, yes. With a cross the color of blood. Be careful, snowman from Ultima Thule [a distant place]. I see a tall, blond scoundrel next to the package card. But I cannot see anymore, no, no. That will be—I will be reasonable—five thousand pounds. Mind you, that's in Block 19 pounds, not those sloppy notes from the Bank of England."

"Nachtstern!" Krebs stood on the threshold of the guardroom and waved to me.

"Keep cool," whispered Luka when I got up.

Marok sat in the guardroom, tilting his chair. Krebs stayed close to the door.

I stood at attention.

Marok took his time to light a cigarette. Now he flicked the match and blew the smoke in my direction.

"Good day, Mr. Nachtstern."

"Good day, Herr Oberscharführer."

"I hear that you took the liberty of being rude to the barracks chief?"

"That must be a misunderstanding, Herr Oberscharführer."

Marok jumped up from the chair and picked up a dog whip from the table. "What? Do you claim that I am telling a lie?"

"I wouldn't dream of it, Herr Oberscharführer."

Fortunately he did not notice that my voice quavered a little.

"That's lucky for you," he said, and tickled my face with the dog whip. "But it's a pity that you couldn't control yourself and show your superiors some respect. Really, a pity. You see, a package has arrived for you. Bring the package, Krebs."

Krebs fetched a Red Cross parcel from a cupboard and put it on the table.

Marok grazed my cheek with the whip.

"Here you can see what you missed out on because you're an impudent lout. You understand, of course, that I can't give you the parcel, don't you?"

"Yes, Herr Oberscharführer."

"Good. Then I will spare you the twenty-five lashes on your backside that I had intended for you. Leave."

Krebs looked maliciously at me when I passed him on my way out of the print shop.

"You got off lightly I see," said Luka when I sat down next to him. "A package did arrive for you, right?"

I nodded.

"Your hands are shaking. Were they that bad?"

"If I hadn't followed your sound advice and kept cool, I wouldn't have been able to sit here now. Had they first started to beat me, they wouldn't have given up until their arms were tired. I saw it in their eyes."

"That's for sure. Those who have a guilty conscience beat you the longest and the hardest. One must say that your parcels give you a lot of pleasure."

I would have liked to say to hell with them, but I didn't. Deep down I did not mean it either. The glimpse I had had of the parcel with its Norwegian stamps meant a lot to me.

"The curse of the rich." I tried to say it lightly.

"Resignation is a precious gift," said Luka sanctimoniously. "But don't be stupid now and tell the others. That would deprive them of the pleasure of having a Red Cross 'prominent' in their midst. It's so interesting to see them suck up to you, I think. But Marok has chosen a far more effective method."

"I think this was Krebs's idea, but I can't understand why he went to all this trouble. He and Marok could have just shared the package and that's that. I need not have known about its arrival at all."

"Oh, it's not that simple. For one or another reason the Germans have not deleted the paragraph that forbids them to enrich themselves on Red Cross parcels. But as we know, there are many ways to skin a cat, and in this case, the appropriate one is called disciplinary punishment. Krebs reports you for being obstinate, and Marok bars you from receiving the parcel as punishment."

"Here now, Luka, don't you think it's contemptible, considering that Krebs is Jewish and a prisoner just like me and all the others here?"

"Jewish or not Jewish, the thief mentality is common to all races. I should know—I am half of each."

"I didn't know that you are half-Jewish."

"Oh yes, I am. In other words, I hail from the same noble ancestry as our soup monarchist. Be careful, here's your friend Marok."

There must have been many delicacies in my parcel, because Marok was in high spirits. He joked and talked to Schnapper and a few of the other men, and even laughed when Schnapper gave him a rather arrogant lesson on the printing of notes. He strutted across the floor for a while, and then he stopped and looked at his watch.

"Pack up the millions, men! We will use the last thirty minutes to have some fun. Assemble in the exercise yard, gentlemen. Krebs, get hold of a stool and a towel."

We looked at each other while we organized the bundles of notes to be handed in. What the hell did he want the stool and the towel for? Had the man thought of a new form of punishment drills, or were we to play blindman's bluff in the exercise yard?

"Quick now," nagged Kurzweil nervously.

Outside in the exercise yard, Marok, in high spirits, rushed at us impatiently. He reminded me of a schoolboy in the upper years who has the noble idea of playing with the school's first-year students. He moved the stool and waved with the towel that Krebs had brought him.

"Hello, boys. Come closer. Stand in a circle around me. As the oldest of this assembly, Springer may sit down on the stool. Look here, Springer, you'll get the towel too."

Marok put the towel into our old paper specialist's hand and pushed him down on the stool. Then he shoved his cap to the back of his head, with his legs far apart. "Now we'll play a fun game called *Schinkenklopfen* [ham-knock]. But you're only allowed to do the slapping with the palm of your hand. Come here, Schnapper, we'll start with you."

"All right," said Schnapper and stepped forward. "But then we must rename the game *Knochenklopfen* [bone-knock], because the *Schinken* [ham] in my trousers is in poor shape."

"You shouldn't be upset about that," sneered Marok. "It will be tough luck for the one who is going to slap you. Bend down so Springer can wrap the towel around your head; you can support yourself with your hands on his knees. That's good, Springer. Now you must watch out that he cannot see anything. Tighten the towel properly around his head. Okay, gentlemen, now one of you can start the fun. Smack him so he can feel it."

Glantzer stepped forward and struck Schnapper on his rear end.

"So, Schnapper, who hit you?" asked Marok.

"Perez," guessed Schnapper.

"Wrong. Continue to stand."

Schnapper guessed wrong the next time, too. Then Marok pulled up his sleeve and slapped him hard.

"Who was that?"

Moritz aged about 13. (PRIVATE COLLECTION)

Moritz and three sisters. There were ten siblings altogether, three brothers and seven sisters. The family moved to the United States and Great Britain in the 1920s, except for Moritz who remained in Oslo. (PRIVATE COLLECTION)

Berg detention camp (also called Quisling's chicken run) outside Tønsberg was established on July 10, 1942 and was under the authority of the Police Department. The camp was not ready when the first Jewish prisoners arrived on October 26, 1942. The "white house" (the commandant's residence) can be seen on the left together with the guards' "casino," located outside the camp itself. In the foreground may be seen part of the camp's barbed wire fence, which was set up by the Jewish prisoners during November 1942. Photo taken in 1944. (NORWEGIAN HOME FRONT MUSEUM)

Roll-call in the Berg detention camp. Norwegian Jøssinger, anti-Nazi, prisoners line up in front. The so-called "Jew barrack" can be seen in the background with Jewish prisoners on their way to the roll-call. Jewish men were the first prisoners who came to the Berg detention camp at the end of October 1942, Moritz Nachtstern among them. Following the selection on the morning of November 26, 1942 Jewish men in so-called "mixed marriages" stayed behind. They were interned at Berg until May 1945. The photo was probably taken in 1944. (NORWEGIAN HOME FRONT MUSEUM)

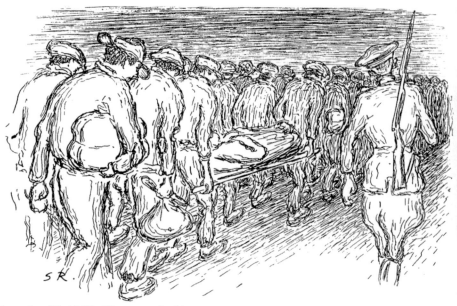

November 26, 1942. After a month of hard work, the Jews who were to be deported were separated from those who were married to non-Jewish women. The drawing depicts the march out of the camp to the railway tracks, where a special train equipped with freight cars waited to take them to Oslo and the death ship SS *Donau*.

The photographer Georg Fossum received a tip from contacts in the Home Front that the Jews were to be deported from Norway. Among others he took this photo of the SS *Donau* as it was towed from the wharf of the America Line at 2:45 p.m. The wharf itself was blocked by German riot squads, but people gathered outside the barrier, most probably friends and acquaintances of the Jews on board, but also others who happened to pass by. (SCANPIX)

kjørte over Tordenskjoldsplass til Gamle Amerikalinjens skur. Der
S/S Donau. K mmet av toget der, fikk vi se grätende kvinner og ba:
faktisk talt jaget ombord. Den natten var det også foregått arrrei
samtlige jødiske kvinner og barn, samt de eldre som var blitt løl
Endel hadde fått nyss om arrestasjonene og hadde stukket seg unda
Det var allerede kommet fanger som hadde sittet på Bredtvedt og oj
blitt hentet på sykehus. De måtte bære sekker med matvarer ombord
som poteter, käl , hälret brød. Samtidig ble det båret opp Smtres
viste seg å inneholde meierismør. Dette skulle selvfølgelig være t
forbruk. Mens lastningen foregikk, jagde tyskerne fangene opp og ne
unner spark og sllag, skrik og brøl hvis de syntes det ikke gikk fo
som stod på bryggen og ikke var blitt oppropt ønda, sto og så på a
Så kem turen til oss. Etter navneppropet ble vi sendt ombord en og
Jog si ett tilfelde hvordan en eldre mann på ca. 80 år på vei op
(denne var lange siden og båten og var meget høi og bratt) nesten
men balansen og holder på å falle ned. To tyske offiserer som sto
relingen, kunne ha hjulpet han ved bare å rekke hånden ut, men de
dig på det, og smudde hodet en annen vei. Og i benärranex henderne
var vi kommet. Mannen greide såvidt å få tak igjen og komme ombord
uniformerte nasister som gikk frem og tilbake på brygga, syntes ak
forøsiet med tyskernes fremgangsmäte. Mange av byens innbyggere ha

Moritz Nachtstern dictated his memoirs to his wife immediately after the war. He describes the boarding of the SS *Donau* on the wharf of the America Line on November 26, 1942. (PRIVATE COLLECTION)

In the records for the day the SS *Donau* left Oslo headed for Stettin, an employee at the Oslo Port Authority made the unusual notation "loading Jews." The ship left with 532 Jews onboard. (OSLO CITY ARCHIVE: FACSIMILE FROM THE *FOREIGN DOCK JOURNAL* OF THE OSLO PORT AUTHORITY 1942)

Stettin, am 30. November 1942.

Übergabeprotokoll.

Am 30. November 1942 wurden 532 Juden aus Norwegen (302 jüdische Männer und 230 jüdische Frauen und Kinder) vom SS-Hauptsturmführer Grossmann an den Vertreter der Staatspolizei Leitstelle Stettin Krim.- Sekretär Schapals übergeben.

Als Übergebender: Als Übernehmender:

G. Grossmann reg.   *Schapals*, reg.
SS-Untersturmführer   Krim. Sekretär.

The first stop on the way to Auschwitz. According to a receipt signed by Klaus Grossmann of the Gestapo in Oslo and Schapals, the secretary of the criminal police in Stettin, 302 men and 230 women and children from the SS *Donau* transport were delivered to the Gestapo in Stettin.

Konzentrationslager Auschwitz   Auschwitz, den 1. Dezember 194 2
Kommandantur / Abt. II

Az. 14 c 4 / 12.42 / St.

Übernahmebestätigung:

Die Übernahme von −532 −Juden aus Norwegen wird hiermit bestätigt.

Der Lagerkommandant
I.A. *[signature]* reg.

SS-Untersturmführer

On December 1, 1942, the office of the commandant in Auschwitz confirmed receipt of the 532 Norwegian Jews. Shortly after their arrival most of the group, including all the women and children, was gassed.

Betrifft : Meldung jüdischer Häftlinge

An die
Kommandanten der
KL Buchenwald. Ravensbrück u. Sachsenhausen

Es sind mir umgehend die im dortigen Lager befindlichen
jüdischen Häftlinge zu melden, die aus dem graphischen
Gewerbe stammen, Papierfachleute oder sonstige geschickte
Handarbeiter (z. B. Friseure) sind.

Diese jüdischen Häftlinge können fremder Nationalität
sein, müssen jedoch deutsche Sprachkenntnisse besitzen.
Bei Abgabe der Meldung ist Nationalität bekanntzugeben.

Termin: 3. August 1942

                    Der Chef des Amtes D II
                    im Auftrage:

                    [signature]

                    ℍ-Obersturmführer

On July 20, 1942, four days after Heinrich Himmler gave the green light for a new attempt to print counterfeit pound notes, Lieutenant Hermann Dorner, of the camp administration's business section, signed an order to the effect that German-speaking Jewish printers and other skilled workers be found among the prisoners in German concentration camps. It was in accordance with this order that Moritz Nachtstern and others were transferred to Sachsenhausen.

American surveillance photo of Sachsenhausen concentration camp. The triangle in the middle of the picture is the main camp. The half-circle is the roll-call square. The camp administration can be seen at the bottom on the left, and half a dozen barracks, mainly for Jewish prisoners, at the bottom on the right. The arrow points at Block 19 where Moritz Nachtstern was when the picture was taken. (US NATIONAL ARCHIVES: COURTESY OF LAWRENCE MALKIN, *KRUEGER'S MEN*)

Block 19 and the area that separated it from Block 18, surrounded by barbed wire. (PHOTO REPRINTED IN SEVERAL EASTERN EUROPEAN PUBLICATIONS AND BELIEVED TO BE IN RUSSIAN ARCHIVES)

Before Bernhard Krüger was appointed leader of the operation, the Nazis had, with little luck, tried to carry out the counterfeiting with German workers in their own print shop on Delbrück-strasse 6a in the Charlottenburg district of Berlin. Moritz Nachtstern and his comrades worked with similar machines. (US NATIONAL ARCHIVES: COURTESY OF LAWRENCE MALKIN, *KRUEGER'S MEN*)

A German worker retouches the negatives of a watermark template in the same manner as the prisoners in Block 19. PHOTO TAKEN BY THE NAZIS. (US NATIONAL ARCHIVES)

A note drawn by Moritz from memory immediately after the war.

An Operation Bernhard £5 note. It is almost impossible even for an expert to distinguish a top-quality *Bernhard* note from a genuine one. After the notes had been aged and crumpled in Block 19, even skilled Swiss bank tellers were fooled. (COURTESY COLIN NARBETH & SON, LONDON)

A genuine £5 note, dated February 1937. (COURTESY COLIN NARBETH & SON, LONDON)

Salomon Smolianoff, called Tovarisch in the book, as sketched by fellow prisoner and artist colleague Leo Haas. Smolianoff was a counterfeiter by profession. It was he who produced the dollar bill that could not be distinguished from a genuine dollar bill. Leo Haas (1901–83) is one of the best known artists who depicted life in concentration camps and ghettos. He was educated at the Art Academy in Karlsruhe and worked as a book illustrator, journal caricaturist and painter until his arrest in 1939. He was imprisoned in several camps before he was sent to Theresienstadt (Terezin). In 1944 he was transferred to Sachsenhausen and Operation Bernhard. (US NATIONAL ARCHIVES: COURTESY OF LAWRENCE MALKIN, *KRUEGER'S MEN* AND © DACS 2008)

Smolianoff works on retouching. SKETCH BY LEO HAAS. (© DACS 2008)

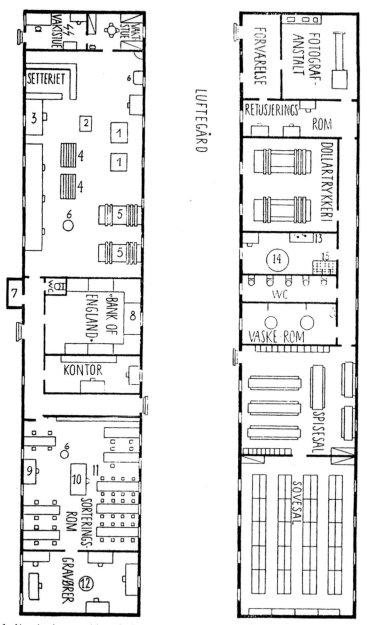

1. Numbering machine. 2. Stencil machine. 3. Barrack chief. 4. Drying rack.
5. Printing machine for pounds. 6. Oven. 7. Generator. 8. Shelves for notes.
9. Foreman's table. 10. Sorting place. 11. Worktables. 12. Engraving machine.
13. Gas table. 14. Centrifuge. 15. Rinse basin.

Sketch of the counterfeiter group in Block 19.

The survivors gathered on the roll-call square in Ebensee on May 7, 1945. The group on the left is waving an American flag. (THE UNITED STATES HOLOCAUST MEMORIAL MUSEUM: COURTESY OF LAWRENCE MALKIN, *KRUEGER'S MEN*)

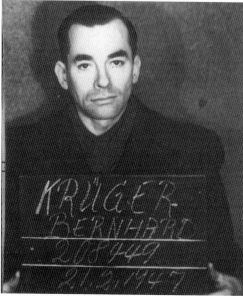

Bernhard Krüger in SS uniform. (US NATIONAL ARCHIVES: COURTESY OF LAWRENCE MALKIN, *KRUEGER'S MEN*)

Bernhard Krüger after he reported to the British occupation authorities in November 1946. They detained him until 1948 and then handed him over to the French authorities. He was never charged. (PUBLIC RECORD OFFICE, UK: COURTESY OF LAWRENCE MALKIN, *KRUEGER'S MEN*)

Seven counterfeiters after they were liberated. First row from left to right: Salomon Smolianoff, Ernst Gottlieb from Vienna, unidentified, Max Groen from Amsterdam. Second row from left to right: Adolf Burger, unidentified, Andries Bosboom from Amsterdam. (FAMILY OF MAX GROEN: COURTESY OF LAWRENCE MALKIN, *KRUEGER'S MEN*)

Moritz met Rachel and fell in love immediately after he came home. On this picture from their engagement, he is still physically marked by his imprisonment in Sachsenhausen. (PRIVATE COLLECTION)

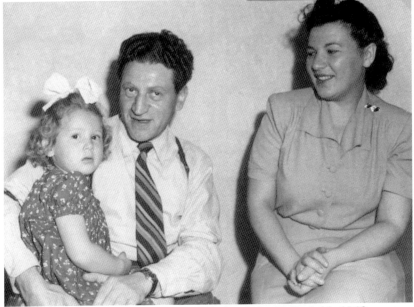

Moritz, a proud father, with his daughter Sidsel and his wife Rachel in 1948, a year before the book was published for the first time. (PRIVATE COLLECTION)

Moritz at work immediately after the war. (PRIVATE COLLECTION)

Moritz enjoys his freedom and a cigarette on Karl Johan (Oslo's main street) after the war. He died in 1969. (PRIVATE COLLECTION)

At the Bæreia Convalescent Home for war invalids. Moritz spent much time here; Bæreia was a refuge for the war invalids. Here they never spoke about the war.

Bundles of Operation Bernhard £5 notes dumped in 1945 are recovered from Lake Toplitz in 1959. (© 2001 CREDIT:TOPHAM/AP TOPFOTO.CO.UK)

Police examine the counterfeit money dumped in Lake Toplitz. (© AKG-IMAGES/ULLSTEIN BILD)

Sachsenhausen today. The oblong blocks shown here commemorate the different barracks; Block 19 is the second last one on the right. (COURTESY FRODE MOLVEN)

The entrance to Sachsenhausen, with the phrase *Arbeit Macht Frei* ("Work Shall Make You Free") set into the gate. This ominous phrase was also found over the gate at Auschwitz. (COURTESY FRODE MOLVEN)

"That was Oberscharführer Marok," said Schnapper without hesitating.

"That's right. Well, then, it's my turn to stand. I'm not one to shy away."

And he actually changed places with Schnapper.

We looked at each other incredulously as he stood there with his rear end up and his head wrapped in the towel. Everybody certainly felt like giving it to him, but Krebs swept us all aside to have enough room. He took off like a hammer thrower and the result left nothing to be desired. It was a terrific slap, and Marok and Springer barely avoided falling down.

"That could only have been you, Krebs," said Marok with a somewhat forced smile when he had straightened up. "And now it's your turn."

"Yes, Herr Oberscharführer," said Krebs, suspiciously polite. "But may I remind you that two new prisoners must be picked up in the quarantine block today."

"Yes, by God, you're quite right, Krebs. But I'm going to remember you when we play *Schinkenklopfen* the next time," he added. He looked relieved, and he probably was. Krebs would not be gentle the next time either.

The rest of us had to continue with this idiotic game until everybody had been in the firing line. Marok took care that no one was too miserly when it was his turn to do the slapping. Of course Josel fared the worst. He had to strike Blaustein's bony rear end until he almost cried. Marok enjoyed himself royally. He would not have been quite so boisterous had he known what was going to happen to him here in the exercise yard the following day. *Schinkenklopfen* was to be Marok's last adventure in Block 19, a 100 percent "Marokish" exit, one could say.

When Marok had finally had his fill of *Schinkenklopfen*, he turned the battlefield over to us and went into the guardroom, presumably to taste the delicacies of the Red Cross parcel.

"I certainly don't love Krebs," said Luka, "but he has my greatest respect for the way he smacked Marok before. I guarantee that the Adonis's arse still hurts from the whack."

"Yes, I'm proud of that plan of action," boasted Schnapper. "I knew perfectly well who slapped me the first few times, but it was Marok I wanted to trap, and I succeeded. I had intended to take him on; by rights it should have been me."

Chapter 15

"OBERSCHARFÜHRER MAROK!"

Two men in civilian dress stood on the threshold of the guardroom. One of them was the man who accompanied Krüger occasionally, walking around in the block and snooping in every corner.

Even Marok's back revealed his fear when he went into the guardroom.

"Did you see the looks of those two in the doorway?" Glantzer let slip in what was almost a loud voice. "I wouldn't like to be in Marok's elegant trousers now. Those two men are Gestapo, that's obvious. They have of course found out that Marok and Weber are messing around with the generals' wives in Berlin. Now both of them will be fired, don't you think? I swear that they'll be sent to the front. It'll be different from playing the big moguls here. Can't you just see them crawling in the mud, Luka?"

"Stop your nonsense," whispered Luka, annoyed. "Do you really believe the gentlemen in Berlin are so stupid that they'd send anyone to the front from this place? There's something called desertion and something called capture. If they are going to punish Marok and Weber, they must either shoot them or lock them up in a place where they won't have a chance to let anything slip about this block."

"I'll be darned, Luka, I didn't think of that. But what will happen to us? What if they decide to close down this entire shop?"

Just then Kurzweil arrived. He had been absent from the print shop for about ten minutes.

"What did Glantzer say, Luka? Speak up."

"Nothing special. We're sitting here wondering what will happen to you and us if they liquidate Mr. Marok and Mr. Weber. Oh, that's right; you weren't here when the Gestapo appeared five minutes ago. You should've seen how pale and weak at the knees Marok was when they called him into the guardroom."

Alarmed, Kurzweil stared at Luka and moistened his lips. "Are the G-G-Gestapo here?" he finally managed to stutter. "Did they arrest Marok, d-d-did you say?"

"For the time being they're dealing with him in the guardroom. Don't just stand there looking like another blockhead, Kurzweil. Take a walk past the door of the guardroom; you'll be able to hear something for sure. We must find out what they want with Marok and Weber. And don't think that your prospects for the future are any better than ours if things start happening in earnest. Hurry up now, and come back afterwards."

Kurzweil swallowed and left. He made several unnecessary trips to the tables and machines before he dared to go near the guardroom. But finally he took heart and crossed the floor directly in front of the guard-room door. I thought I could see his ears, big already, stretch and grow. Now he turned and walked back the same way. This time he was bold enough to stop for a moment in front of the door.

"God help me, he's such a daredevil," said Glantzer appreciatively. "If only he doesn't forget to come back and tell us what he's heard. No, by God, here he comes. Bravo, old man!"

We looked at him anxiously.

"Did you hear anything?"

He shook his head.

"I couldn't make out the words, but there is something wrong. I have never heard Marok being so meek before. He was explaining something, but I didn't understand what it was." Suddenly Kurzweil thought of his position. "Well, this isn't something that concerns you. Look after your work, men, and get on with it now."

A door was shut with a loud bang somewhere. Kurzweil was startled. "What was that?"

Luka nodded toward the guardroom.

"I think it was the door to the exercise yard."

Soon thereafter a furious voice reached us through the thin outer wall: "Damned dog!"

Every man in the print shop sat as if paralyzed and listened.

Glantzer, whose place was near the window, pressed his face against it. He had scraped a thin stripe in the paint of the glass to be able to follow what took place in the exercise yard during the workday.

"Did you hear the smack? It was Marok's face that was slapped. Oh, hell. Now they're tearing the decorations off his uniform. It's that sneak, you know, who's doing it. And now it's Weber's turn. Poor devils, they must be suffering now. The cold sweat is running down their pale faces. Krüger is there, too, but he doesn't even lift his little finger to help his disciples. His face is cold and hard like stone. I've never seen him like this before. Now both Marok and Weber are being led out through the gate. Oh, hell, how wretched they look, stripped of their medals."

We could hear a car start outside the board fence.

The air in the print shop was loaded with nervous tension bordering on desperation. Kurzweil scurried around between machines and tables and begged us to be quiet and work. No one paid any attention to him.

I had the scary feeling of sitting on a powder keg, watching the match come closer and closer. What if they closed down the entire print shop after the incident with Marok and Weber?

I could not control myself; I had to find out what Luka thought about this.

He looked at me furiously. "Damn you, shut up, man. Talk to whomever the hell you want to, but leave me alone."

"*Achtung!*" called Kurzweil.

Krüger was serious when he greeted us, but not unfriendly.

"Good day, gentlemen." He looked us over carefully. "I regret to inform you that Oberscharführer Marok and Oberscharführer Weber have proven to be unworthy of the task with which they have been entrusted. They have committed a serious crime and they will be punished now. This is what happens to those who break their promises and forget their duty. For you, gentlemen, this affair will not have any consequences. Of course not. As long as you carry out your work conscientiously and comply with the rules and regulations that are in force here at all times, you are under my personal protection. Well, gentlemen, that is what I wanted to tell you today. Good morning."

Krüger took the huge leather briefcase that Kurzweil had filled with bundles of notes and returned to the guardroom. Five minutes later we saw Krebs go in to see him. The barracks head still looked scared.

Krüger's short speech had a calming influence on us. After all, he had said that we would not have any trouble because of Marok's and Weber's downfall.

Glantzer shook his head. "I'll never understand Krüger, so help me if I will. Here he comes and gives us a report about the two idiots, so to speak, as if we were attending some kind of board meeting. Why?"

"Because Krüger is a sly devil," said Luka, back to his old self again. "He was aware that we knew everything that took place outside in the exercise yard. He noticed it as soon as he came in here. So he played board meeting with us until he saw that we were safe and submissive again. There is only one thing in the whole world that Krüger is afraid of, and that's that a spark will fly into this powder keg and blow up his dearly beloved counterfeit workshop. And being the modern employer he is, Krüger also knows that nervous and tense workers cannot be as productive as they should be. In our sophisticated and demanding profession, only excellent results are acceptable. If he were able to, he'd surely provide us with the women he talked about once, as well as many other things that would serve to energize us. Not for our sake, but for his own and that of his holy undertaking."

"What did Luka say to you, Glantzer? Speak up." Kurzweil's tone of voice was tougher and his forefinger angrier than ever before.

Krebs came out of the guardroom. He not only looked relieved, but as if he had just been promoted to Oberscharführer.

Although everything was seemingly back to normal, it was not, because even though we had, more than once, wished that both Marok and Weber would be sent to a certain place, we were fully aware that those who would replace them might be ten times worse.

But during lunch break that day I had a pleasant surprise. A man came over to me and shook my hand. "I hear that you are Norwegian," he said.

A few seconds must have gone by before I realized that the man was speaking Danish and not German.

"Are you really Danish?" I asked in Norwegian. "When did you get here?"

"Yes, I'm Danish, and I got here half an hour ago. My friend Levi and I were supposed to be picked up from the quarantine block yesterday, but obviously something got in the way."

Then I remembered that Krebs had mentioned he was to pick up two prisoners from the quarantine block.

"What's actually going on in this mysterious house?" he asked, looking at me curiously.

I shrugged my shoulders. "You'll find out soon enough. Where are you from?" His appearance, and the way he said *house* instead of *block* revealed that he had not been in any concentration camps before coming here.

"I came straight from Copenhagen. My name is Hoffgaard."

"Are you a printer?" I asked. It was great to be standing there speaking Norwegian to someone who understood what I said, almost a countryman.

He shook his head. "No, I am a bank employee. Why did you think I was a printer?"

"Because this mysterious house, as you call it, is a print shop. Please do not ask me what we print here. Both of us can only get into trouble if I tell you. Anyhow, you'll find out in about half an hour."

Krebs strutted past us with a big, pleasant-smelling cigar in his mouth.

The Dane looked after him, frowning. "What a scoundrel," he said furiously. "That's my cigar he's enjoying. I had a whole box with me when I got here. I'm going to demand it back, so help me God."

"No, don't do that." I grabbed his arm. "If you mention so much as a syllable about the cigars he will torment you to death. I have been here long enough to know what I'm talking about, and I only mean well."

"Damn it," he mumbled savagely. "Tell me one thing: Why are there only Jews here?"

"Well, I suppose they might have had the idea that only half-Jews or 100 percent Jews should be in this block."

"In that case they are not very consistent—considering they are Germans—since for my part, I'm only 25 percent Jewish."

I looked at him in surprise. "They also arrest people who are 25 percent Jewish in Denmark?"

"Not as Jews. They arrested me because I tried to escape to Sweden with my wife and children. My wife is 100 percent Jewish, so she and the children were sent to the concentration camp at Theresienstadt."

"To work!" called Kurzweil.

I was completely confused when I sat down to scrutinize the pound notes again. What could it mean that Hoffgaard had ended up here? Could it mean that we who were in this block also had a chance to survive? No, that thought was too optimistic, considering what we were doing here. But why did they send a man to us who was only 25 percent Jewish, and whom they themselves did not consider a Jew? If he had been a specialist in one or another typographical area, it might make sense, but after all, he was not . . . Had they wanted to get ahold of an ordinary bank employee, there were surely hundreds of 50 percent and 100 percent Jews to choose from.

Luka pushed me with his elbow. "Are you pondering over the trisection of a triangle?"

I told him about the Dane.

Luka looked at me sympathetically.

"Have you never met people who walk around asking if anyone has seen their glasses when they are on their forehead? You are one of them."

"Nonsense; I don't wear glasses, and you know it very well."

"No, but you belong to the chosen people who receive Red Cross parcels, and so does the Dane, and you can be sure that Marok was aware of this. He probably thought that your parcels were not enough, so he maneuvered this bank employee into Block 19. You'll see that he will be appointed head cashier of our Bank of England. Too bad that Marok will probably never enjoy the fruits of his clever plan! No wonder Krebs is walking around smoking cigars and looking overjoyed! As for you, you'll have to share your 'prominent position' with the newcomer. My condolences."

In the beginning I thought that Luka's theory was too far-fetched. I did not think for a moment that Marok would be reluctant to risk a prisoner's life on account of a few Red Cross parcels—I had seen Germans beat prisoners to death for less than that. It was the practical side of the situation that I found so unreasonable. According to the Germans' own regulations, the Dane was not to be treated like a Jew. How, then, had Marok managed to persuade the camp commandant to turn Hoffgaard over to a kommando such as ours, which was clearly strictly Jewish? The camp commandant must have known that we in this block were a group of prisoners who were doomed to death. Had the Dane been an essential specialist or Marok a high-ranking influential officer, I might have been able to understand it.

Luka moved his head irritably when I voiced my objections.

"I'll reconstruct the whole course of events for you. Okay, Marok finds out—how is immaterial—that a 25 percent Jewish Dane has arrived, or will arrive, in Sachsenhausen. He is looking for such a man—that is, for such a man's parcels—either for his own sake, or perhaps because a little Cleopatra in Berlin has become wildly excited about the contents of a certain person's Red Cross parcels. Let us stick to the latter alternative, so as to get a whiff of classical eroticism in this story.

"So what does Marok Antonius, who is up to his ears in love, do now? He goes to see Krüger, the man whose only and all-consuming passion is this counterfeit mint, and tells him that he knows of a Jew—he mentions neither 25 percent, 50 percent, nor 100 percent—who would be of vital use in Block 19. Krüger immediately telephones the camp commandant, and in the course of five short minutes our Antonius's wish has been fulfilled. Because you surely don't believe that the great camp commandant bothers to find out if the prisoner is one-quarter, one-half, or 100 percent Jewish. Conclusion: One man's death is another man's bread."

It turned out later that Luka's theory was correct. Hoffgaard had ended up in Block 19 simply because Marok was after Red Cross parcels.

I dreaded meeting Hoffgaard when we were all in the dayroom at the end of our working day. The man had to be completely depressed after what he had seen and heard since we had talked to each other a few hours ago. To my great surprise, nothing about him suggested that when I met him.

"Why that strange look, Norwegian?"

"Well, to be honest, I expected to find you quite depressed."

"Oh shit, we'll get through this, you'll see. As long as there is life, there's hope, you know. It will be worse, once I am home in Denmark, to persuade my respectable father to accept the fact that I was involved with something as horrific as making counterfeit money. But those notes would have gone like freshly baked Danish pastry in my bank. Well, perhaps they do, for that matter."

Hoffgaard was and always would be the great optimist among us.

Marok was shot. Weber was sentenced to fifteen years in prison. Krüger came in person and told us a few days after the arrest. Of course, he did not fail to emphasize that this is what would happen to all those who violated the strict but just regulations in Block 19, while those who did their duty and whose conduct was honest had nothing to fear.

During the three- or four-day interval until a new SS man arrived, Krebs was the highest authority in the block, a fact he did not let us forget for a single minute.

Chapter 16

Hauptscharführer Beckmann, alias "Wild West," stood on the floor with his feet wide apart and juggled a large-caliber pistol. It was the constant pistol-juggling that gave him his nickname.

"Look at this here shooter, fellows. If I had a penny for each Russian I sent to the happy hunting grounds with this pistol, I would be a rich man. The Russian hordes were seized by wild panic when they saw the two of us. Light a cigarette, Kurzweil, and I will shoot its tip off so easily and accurately that you won't even notice it."

"I don't have any cigarettes," stuttered Kurzweil.

"That's too bad," said Wild West, putting the gun back into its holster. "Today I'm really in the mood for a champion shot." He blinked gruffly beneath his bushy, yellowish-white eyebrows and smacked the leather case with his hand.

Wild West was a fool, but a dangerous one. His hearing was like a dog's, and his eyes were like those of an Indian on the warpath.

"No, my dear Springer, don't straighten up now. There are still five minutes left until dinner. I won't tolerate any of you shirking at work, remember that, all of you! You won't get anywhere with me, no, sir. You'd like it if I were to end up the same way as Marok and Weber, right? You can be sure that tough Helmuth Beckmann, or Wild West, as you call me, is not that dumb. That shocked you, I guess. You probably didn't suspect that I knew it. Oh yes, I know this and much more.

"But as I said, you won't see Hauptscharführer Helmuth Beckmann ending up the same way as the two idiots who were here before. I, too, have a good time with the girls in Berlin, good heavens—but I keep my head clear and don't blabber about everything. So help me, a man in my uniform cannot walk the streets of Berlin in peace. The women buzz and hum around me like mosquitoes around a trout fisherman. Did you hear that? By God, it was well said, huh? They all want to get married, whether they are married already or not. But old Helmuth is too tough to be tempted more than he wants to be. Kurzweil, I need two men to pick up the food."

Glantzer and I were chosen this time. Wild West walked ahead of us, and we followed him outside to the gate in the board fence. He unlocked the gate and the soup bucket stood outside, waiting for us as usual. It was brought there by prisoners from the camp.

Wild West lifted the lid. A stench rose from the gray-green mixture. "Ah, spinach soup," said Wild West, but he quickly replaced the lid.

The big soup bucket was heavy, and the prisoners in Block 19 were in poor shape. We usually put down the bucket and rested two or three times before we brought it into the mess hall. This time Wild West made sure there was no way for us to rest at all.

"Hurry, hurry!" he nagged nonstop as he pounded our backs with his hard fist. We were completely exhausted when we dragged, more than carried, the bucket into the mess hall. Wild West followed us all the way. Of course Güting had to show him how important a Stubendienst he was, and scolded us angrily. He almost deprived us of participating in the subsequent feast.

Lately the soup had become worse each day. Today it was worse than ever. It was not only the terrible odor and taste that made it inedible; it was also full of sand, which grated between our teeth.

"You're much too well off here," said Wild West, who enjoyed our grimaces. "Imagine getting such tasty spinach soup on a weekday."

The only one who had no problem swallowing the mushy gray-green soup was, as usual, the monarchist from Vienna. His stomach would have been an interesting object of study for medical science.

I happened to look at Bober just as he flung his spoon down on the table. Then he took his false teeth out of his mouth and threw them into his soup dish.

"Eat by yourselves," he said dejectedly in a loud voice. "Damn it, I can't swallow it."

Suddenly Wild West was in a hurry to leave.

That day there was so much soup left over in our dishes that the monarchist barely managed to get up from the table. I imagined that I could see the green stuff oozing out of his ears.

"The first day I am a free man, I won't do anything but eat beef from morning till night," said Hoffgaard when we went back to work. "And the meat will be tender and delicious, you can be sure of that."

"Then you might just as well order an ambulance for dessert and coffee," Leib Italiener advised him cheerfully.

I envied those two. Here they talked as if it were just a question of time as to when they would be free. Of course, the fact that neither of them had been in a concentration camp before they got here explained their irrepressible optimism. Had the way to this block been through an inferno such as Auschwitz or Buchenwald, their opinions might have been somewhat different. They had heard about the atrocities in these and other camps, but they had never experienced them personally. This was why I envied them: They had not yet lost the ability to believe in a miracle, as I and the other prisoners here had.

Or was there perhaps a tiny bit of hope left in us too? Not a single man had committed suicide. Therefore, there had to be a spark of hope in us that defied all experience and common sense. Wasn't this proof enough that miracles could happen? Even old, wise, and level-headed Springer thought that such a possibility could not be completely disregarded.

And when all was said and done, was it not a small miracle that I was sitting here now? One more day of carrying cement would have been more than I could have survived, as ill as I was. Why was I spared?

Because Nachemsohn had stepped behind me in the tattooing line. Why was I the only Jew who was sent back to Block 11 in Auschwitz? Because the doctor had loved Norway, and because by chance he had asked me where I was from. *By chance?*

Why had Bernhard Krupp asked me to bring regards to his fiancée at home in Norway? There were other Norwegians there then. "I know that you'll make it home, Moritz," he had said, just before he died. Those were the words that had helped me bear up in Monowitz and Auschwitz during the terrible times that followed—the words that had forced me to endure. Maybe they could help me and force me to get through this too. They had to.

What if all the other Norwegian Jews were already dead? Who would then tell about the hell we had been in? I had to get back. I had to believe in a miracle. And when the miracle happened, I had to be in good health and of sound mind to bear witness.

I was so busy with my thoughts that I did not notice Krebs until he was standing directly in front of me. He must have seen that I was "sabotaging" the work, but he pretended that he did not.

"You are supposed to go and see Beckmann," he said in a friendly voice. "A grand package has arrived for you," he whispered confidentially when I got up. Krebs's behavior toward me had become entirely different since Beckmann's arrival. The reason for this was not hard to understand. As barracks chief he still had many advantages over the other prisoners, but he could no longer take the same liberties as he had in the days of Marok and Weber.

The package that stood on the table in the guardroom broke all records in Block 19. It was a Swedish parcel.

"Well, that's some package," said Beckmann after emptying its contents on the table. "Don't you agree?"

"Yes." It slipped out. I was so anxious to find out if I would be able to keep part of the treasure that I could barely stand still.

Beckmann looked at me quickly.

"You don't think that I've stolen anything?"

"Absolutely not, Herr Hauptscharführer."

"A German soldier never steals from a prisoner," he said, and fingered a brand-new set of fine underwear that this unbelievable dream of a package also contained. "It's a different story if you feel like giving me something. This set of underwear, for example, would fit me better than you. Besides, I suffer badly from rheumatism. Of course, I will give you another set. It is a bit thinner and maybe somewhat worn, but you are only indoors. Of course, you may keep the rest of the package for yourself."

I did not believe my own ears. Was he really serious that he would only keep the underwear?

"You are quite welcome to the underwear," I stuttered.

I thought I was dreaming when I left the guardroom with the package under my arm. So did the men in the print shop. They stared at me as if I had grown wings on my back.

But in the dayroom Krebs was waiting for me.

"May I see it?" he asked furtively, standing in front of my cupboard.

For a moment I thought of saying no, but the expression on his sly face warned me. If he felt like it, he would not hesitate for a moment to strike me down and then accuse me of having attacked him. The result would be punishment drills and not a bite of the contents of the package. I held the package out to him. "Taste the stuff, Krebs." I actually managed to be so believable when I pretended to be the happy giver of gifts that he became confused. But when I thought he had had enough, I resolutely put the package into my cupboard.

"Wild West gave me strict orders to report to him if so much as a crumb disappeared from the package. He's after somebody—that's obvious." I took a chance on the bluff because I knew that Krebs was scared of losing his job.

His hands must have tingled but he did not hit me. "Don't stand there and talk nonsense," he grumbled. "See that you get back to work."

As usual I confided in Luka.

"This will work," he whispered. "For once you've really acted with your head. Risky, I admit, but a hundred percent correct. Like all thugs, Krebs is a cowardly wretch when it comes to his own skin, and he's felt insecure and afraid ever since Marok's downfall. I would imagine that he has reason to. But as I said, your bluff will work. I'm willing to swear on my Jewish-Roman head that you'll find the package untouched in the cupboard."

"Achtung!"

A serious Krüger came in with Wild West at his heels. "Good day, gentlemen." He said nothing more until Wild West had brought in Krebs, Güting, and the others who worked in the engraving shop. Now we had no doubt that something serious was amiss. It was deathly quiet in the large room.

"Lauber."

Lauber came forward.

"Tell us about the gold that was in your mouth."

Lauber cleared his throat, confused. "Do you mean the gold bridge that was in my mouth, Herr Sturmbannführer?"

"Exactly, Lauber. What happened to it?"

"I had an infection in my jaw and asked Marok to take me to the doctor. The doctor decided that the big gold bridge had to be removed, which he did."

"What happened to the gold, Lauber?"

"Marok took care of it."

"That's right—Marok confessed to this during the investigation. But where is the gold now, gentlemen? It is neither among Marok's belongings that he left behind, nor in the guardroom. It must be somewhere, don't you agree, gentlemen?"

I broke into a cold sweat. It was Güting who had packed Marok's things, and I had helped him.

Then Güting stepped forward. "Herr Sturmbannführer, I took care of the gold when I found it among Marok's belongings, because I knew that it didn't belong to him. It's now in my cupboard; I can get it right away."

"Go ahead, Güting. But why did you not hand it over before?"

"Herr Sturmbannführer, I took care of the gold at the time. Of course it's unforgivable, but I simply forgot all about the gold bridge."

"I understand, Güting. Fetch the gold and let's bring this affair to a close." Krüger sounded relieved.

Güting looked just as relieved as Krüger when he came back with a small package. Krüger put it into his pocket. With Wild West at his heels, he then went into the Bank of England to fill his briefcase.

For my part, I felt as if I had awakened from a nightmare when I sat down at the worktable. I knew this much about Güting: If he had managed to hide the gold in a safe place, he never would have confessed anything about "having taken care of it."

"Do you really think he'll get off that easily? Krüger cannot be so dumb that he believes Güting's lie?" I said.

"No more than you and I," said Luka. "He just doesn't want any more executions than are strictly necessary. It might damage the concern's reputation."

"I think I'm dreaming," sighed Glantzer. "Here we have God knows how many millions of pounds in current notes, and yet there's such an upheaval about Lauber's poor gold bridge. What would happen if any of those pieces of paper disappeared?"

"Then I believe you'd see a different Krüger than the one we saw today."

"Be careful—the bank robber is coming. Look at Wild West; he's barely managing to carry the bag. The old man is getting greedier and greedier each time."

Krüger stopped in the middle of the floor.

"Gentlemen, as I have told you before, and as you know, we are engaged in some very important work. Thanks to the admirable results we have achieved, I have been assigned the task of carrying out major extensions. Block 18, our neighboring block, will be placed at our disposal, and our workforce will be increased accordingly. Not only will we increase production, but we shall also extend it to include several different 'articles.' I daresay there will be many interesting tasks ahead of you. Moreover, the guards will shortly be reinforced by three men: Hauptscharführer Hoffmann, Oberscharführer Werner, and Oberscharführer Bauer. I hope that you will not give any of these gentlemen reason to complain. Good-bye, gentlemen."

Wild West followed Krüger outside with the heavy briefcase in his hands.

"Oh hell," Glantzer let slip. "We're going to set an unbeatable record in money forgery, fellows."

Luka had a bright sparkle in his eyes.

"It means much more than that for us. Dear God, man, don't you understand that we can feel safe now that the print shop will not be discontinued, and we won't be sent to a certain place? For us, time is of the greatest importance. This is the first good moment I have had in this hellhole."

"You're right," Glantzer exclaimed happily, "but what do you think these new 'articles' might be?"

"Quiet, for God's sake, quiet," hushed Kurzweil, flexing his thin arms. It was not only at our table that the big news had created a stir. He barely managed to calm us down before Wild West came back.

We breathed a sigh of relief when we saw Wild West pull out his pistol. So he had not noticed our impudent behavior. He strode around the print shop, feet wide apart, juggling his revolver. The scene reminded me of the saloon episodes in the cowboy films from William S. Hart's days. It was strange that we did not put up our hands!

"Three more men are coming. You heard it. You will find out what it means to work under supervision, you can be sure of that," said Wild West.

Just then Bober came in from the engraving workshop. He marched solemnly over to Wild West and clicked his heels. "Herr Hauptscharführer,

Sturmbannführer Krüger ordered me to print a poster with certain type-faces. The fonts are ready to be picked up in the camp."

Wild West scratched his ruddy neck. "Must it be today?"

"Herr Hauptscharführer, Sturmbannführer Krüger ordered that the poster be ready tomorrow. The package is in the canteen."

Wild West put his pistol determinedly into the holster. "Well, I will take care of the matter. Get back to work."

Bober clicked his heels and about-faced like a well-trained recruit.

Wild West looked after him appreciatively and nodded with satisfaction. Then he pulled down his uniform jacket properly and left the block. A little later we heard the gate in the board fence slam shut.

Then Bober came back. He looked at the clock on the wall and walked quickly toward the guardroom.

Kurzweil came limping from the other end of the room. "Where are you going? Stop!"

Bober threatened him with his fist and slipped into the guardroom.

Kurzweil did not dare follow him further than to the door. He remained standing there and washed his hands in cold sweat. "Is he raving mad? Does he intend to play with Wild West's uniforms too? Even in broad daylight?"

Scratching sounds suddenly came from the loudspeaker underneath the ceiling. We rarely heard anything through this, our reward from Krüger.

One and all stared at the loudspeaker with wide eyes.

Then we heard it—the German news broadcast from London.

"This is London. Since the battle of El Alamein in October last year and the defeat at Stalingrad in February this year, the Germans have retreated on all fronts. In Russia our courageous allies have, among other things, recaptured Kiev, and von Manstein is retreating from the Asovsk Sea to Isjum. In Italy, Naples fell on September thirtieth, and since then our troops have slowly but surely fought their way toward the north. Kesselring is fighting like a wounded tiger, but the outcome of this tough battle can only be one. In Germany the remnants of what was once the powerful Luftwaffe fight a futile battle to prevent our bombers from reaching the cities and other military targets with their cargo. We are becoming stronger and stronger in the air, which Hitler and Co. will soon find out."

We stared gratefully and with admiration at Bober when he came out from the guardroom. We came close to giving him a big cheer, and some made an attempt, but Bober stopped them with a hand movement. "Don't ruin my beautiful moment. Wild West may be here any minute. Now things are going well in the world."

Five minutes later Wild West returned. He probably had an inkling that something had happened while he was gone, because he walked around sniffing and looking everywhere for quite a while before he went into the guardroom with the little package he carried in his hand.

"Good Lord, what a day," said Luka seriously.

Glantzer shook his head. "What tremendous luck that we were able to listen to the German broadcast just then. It must have been a fluke."

"A fluke? You can bet your life that it wasn't. Didn't you see that Bober looked at the clock as soon as he came in here? Ask him tonight."

Glantzer was not the only one who wanted to find out more about this incident that evening.

Bober smiled patronizingly at those who talked about a fluke.

"Don't be so dumb. I knew where on the dial I would find the right station, and of course I also knew the exact time of the transmission. My God, what a wonderful cigarette, Norwegian!"

In honor of the occasion I had given away more of the contents of the parcel than I had actually wanted to, and Bober had gotten the well-deserved better part.

"But where the hell do you know all that from?" pried Schnapper.

Bober blew blue smoke into Schnapper's curious face. "That's a state secret, you seal. I suppose you have seen a picture of a seal, Schnapper? It's just as round and baldheaded as you."

"Kiss my arse," grumbled Schnapper threateningly. But then he thought about what he had heard about the bombing of the German cities. "Did you hear what he said? We're getting stronger and stronger in the air, and the Germans will soon notice it, he said. They are not enjoying themselves in Berlin nowadays, but I think they will be quite a bit worse off when the Americans and the British get the ball rolling in earnest. We'll probably notice it here in the block too, but so what? I prefer getting killed by an Allied bomb to dying in a gas chamber." He pushed Cytrin with his elbow. "What's the matter with you, old man? You look as if you've received bad news."

Cytrin shrugged his shoulders. "It's just that the sooner the Germans go to hell, the closer we get to the gas chamber you talked about."

"Stop this talk, man!" called Leib Italiener from the other end of the table. "You know what we agreed on at the worktable. You and I are going to Palestine when the damned Germans are on their knees in their ruins and begging for mercy. Begging, the way only a cowardly German can do it."

"Hush, hush," said Kurzweil meekly.

"Ah," scoffed Blaustein. "Wild West is in Berlin smelling the whores. Italiener is right; Palestine is the place for us. What's left for us in Germany, Poland, Czechoslovakia, or wherever we're from? They have killed our women and children, and what earthly possessions we owned do not exist anymore. What then? Let us do as Italiener says: Let's go to Palestine and dig so deep into the soil there that no one can budge us. Someday we Jews have to see to it that we can settle down."

"Ha," said Cytrin. "You talk as if it were just a matter of going to Palestine and settling there. First we must get away from here alive."

We talked, discussing the events of the day long into the evening.

Chapter 17

WE WENT OUT TO THE EXERCISE YARD DURING THE LUNCH BREAK. LUKA and I talked about the two SS men who'd arrived a few days earlier. We agreed that no matter what, they were an improvement on Wild West. One of them had been in Norway several times during the war. Among other things, he insisted that Stavanger was the most beautiful city in the country. As an Oslo native I sided of course with the capital, which he did not want to hear. But he drove me into a corner because I'd never been in Stavanger.

Just as we were about to turn around at the gate in the board fence, it was opened by a dry-looking man in SS uniform who was about six and a half feet tall. When he had locked the door behind him, he continued toward the block entrance without so much as looking at us.

"Ugh," said Luka. "There you see the prototype of a Himmler disciple, a fanatic through and through."

"Poor us," said a fellow next to us. "If this devil is going to stay here, we'll be in for trouble."

"Do you know him, Felix?"

"Yes, unfortunately. He was the camp chief in Dachau while I was there, if I'm not completely mistaken. But I could be wrong; I hope so, for our own sake."

"What was the name of the man in Dachau?"

"Werner."

"Then it's him. Krüger mentioned the names of all three who were to come here. Hoffmann and Bauer are already here, and the third name was Werner, Oberscharführer Werner."

Kurzweil appeared on the block steps.

"*An die Arbeit* [Get to work]!"

We had hardly sat down to work with the endless paper pieces when Kurzweil called out his equally endless *Achtung!*

Wild West came in to introduce the new SS man. He put his meaty hand on the pistol case and looked around the print shop with a fierce expression. The new man stood next to him and scrutinized us with a narrow look typical of the "master race."

Wild West cleared his throat before he said: "This is Oberscharführer Werner!" He looked at us as if he expected us to greet the newcomer with a resounding *Heil Hitler.*

Werner took a step forward. "Have any of you been in Dachau?"

Those who had, answered yes.

"Well, then, you know me."

Then they both went back into the guardroom.

"So help me, one wouldn't know that Wild West has a higher rank than the new smart aleck," said Glantzer.

It was the first time Werner showed up in the print shop. We would see more than enough of him, both in the shop and many other places. He did not leave us alone until the Americans had, so to speak, cornered him.

"A black angel just walked through the room," said Luka somberly.

We worked without talking for a long time.

I forced my thoughts to escape the present. They whirled around the dangerous topic like moths around a naked lightbulb. Finally I managed to banish them into one of the "safe drawers" in my mind. This time the drawer was called Stensbak A/S, where I had had my first job, consisting of sharpening razor blades on a clever but definitely not entirely safe machine. After my first day at work I sat down at the dinner table without washing my hands. My mother was both shocked and angry at my outrageous behavior and gave me the choice between washing or going without dinner. With an empty stomach and a heavy heart I chose the latter, because I did not dare to show her my fingertips, which resembled miniature chopping blocks. Had she seen them, she would no doubt have forbidden me to go back to the grindstone. Where would I then get the day's half-crown? I was all of thirteen years old at the time, and at that age a boy does not like to be without any coins in his pockets.

I also remembered another upsetting incident from this job. The grindstone stood in the basement, and on one of the shelves lay a knife, just the kind of knife my heart yearned for. It was not totally unblemished, but a bit of rust and a broken tip were of course easy to fix for a master sharpener like myself. This ill-fated knife caused me much more trouble than did all my chopped-up fingertips. The result was, sadly, that the knife was in my pocket one evening when I went home. The night that followed my crime was the first really restless night of my life. I dreamed and fantasized about court cases and the ordeal of carrying hot iron until I woke up, because my whole family stood around my bed staring at me fearfully. I felt like a purified and undeservedly lucky person when, on the following day, I was able to put the knife back on the shelf without being discovered.

I must have jumped up from the stool when the air-raid warning sounded. According to instructions, everybody began to collect all the notes and paper. Kurzweil already stood near the cupboard, an ordinary wooden cupboard, and signaled to us fearfully and impatiently. Wild West and the other SS men came rushing out of the guardroom, their gestures nervous. They nagged and rushed us and forgot completely that they were representatives of the death-defying "master race."

As we handed in bundles of the finished or semi-finished product, we were ordered back to our places. They themselves were not slow in getting out to the bomb shelter the second Kurzweil had locked the door of the cupboard.

So there we sat waiting for the noise to begin. Until now no bombs had fallen on the camp, but we did not have any guarantee that this would never occur. However, it was obvious that the Allied planes came in increasing numbers and with bigger and bigger cargoes of bombs intended for Berlin.

The sight of the bent and motionless shapes at the tables seemed eerily unreal. It was like looking at a field of wheat moving in the wind suddenly turned to stone.

Little Italiener—it was an attack of polio that had left him crippled—came calmly strolling in from the engraving workshop. He stopped and looked at us for a while in surprise. Then he shook his head and laughed gleefully. "But in God's name, men, what's the matter with you? So help me, I thought for a minute I'd come to a monastery in the middle of devotions."

He went over to the cupboard with the locked-up notes.

"Are these Germans not an amazing people, or what?" he said, and hit the knuckle of his forefinger against the thin board door. "They take good care that all compromising papers are locked up to prevent them from blowing out into the camp in case a stray bomb comes to visit us. Did you ever see anything like this bombproof safe?"

Just then things started off with a bang in Berlin. It was as if all the antiaircraft guns the city owned were fired at one and the same time. Then the heavy, muffled booms of the bombs followed. I felt the earth tremble underneath the block. Several of the prisoners instinctively threw themselves under the tables, where they remained curled up with their jackets firmly pulled over their heads. Italiener walked around and comforted them with encouraging words and a well-meant kick in the rear end.

No bomb fell on the camp this time.

But in the evening I got a foretaste of what could happen. Ever since the Allied planes had started to come at night, all the prisoners in the block had had to take turns as guards. That evening I was on guard duty in the exercise yard when the planes arrived around 10:00 p.m. The myriad tracers from the antiaircraft fire and the light clusters from the countless beams of the searchlights were an amazing sight. It seemed like a miracle that any planes could avoid being hit. But the small silver birds sailed calmly and undauntedly from one light cluster to another. One would have thought that they were invulnerable.

But suddenly I saw something that overturned that theory. A burning plane swerved downward and in the direction of the camp. It resembled a giant torch that one or another god had thrown away in a fit of rage. I squatted down instinctively. I had a chilling feeling that a flaming apparition sped above my head. It was bright and warm around me as if on a midsummer's day. The plane ended up crashing with an earth-shattering bang just outside the camp area, and a gigantic fan of fire leapt toward the black sky in the north. The pressure from the explosion was so strong that I was sure all the blocks would be pressed together into a single big pile of splinters. I closed my eyes. When I opened them again I saw to my joy and surprise that both the board fence and our block were intact. And nothing had happened to the other blocks either. But what was it that came falling down from the sky? It turned out to be four or five parachutists, and there was no doubt that at least half of them landed inside the camp. If they were alive, they would not be pleased to discover that they had jumped from a burning plane into a witches' cauldron.

When the all-clear signal sounded I went into the block. On the threshold of the dayroom I stopped, dumbfounded. Had the men gone raving mad? What could it mean that they had covered their faces with soot? I looked curiously at Schnapper, who sat on a stool and hiccuped with laughter.

"Oh, that blasted sneaky Italiener," he grinned, hitting his knees. "While it was dark here and the men were the most terrified, he pretended to be the great comforter. He spoke to the boys encouragingly and patted and stroked their cheeks to no end. You should've seen the men when the light came on a few minutes ago. One pointed at the other and they laughed themselves sick at the soot-smudged faces. I haven't had so much fun since I went to the circus. What the hell are you sneering at?" Schnapper looked at me suspiciously.

I stroked my forefinger alongside his hairless pate and stuck it underneath his nose. It was black with soot. Schnapper stared at the soot in disbelief. Then he touched his forehead with both hands and ran his palms backwards.

"The damned scoundrel," he snarled savagely, and stared at his black palms. "Where is he? I'll teach him to behave himself, he can be sure of that."

But Italiener was nowhere to be seen.

———

Hoffgaard shook his head when he returned from the office in the camp.

"What did they want with you?" asked Shurak curiously. "I saw Wild West take you out to the camp a while ago, and so help me, I began to wonder about all sorts of things."

"Some good friends in Copenhagen are working to get me released. It's nice to know that one has friends who really make an effort to help. It's just a pity that the attempt this time is doomed to failure beforehand. Had I not, because of one idiotic misunderstanding or another, ended up in this elite colony, I would probably have been sent home a free man. In any case, this is what I understood in the office a while ago. For obvious reasons they cannot send me home now with my head on my shoulders, and I'm actually not interested in making the trip without it."

"You can thank blessed, departed Marok for this misunderstanding," said Shurak.

Hoffgaard gestured with his hands. "Oh well, here I am, and here I must stay for now. There is nothing I can do about it. You'll see that we'll get through it, Shurak."

"*Achtung!*"

Werner let us stand to attention while he walked around, peeking and snooping. He did not find anything to swoop down on until he came to Hoffgaard's cupboard, where he discovered a speck of dust in a corner.

"Who owns this cupboard?"

Hoffgaard came forward. "I do, Herr Oberscharführer."

"You are a pig—you cannot keep your cupboard clean."

"But I have . . ."

"Keep your big mouth shut!" Werner interrupted him furiously and raised his hand.

Then Hoffgaard made the fateful blunder of raising his arms to protect himself. He had to pay dearly for this shameful violation of discipline and propriety.

When Werner had satisfied his need to beat a defenseless person, he went into our dormitory. At a signal Krebs followed him. They stayed there for quite a while.

"Such a lout," mumbled Hoffgaard when he went out to the washroom to take care of his bruised face.

Werner left us without a word when he emerged from the dormitory. But Krebs went over to Italiener to tell him that he was not allowed to smoke for two weeks, because his bed had not found favor in Werner's critical and priggish eyes.

Italiener put a highly injured expression on his face. "But I sleep well in my bed as it is. My particular shape simply demands a hollow here and a lump there."

Krebs sneered. "Go to Werner and tell him that. I'll give you twenty cigarettes if you dare."

"All right," said Italiener, and left.

"What—he went?" Cytrin let slip, surprised.

"I think you'll find him on the toilet, if you want to get ahold of him," said Krebs.

"I'm not so sure about that," said Bober thoughtfully. "Anything can be expected from that man. I would not be surprised at all if you lose the twenty cigarettes, Krebs."

"Such nonsense," scoffed Krebs, cocksure.

However, he looked anything but cocksure when Werner and Italiener came through the doorway five minutes later.

"Krebs," said Werner slowly, standing with his feet wide apart in front of Krebs. "Italiener insists that you promised him twenty cigarettes if he dared to tell me that he slept well in his bed just as it is. Is that right? I advise you to tell the truth."

Krebs hesitated for a brief second. "That's right, Herr Oberscharführer, but it was just a joke on my part."

"Is that so? But Italiener took the bet seriously and has won it. Let him have the cigarettes right away."

Krebs's face turned red with fury at the disgrace. However, he had no choice but to get the cigarettes to give to the winner.

Gloating, Italiener put the prize into his pocket.

"Stop for a second, my foolhardy man," said Werner shrewdly. "You are not permitted to smoke, so you have no use for them. Divide them among your friends and hurry up now."

With a disappointed look on his waif-like face, Italiener began to hand out the valuable prize. His movements became slower and slower with each cigarette. In the end he had only one left in his hand. Then he turned and looked imploringly at Werner.

"That one too," said Werner mercilessly. Just as he was leaving he turned to Krebs. "If you want my advice, don't get involved in such bets again. Understood?"

"Yes, Herr Oberscharführer."

Werner had hardly left before Krebs chased us out.

"See to it that you get back to work, you confounded lazy people. The lunch break was over several minutes ago."

Glantzer chuckled with satisfaction when he reached for the first note of the bundle. "So help me, this served Krebs right. But poor Italiener—he'll have to go through a lot for a long time."

"I don't think you have to worry about that," said Luka.

"What do you think, then? Do you believe that Krebs will suddenly change into a nice and forbearing Joseph in Egypt, or what?"

"Oh no, that's the last thing I believe. I simply think that he will be fired as barracks head one day. The stakes he plays for are too high even for a shrewd player like him. Ever since Werner arrived, Krebs has used all kinds of tricks to stir up trouble between Wild West and him. He knows that this is the only way that he can gain some influence, and so he tries the old tactic of dividing and conquering. Had both men been like Wild West, his plan would most probably have succeeded. But he won't get a man like Werner to wriggle on the hook with an ordinary worm. If he has not understood it before, he ought to after this episode with Italiener."

Glantzer glanced irritably at Luka. "Could you not just as well explain to me how Krebs manages to stir up trouble between Werner and Wild West? But don't give me your usual roundabout talk."

"Well," said Luka, "one fine day Krebs will click his heels and say, 'Herr Hauptscharführer, I ask permission to move table number six a few feet forward because of the light.' Wild West will look at Krebs's irreproachable posture and think, 'By God, I could make an excellent soldier of this man.' So he answers, 'Just you move the table.' But Krebs does not move the table right away. He waits until Werner has relieved Wild West in the print shop. Not only that, but he also makes sure that the table is moved the moment he sees that Werner is furious for one or another reason. That's when he asks the men who work at table number six to carry out the well-calculated operation.

"Of course, Werner comes running like a taunted bear and asks what in hell they are doing. 'We are moving the table a little because of the light,' says Krebs in the world's most innocent voice. 'Damn nonsense!

The table must stay where it is, end of story!' Only then will Krebs say that this is an order from Beckmann, from Hauptscharführer Beckmann. A situation like this is highly unpleasant for a man like Werner. He can't very well neglect an order from a superior just like that, but it is almost as hard for him to call off his own clear-cut order to the slave Krebs. Whichever alternative he chooses, this story of the table ends with a warm confrontation in the guardroom.

"Next time, the disagreement may be about a cupboard or a machine. Werner and Wild West will fight bitterly about the position of leadership here, and it is easy for a bright man like Krebs to stir up trouble between such people. But if his ploy is discovered before the two antagonists have spoiled their chances in Krüger's eyes, he is finished. Wild West will never see through him; however, Werner most probably will, if he has not already done so. Well, Glantzer, hopefully you do not need another earful."

Glantzer gave Luka an ugly sideways look. "What kind of nonsense are you talking about? Anyhow, you're just sitting there stirring the mush of your brain, man. So help me God, I feel like telling Krebs what kind of nonsense you're dreaming up about him. I suppose you'd have to eat your words."

"Hush, here comes the quartet."

All four SS men came in from the guardroom and settled down at the inspection table, where they began to play cards. Werner looked up from the cards incessantly to make sure that no one in the print shop had the audacity to straighten his back for so much as a second. It obviously spoiled the game for his partner. Wild West's face became redder and redder. Finally he threw his cards on the table with a bang and started to argue with Werner, who was generous enough to answer in kind. We could not hear what they said, but judging from their facial expressions they were not exchanging niceties. In the end, Wild West pointed at his distinctions with one hand and at the guardroom with the other. It was a request that a soldier on duty could not get around, and Werner obeyed the order. His long, thin legs twitched with tension as he strode off to the guardroom. The other three continued to play cards, and now they were almost relaxed. Of the three guards the only one who was dangerous was Wild West, but he was too busy with the cards to bother with us.

"At any rate, you're right that Wild West and Werner are not best friends," admitted Glantzer magnanimously. "In the meantime, I'm sitting here thinking what we could have done if we'd had some invisible ink."

"Sent a message to Churchill and asked him to be kind enough to drop a few bombs on the block," said Luka drily. "You're the man with the really great ideas, Glantzer."

"Oh, go to hell, you double pessimist. Besides, I prefer a bomb to the gas chamber. You are the only one who wants to go up through the chimney so badly. The air of the crematorium smoke will be sour that day, dear Luka."

I saw that Luka's hands began to tremble and he pushed Glantzer hard. "Do you remember the Bald Heads club, Glantzer?"

It worked immediately. Glantzer did not say another word.

Hammering and knocking came from Block 18, where the carpenters from the camp were working on our new workshops. From Krebs we knew that sixty men were in quarantine, waiting for us to be able to receive them.

Everyone was gathered in the print shop. We stood in a group waiting anxiously for what was going to happen next. We realized that it was something special.

Werner appeared in the doorway with a paper in his hand. He looked at us for a moment, then announced, "As ordered by Sturmbannführer Krüger, today Leo Krebs and Herman Güting have been removed from their positions as barracks chief and Stubendienst, respectively. At the same time Arthur Levin has been appointed as the new barracks head and Alfred Pick as the Stubendienst. *Achtung!*"

It was Krüger who appeared on the scene, with a serious expression on his face. He carried a long, beautifully ornamented dagger. "Good day, gentlemen."

I looked over at Krebs. He was staring at the dagger with wide eyes. Suddenly his knees gave way and he fell to the floor. Both Krüger and Werner pretended nothing had happened.

"As you have already heard," Krüger continued, unconcerned, "I have considered it necessary to make a few changes here. Two of my trusted men have betrayed my confidence in them and must accept the consequences. I hope that I do not have to repeat again that no one, absolutely no one, can count on my support if he disregards the rules of this establishment." Krüger pointed to the unconscious ex–barracks chief with the dagger. "Carry him into the dormitory. He will be given two weeks' vacation to recuperate. I will go out of my way as much as I possibly can for my colleagues. Good-bye, gentlemen."

Werner opened the door for Krüger and saluted as if it were Himmler himself who stood in front of him.

The two newly appointed spokesmen remained standing on the floor while the rest of us went back to our workplaces.

"One must admit that here, too, a little something happens once in a while," said Luka drily as he cleaned his glasses.

"A *little* something?" Glantzer had trouble keeping still on his stool. "Was it a *little*, you said? So help me, I think I'm going to quit and leave before I go completely mad. When an intelligent man like Krüger begins to play with eighteen-inch-long daggers and Krebs, who is as strong as a bull, collapses like a calf about to be slaughtered, just because he is being fired as barracks chief, then I think the end is near. Tell me, is it me who's completely nuts?"

"Ask Moritz. He can explain to you the connection between the beautiful dagger and the fallen Krebs."

I could. I knew, because Cytrin told me, that Krebs had stolen the dagger from among Marok's belongings before they were sent to Berlin.

Cytrin had caught a glimpse of it in Krebs's cupboard. He recognized it because he was the one who had made its beautiful ornaments.

Glantzer looked at Luka.

"I don't like to say it, but I must admit that there's something to your prophecies. It's obvious that it was Werner who sniffed out this dagger in Krebs's cupboard. Now I understand why Krebs blacked out when he saw it. What I can't understand is that he gets off so easily. In any other camp both he and Güting would have been hanged on the spot. Krebs is even going to have a two-week holiday. A holiday? So help me, I'm going to steal Krüger's trousers when he comes here next time. At the very least, that would get me a month's stay at a mountain resort, right? Güting steals gold and Krebs a valuable dagger from the German state without being punished other than losing their jobs. No, I'm going home to bed. Do predict something, dear Luka."

"Everything must be quiet in the Schipkapass [important mountain pass in the Bulgarian Balkan Mountains]. It's that simple. Besides, it was Krebs who managed to overcome the last difficult details of the pound cliché when everything almost came to a standstill for us. You can imagine what this meant to Krüger."

"God, yes. The man would lie naked with his counterfeit operation if it were possible. I'd swear that he could also manage to have children with it. No wonder he gave midwife Krebs a two-week holiday."

"He did that to show Krebs he's not let him down completely. He knows that a desperate Krebs could think of something that could kill the whole institution. You can be sure that nice Uncle Krüger will never do anything without a reason."

"Yes, damn it, that's it."

"What was it Glantzer said, Luka? Speak up!"

"He said, 'Yes, damn it, that's it.'"

"Correct, I heard it well. What was it about?"

"Work, of course. We never talk about anything other than work. You know that very well, you twerp."

Chapter 18

"WE STOOD IN THE GAS CHAMBER LINE AND CLUNG TO EACH OTHER IN order to be able to stay on our feet. We knew that we had less than an hour left to live judging by the length of the line. Most of us were Musselmän-ner, and for us this was no reason to be seized by panic—we were too apathetic. Do you see the man on the right at the farthest table? He went alongside the line, begging for pieces of bread. He ate the awful black crumbs he received with a voracious appetite. One would have thought that he had thirty more years to live and not that many minutes. Some prayed; others talked together quietly. Strangely, I for my part felt like singing one of my old cabaret songs, but I decided not to; firstly, because I thought it would smack of too much theater, and secondly, because it was doubtful that the orthodox victims in the line would have appreciated being followed to the grave by 'Valentine' and 'Ferdinand.'"

I looked at Max, the young Dutchman who had been sharing his story with us. "Are you a cabaret singer, then?" I asked.

"I'm a little of everything: cabaret singer, memory artist, mathemati-cian, and film photographer. I'm only twenty-eight years old, but then again, I started when I was just a young boy. I have managed to appear as a singer on the radio programs of several countries, and I've performed on the same street in Paris as Maurice Chevalier.

"But coming back to the line—the insatiable, gaping mouth of the gas chamber had come perilously close to me and the other sixty men here, when something happened that we people called a miracle. A couple of German officers came over to the line. The pleasant man, who is the chief here, began to inquire about our professions and ages. The first prisoner whom he spoke to was a tailor. Krüger, which, as you know, is the name of the pleasant man, nodded and continued to ask questions. The next man was a carpenter. Krüger told the man to get out of the line and stand behind him. This is when I realized that there was a chance in the air to be saved from the gas chamber.

"As the officers chose people with the most varied professions, I decided to mention all of mine," Max continued. "Good God, my very life was at stake. When it was my turn, it poured out of me: cabaret singer, memory artist, mathematician, and photographer. I had been rather steady on my feet in the line, yes, I had, but when the officers signaled to me, it was as though my balancing nerves refused to cooperate. I must have staggered badly when I left the line. You'll undoubtedly find it ridiculous when I tell you that I was scared to death that the officer would stop me and tell me he had no use for people who drank. Had you been in such a line, you would understand.

"That day the gas chamber—and there are many of them in Auschwitz now—was cheated of sixty temporary guests. I don't think any of us really understood that we had been saved until we were sitting on the train that brought us here—in ordinary passenger compartments, if you please. Maybe you don't believe it?"

"Oh yes, we traveled the same way, in passenger compartments."

"Did you really? Wasn't it a wonderful feeling to sit on a bench in a passenger train? I haven't enjoyed myself like that since I was a little boy and rode on a roller coaster for the first time. When we arrived here in Sachsenhausen seven weeks ago, we were placed in a quarantine block. Those weeks were like a dream. The food was brought to us and no one chased us out to work. Since you yourself have been in Auschwitz, you know how it felt to come here. My God, just look at the wonderful clothes we got. I didn't feel nearly as well dressed when I performed in white tie and tails, that's for sure."

Epstein, who had been listening to the Dutchman, interrupted Max. "Are you saying that you can sing 'Valentine' in French?"

"Yes, of course."

Epstein looked at him imploringly. "Could you please sing it to an old Parisian?"

"With pleasure." Max got up and waved to a man who was sitting at the other end of the room. "Come here, Harry."

Harry, a dark-haired young man in his late twenties, came over to us. "Is there something you wanted, Max?" he said.

"This is Harry from Brussels," said Max. "He plays all existing—and imaginary—instruments, and he's as good a dancer as Fred Astaire. Harry, we have a genuine Parisian here, and he's asked me to sing 'Valentine' to him in French. You know that I'm happy to do it, and I hope you'll accompany me. I think the saxophone will do."

"Saxophone it is," said Harry, and pretended to sling the strap over his head. He stretched his neck and wriggled his head, to sort of adjust the strap before he curled his fingers around the pretend instrument. Then came a series of saxophone sounds, so natural that we were completely taken aback. Instinctively we looked closer to be sure his hands were actually empty. In the past I had been much too frequent a guest at the Mølla in Oslo, where I had heard all kinds of music, but never anything like this. Harry was simply a wizard. How could this mistreated and starved human being produce these phenomenal sounds? Harry went on to approximate the well-known melody. Then Max began to sing:

> On se rapelle toujours sa première maîtresse
> J'ai gardé d'la mienne un souvenir plein d'ivresse
> Un jour qu'il avait plu tous l'deux on s'était plu
> Ensuite on se plut de plus en plus
> J'ai d'mandé son nom, elle me dit "Valentine"
> Et comme elle suivait chaque soir la rue Custine

Je pris le même chemin
Et puis j'ai pris sa main
Je lui pris tout enfin:
Elle avait de tout petits petons, Valentine, Valentine
Elle avait de tout petits tétons,
Que je tâtais à tâtons, ton-ton-tontaine
Elle avait un tout petit menton, Valentine, Valentine
Outre ses petits petons, ses p'tits tétons, son p'tit menton,
Elle était frisée comme un mouton.
Hier sur l'Boul'vard, je rencontrai une grosse dame
Avec des grands pieds, d'une taille d'hippopotame,
Elle me sauta au cou et cria "Bonjour, mon loup"
Je lui dis "Pardon, mais qui êtes vous?"
Elle me répondit: "Mais, c'est moi, Valentine!"
Devant son double menton et sa triple poitrine
J'pensai rempli d'effroi
"Qu'elle a changé, ma foi!"
Dire qu'autrefois:
Elle avait de tout petits petons, Valentine, Valentine
Elle avait de tout petits tétons,
Que je tâtais à tâtons, ton-ton-tontaine
Elle avait un tout petit menton, Valentine, Valentine
Outre ses petits petons, ses p'tits tétons, son p'tit menton,
Elle était frisée comme un mouton.

None of us had ever imagined that we would hear anything like this in Block 19. Epstein had tears in his eyes, and the rest of us sat in solemn gratitude, as quiet as mice.

Someone suddenly shouted *Bravo!* behind us.

We turned around, surprised. Krüger and two high-ranking SS offi-cers stood in the room, all three clapping enthusiastically.

Krüger signaled to us to sit down again on the stools. "I'm happy to hear that you have two such capable artists among you now," he said. "They will surely be able to provide you with many pleasant moments. Anyhow, I have come to tell you that we will put the neighboring block to use in the coming days. And then, gentlemen, we will go ahead with our really important work."

"'There are more things in heaven and earth, Horatio,'" said Reussen, a lawyer from Lemberg, quoting from *Hamlet*.

While some of us discussed the concept of fate and other more or less supernatural things, I thought of something that had happened to me more than twenty years ago, at Café Regent on Hausmannsgata. One evening as we were playing chess, a strange fellow had come in and insisted that he was a fortune-teller—for money, of course. I, among others, thought it might be fun to find out a bit about what the future had to offer. He looked at my hand for a long time before he told me that I would have a long life. "But," he continued, frowning, "you'll have hard times and you'll be in great danger in your forties." At the time, with the arrogance of a seventeen-year-old, I had laughed at the man, and had never thought of his prophecy until just that evening.

All of Block 19 and half of Block 18, about 300 square feet, was put to use for the manufacturing of the counterfeit operation's products. The other half of the new block was occupied by our mess hall and dormitory. We were now more than a hundred men from thirteen or fourteen different countries, and among us were all the different specialists that a well-equipped, ultramodern print shop required. Experienced installers, electricians, and carpenters made sure that the machines and instruments were in tiptop condition all the time. For record-keeping and other office work, Krüger had chosen lawyers and other more than qualified functionaries from the gas chamber line at Auschwitz.

But even as our workforce was growing, one SS man after another was being sent away. Eventually there were only sixteen guards left, most of whom were war invalids who were missing an arm or a leg.

One of the new prisoners died only two days after he had arrived in the block. We watched as his friends carried him out.

"Lucky duck, able to go naturally," said Schnapper almost enviously.

"You can just believe it," grumbled Glantzer sardonically. "I think they gave him an injection when they realized he would not be fit for work."

"Let it go. At least now he is spared from being sent to the gas chamber. None of us in this death gang will get much closer to a natural death."

Levin, the new barracks chief, waved me over to him. "You have to come with me out to the camp to pick up some tools." He looked around carefully. "If one of the enlisted men accompanies us, I'll try to finagle a stop in the Norwegian block, so you can ask about a parcel."

It was one of the enlisted SS soldiers who escorted us.

When we crossed the large square, something happened. I recognized one of the prisoners who was walking around there. It was Olav Røgeberg, who had been the editor of the daily newspaper *Dagbladet* for some time while I worked in its print shop. He also seemed to recognize me. To be on the safe side I shook my head, warning him. I would so much have liked to say hello to my old boss, but I knew that it was impossible for a "leper" like me.

But Levin actually managed to maneuver us into the Norwegian block. He fooled the SS soldier, who was new in the service, by telling him something about a pipe wrench in Block 2. It was like coming to a piece of Norway. A blond fellow in his thirties came over to us. I could not contain myself.

"Hello! Where are you from?" I asked in Norwegian.

"Drammen. And you?"

"Oslo."

"Speak German," the soldier said angrily.

Levin inquired about the pipe wrench.

Of course we did not get any pipe wrench. But when we left I had been promised a package. Even though I had not been able to exchange many words with the pleasant man from Drammen, it had been an enjoyable interlude. It was more than a year since I had last talked to a Norwegian.

"You will, of course, remember me when you get your package," said Levin.

"Definitely."

The big loudspeaker on the square announced that Sonja Henie and Maurice Chevalier had fallen victim to the Jewish plutocratic system. We did not believe this any more than the daily reports about the Wehrmacht's invulnerability. The highly praised elastic warfare was beginning to be much too elastic. That we in Block 19 would most likely not be able to enjoy the developments on the battlefronts was another matter. (This was in the spring of 1944.)

A private car stood outside the gate in the board fence. The uniformed driver looked at us curiously as we passed by.

"Krüger's car," whispered Levin.

And so it was. Krüger, smiling more than usual, stood in the print shop chatting with Werner. Two well-filled leather bags stood on the floor next to him. At a nod from Krüger, Levin went over to him. Werner took one bag in each hand and left. The bags were heavy in his long, thin arms.

"Did you hear anything new in the camp?" asked Luka eagerly.

"We didn't get a chance to ask about forbidden matters. But I think I'll get a package soon."

"Again?" said Glantzer enthusiastically. "You received a parcel no more than two weeks ago, and on top of that, it was untouched."

It was true. Both Hoffgaard and I had each received a plentiful package quite recently.

"I wish that I too had chosen a polar bear couple as my parents," Luka teased me good-naturedly. On the whole he had returned to being his old, cheerful self since the sixty newcomers, headed by Max and Harry, had arrived. The two indestructible and talented performers had also managed to improve the mood among the rest of us by several degrees. At the moment they were working hard to arrange a cabaret performance, the premiere of which would take place shortly. They had already obtained Krüger's permission and blessing. He had even promised to attend the big event.

"Now, look at Levin," whispered Glantzer. "Just look at him, how he's fumbling with his hands like a schoolboy. What the heck did Krüger say to the poor boy?"

Just then Krüger left with his usual: "Good-bye, gentlemen!"

Luka waved to Levin. When he had come over to our table, Luka pointed at him with his forefinger and imitated Kurzweil: "What was it Krüger said to you, Levin? Speak up!"

Levin smiled and bent down to us. "Oh hell, this is the most embarrassing thing I have experienced. Can you believe that the man stood there, completely serious, and offered me a half-hour's pleasure with one of the bordello girls?"

"Now you are lying," scoffed Luka. "What did you say?"

"I said 'No, thank you,' although I would've liked to do it."

"Dear God," wailed Glantzer. "I should have gotten such an offer."

"You? You are stiff in your big mouth, but that's the only place, you eunuch," said Luka. "Suppose you *had* been man enough to sleep with a woman—would you have wanted to do it with an SS man sitting on the edge of the bed? Because you can't believe that one of us would be allowed to be alone with anybody outside these walls." Then, after a pause: "See to it that you work faster, men!" he said, in a loud, harsh voice.

Werner was standing in the doorway.

Chapter 19

BERLIN BECAME EVER GREEDIER FOR POUNDS. WE WORKED IN TWO shifts, day and night. Werner, who had become Krüger's right-hand man, increased the pace from one week to the next. In Marok and Weber's day this had not happened. They thought only of their own comfortable existence, and were not interested in speeding up the printing. They knew as well as we did that the day the demand for pounds in Berlin was met, the print shop would be discontinued and they would end up in one or another dangerous spot. That we prisoners would be sent to the gas chambers was, of course, something they could not have cared less about.

But Werner was a completely different type. He was a zealous fanatic who thought only of his career, apart from the fact that he was a convinced and devout Jew hater, as advocated by Hitler and Himmler. When he did not stand over us in the print shop, he liked to stand behind a wall and spy on us through a hole in the wood. It was through such a hole that he saw me once when I turned to Luka and said something. I thought everything was okay, but then he suddenly stood directly in front of me.

"You are talking instead of working, I see."

"I—"

"Stand up when I am talking to you."

I got up, eager to explain that I had asked Luka to lend me a special needle we used to remove the fiber-fine splinters that could, once in a while, be found in the pieces of paper.

"Keep your big mouth shut; you have become conspicuous, my man."

This meant that from here on out, I had to be prepared to suffer for the slightest offense or mistake on my part. All the guards would be instructed to watch me night and day.

"Come with me, my man."

As expected, we headed for the exercise yard, where Werner personally supervised the punishment drills. And he did so thoroughly. In short, he did not give up until I lay on the ground flat like a toad, like a knocked-out boxer. Actually, he did not give up then either. He drew his revolver and pointed the muzzle at my neck.

"Get up. You have five seconds to get back on your feet."

I had a valid excuse for not complying with his request.

Then he put his pistol back into its case. "Well, now you can go back inside."

Go inside, he had said. It would have been nice if I could have gotten up to walk then. Although even if I had been able to, I would not have committed such an idiotic blunder. Had I been given my freedom plus a million pounds for my achievement, I would not have been able to get back on my feet at that moment. Instead, I wiggled into the block on my elbows.

Glantzer had watched the scene through the scratch in the window paint. "I was sure he was going to shoot you," he whispered.

———— ✦ ————

"Glorified and sanctified be God's great name throughout the world which He has created according to His will. May He establish His kingdom in your lifetime and during your days, and within the life of the entire House of Israel, speedily and soon; and say, Amen.

"May His great name be blessed forever and to all eternity.

"Blessed and praised, glorified and exalted, extolled and honored, adored and lauded be the name of the Holy One, blessed be He, beyond all the blessings and hymns, praises and consolations that are ever spoken in the world; and say, Amen."

Serious-faced, the men in the little group parted.

The prisoner who had read the prayer passed the table where Schnapper and I sat.

"Was it your father you said Kaddish [prayer for the dead] for?" I asked.

"Yes, he was beaten to death in Auschwitz a year ago today," he replied.

———

I was house-cleaning in Werner's private apartment in a building just outside the camp. Had Werner known that it was me the Stubendienst had chosen for this job, he surely would have vetoed it, because I was still conspicuous.

There was a big picture of a woman on the table. I looked at it while I pretended to dust the frame. She had a pointed nose and a mouth as straight as a line. In the corner at the bottom of the picture was written in ink, *To Kurt from Trudel.*

You must have caught a real shrew there, my dear Werner, and it serves you right, I thought. Next to the picture lay a book with the same inscription, whose title was *Beyond,* a novel by John Galsworthy. If anyone had told me then that I would come to own this very book, I would probably have looked at the person with pity. But it actually did happen.

"Finish quickly," nagged Psoch, one of the two Unterscharführers (junior squad leaders) who were responsible for my precious person.

A big picture hung on the wall that said a good deal about Werner, the fanatic. The picture showed Hitler himself shaking hands with a young cadet. The cadet was Kurt Werner. He was standing on the farthest flank of a straight line of young cadets, probably Hitler Youth.

Even though it was the despicable Werner who lived in this studio apartment, it was still wonderful to be there. I had not been in a proper dwelling since I had been arrested in my own studio apartment on that fateful morning back in 1942. I would not be surprised if there was another Werner who was ruining my home now.

"Get away from the picture!" shouted Psoch when I tried to dust it off.

"I see everything." This was the constant refrain of Unterscharführer Apfelbaum. He was actually one of the guards who saw the least. Now he came over to our table.

"Here's a cigarette for you," he said condescendingly to Glantzer. "Tell me a bit about the notes you are working on."

"Yes, Herr Unterscharführer," said Glantzer contentedly, and put the welcome cigarette behind his ear. "Would you like a five-, ten-, twenty-, or fifty-pound note?"

"It doesn't matter. They're all the same."

Glantzer picked up a five-pound note and put it on the glass disk. He turned on both lights and began to explain: "Look here at the lady's right hand. It has five dots—secret markings. Also, one has to make sure that she sits properly in her oval. The lines in the watermarks must not 'swim,' as it's called in the technical terminology. Neither should they be too high up on the bill. Only the Bank of England can take such liberties, but we cannot."

"Hmmph," grumbled Apfelbaum. "Continue."

"Of course. While I'm talking about these confounded dots, I might as well explain the others at the same time. First of all, there are three next to the nice pound sign here, and secondly, you can see that there are two such flyspecks under the name of the head cashier too. Important specks, Herr Unterscharführer. If a single one is missing, there's hell to pay. Then we have the notches—also secret markings. You, Herr Unterscharführer, who can see so well, have probably discovered that there is a little notch here in both the 'i' and the 'f.'"

"Of course, but what kind of markings are these?" Apfelbaum put a fingertip on the note.

"You have good eyes, Herr Unterscharführer. Those are not markings, but quite simply a mere splinter. This note will not end up with the good ones, but on the shelf for the airdrops, you know. But don't think they are bad; the Bank of England sends out notes that are of much worse quality than these. All in all, Herr Unterscharführer, counterfeit notes are much more genuine than the genuine ones."

"Hmmph. But where the hell does the splinter come from?"

"From the type of wood that the paper is made of. Sturmbannführer Krüger himself has explained this to me. He told me that the British make the paper for their notes from a type of wood they get from India. This type of wood is so delicate that there are never any splinters in the paper. But you must make the paper from different types of wood, and therefore it happens that we find a splinter like this in the notes when we examine them under a light. If they are bigger than this one, the notes are thrown away. If not, we remove the splinters and pass the notes as *Abwurf.*"

"Yes, of course," said Apfelbaum, as if this was something he knew only too well. "And you are making the secret markings so that you'll be able to recognize the notes, right?" He was completely serious when he said this.

And then came another air-raid warning.

We had become so used to these disruptions that we considered the gathering of notes and paper part of the usual work. We were no longer afraid of these air armadas, which Luka and Max insisted were made up of more than a thousand planes at one time. When it was dark, the first planes surrounded the entire camp area with green spots of light, and during the day they waited to drop their bombs until they were over Berlin.

But on this day, something happened that upset both Germans and prisoners alike.

I was on my way back to my place at the table when the bang came.

"We're being bombed!" someone shouted desperately.

At that moment the men who worked in Block 18 came into our barracks.

"We're finished. Block 17 is in flames, and our block has started to burn too."

Wild panic seized us as we rushed toward the exit, but Werner stood there with his men, all of whom had drawn their pistols.

"Stay where you are! If you try to get out we will shoot you down like dogs. The camp is not being bombed; it is only a firebomb which has accidentally landed here. The firefighters have contained the fire, and there is no danger to any of our barracks. Use your sense, people." Werner was probably not as cocksure as he appeared to be. The hand holding the pistol was not quite steady.

Two young boys stood next to me with their arms around each other's waists. They were too scared to bother hiding how they felt about each other. Luckily Werner was too busy with other things to notice the boys' highly irregular conduct.

Wild West came in from Block 18. Beads of sweat had formed on his ruddy face.

"All's well," he said, trying to look calm and composed. "The firefighters have mastered the situation, and there is no longer any danger."

Werner put his pistol back into the holster. He looked relieved. "Well, people, back to work."

We went back to our places.

"Something almost went wrong," said Luka.

"So help me, I thought the British had found out about this print shop and come to destroy it," mumbled Glantzer.

"All of us thought so, but if this had been the case, they would not have used a firebomb—at any rate, not just one. Watch out, Wild West is coming."

Wild West came striding across the floor with his hand on the pistol case.

"You were scared out of your wits, you cowards. Had you been on the front when the action was at its hottest, I think you would have run away. You are completely spineless, to get so hysterical because of a mere firebomb. You were thinking of running away. Where to, if I may ask?" He pulled out his pistol and swung it around. "Even if you had managed to get out to the exercise yard, I would have shot all of you down with this by myself. But just wait until you finish work today. You will find out what punishment drills are like, you can bet your lives on that. You made your bed—now lie in it. You are much too well off here, that's what's wrong. You think you can take all kinds of liberties, don't you?"

"*Achtung!*"

Krüger and Werner came in from the guardroom. Krüger did not have any briefcases with him today, and it was obvious that he had raced all the way from Berlin.

"Sit down, gentlemen. It was a regrettable incident that occurred here today, and I can well understand that you became nervous, as I myself did when I heard about it. But I can assure you that it was a mishap and absolutely nothing else. The firebomb came from a damaged plane. You know as well as I do that bombs are never dropped on prison camps. Now you can pack up and take the rest of the day off. I am sure you will find something pleasant to do. By the way, a new man will arrive here sometime today. Good-bye, gentlemen."

The only one who looked dissatisfied was Wild West. He stared angrily after us when we went into the dayroom. The room was filled with the sour smell of smoke.

"There's not a splinter left of Block 17," called Schnapper, who had climbed up to a window ledge and looked out.

"To hell with it," said Bober. "Let's think about having some fun instead. According to Uncle Krüger, a new man is supposed to come here today. Does anyone have a good suggestion for a dignified reception ceremony? No? Then I suggest we initiate him into his new calling in an elegant manner, and for this purpose, only printers' ink can suitably be used as 'holy water.' A man whose arrival has been announced by Krüger himself demands it," he ended solemnly.

Half an hour later Levin came with the new man, a Russian. Tovarisch was skin and bones and ragged like all newcomers, but there was something about him that showed he was somewhat out of the ordinary.

"Good day, fair-haired gathering," he said pleasantly.

"Take off your rags," ordered Levin harshly.

When the man was completely naked, Bober, the master of ceremonies, went over to him. "Welcome to our clan, Tovarisch." He took the Russian by the arm and led him over to the nearest table. "Climb up so I can anoint you and initiate you into your important task."

"Thank you for this great and undeserved honor," said Tovarisch, in the same tone. Calm and smiling, he put up with Bober's craziest idea—a brush and printers' ink.

"Now you are anointed and initiated, and you're one of us," said Bober, when there was no more printers' ink left in the box. "Tell us who you are and where you come from, brother Tovarisch."

The Russian was a grotesque sight, his emaciated body smeared with all kinds of mysterious signs. But he bowed and smiled, seemingly pleased.

"Dear brothers, I am completely overwhelmed by the royal reception you have given a humble person like me. I come from the famous holiday spot Mauthausen, picked up by special envoys to work here. I don't know what you are doing, but I suspect a great deal. I am a counterfeiter by profession, and I have references from diametrically opposed sources that I am an artist in my line of work."

It was no boast; Tovarisch was an artist in his profession. A few months later he saved all of us by producing a dollar bill that made the Nazi leaders in Berlin gasp.

Chapter 20

As soon as the radio was turned on, this is what we heard:

"The henchmen of Bolshevism have attacked Europe from the west. The German defense will repel the onslaught with fanatical determination and fervent passion. Last night the enemy began its assault on Western Europe, for which it had prepared a long time, and which we had long expected. It began with major attacks on our coastal fortifications, followed by parachutists that were dropped in several places on the northern French coast between Le Havre and Cherbourg. Simultaneously, enemy forces were put ashore from the sea, supported by strong naval forces. Furious battles are under way in the coastlines under attack. The losses of the invasion forces rise from hour to hour. Enemy attacks east of Rome have collapsed. There are continued German-Rumanian advances near Jassy. The center for Tito's gangs has been destroyed."

Suddenly the loudspeaker below the ceiling became silent.

One could almost hear everybody start to breathe again. But no one said a word, because Werner and Wild West were standing at the door of the guardroom, carefully looking around the room to find a pretext for chasing us outside to the exercise yard. Lately punishment drills had been, so to speak, the order of the day. As a rule it was Wild West who tormented us, while repeating his everlasting "You have made your bed, so lie in it." But today the gentlemen did not have a chance to pounce on us.

A pair of swallows threw themselves boldly and elegantly toward the cloudless sky, as though flying between invisible trapezes. In a green field below them shrieked a pair of magpies. And here and there stood slim birch stems that shone like fresh stripes of chalk against the dark green "blackboard" of the evergreen. The sight was like a fairy-tale setting.

"So help me, it will be interesting to see how things are in Berlin nowadays," said Luka, pulling his feet comfortably underneath him.

Ten of us prisoners sat in a truck headed for Berlin to pick up new machines for our money factory. Just before we arrived we passed many newly constructed wood barracks.

"Houses for the bombed-out residents," said Schnapper drily.

I had last been in Berlin a year and a half before. Berlin, where the houses had been intact, the store windows well filled, the people on the pavements well-nourished and well-dressed, and the children in the parks round-cheeked. Was this the same city? Where were the undamaged houses, the arrogant and cocksure people? Ruins and filth and gray, subdued people were everywhere.

"It's only this section of the city that looks like this," one of our guards thought he should tell us. "The rest of the city is as good as intact. But this is nothing compared to how it looks in London. The whole city is like a big bomb crater."

"Ask him if he was in London recently," said Schnapper sardonically.

"Soon there won't be anything left of their shit island," continued the soldier. "Our new weapons rain down day and night. Our airmen say that the whole population runs around like confused bedbugs. They might as well jump into the sea right away, because worse things are facing them."

"And for the poor wretches who have landed in France it is surely not pleasant," said Luka hypocritically.

"No, that's for sure. We let them come ashore and then we do away with all of them. Just let them come; it suits us fine, as then we don't have to go to them."

The truck stopped outside a large, damaged workshop building.

The stage floor was made of the boxes in which the precious paper was sent to us. Wool blankets served as a curtain. The SS men, headed by Krüger himself, occupied the orchestra seats.

The master of ceremonies, Bober, opened the show.

"Gentlemen and honored audience members. First of all, I want to welcome you to our little show. I can assure you that we're very flattered that connoisseurs from all over Europe are present here. I daresay that few artists have ever performed in front of a more cosmopolitan audience. But I also daresay that we can offer you something that most of you could not have imagined possible."

"Bober is so wonderfully bold that he can do almost as he pleases," whispered Max enthusiastically.

"As long as he does not blow up the talent," mumbled Harry. "If Krüger or any of the others smells a rat, all hell will break loose, and it's good-night for us."

"Take it easy," said Max, trying to calm his friend. "If there's a stubble-necked German who is *not* taken in by a man like Bober, he surely doesn't wear an SS uniform."

Max, Harry, and I stood behind the blanket and looked down at the room.

"Well, gentlemen," continued Bober, as if he had never done anything other than appear on a stage. "The first item on this evening's program is accordion music, to be performed by the well-known virtuoso, Hans Blass of Vienna. The exquisite instrument he plays has its, shall we say, tragic story. A certain Mr. Weber received it—at least, that's what he said—as a gift from one of his Jewish admirers. To say the least, he abused the gift in every way. But as we know, Nemesis runs through our fragile world, and this gentleman had to pay dearly for his misdeeds and his frivolities.

'You made your bed, now lie in it,' to quote one of this establishment's energetic and observant chiefs."

"Look at Wild West," said Max. "Trust me, he's enjoying himself."

"And so, gentlemen, the well-known accordion virtuoso, Hans Blass!"

Hans Blass slipped in front of the blanket with the song "*Alte Kameraden*" ("Old Comrades") coming from the instrument at full strength. It sounded as if an entire well-trained orchestra was at work.

"It's going well," said Bober, who was behind the blanket now. "Stein and Pick have only a few steps left to the guardroom. What's important now is to keep it going nonstop, so none of our guests of honor will have time to turn around. This is a tense business, but I think Pick and Stein will have some British news to give us when we have finished this confounded show."

"It's a hell of a risk," said Harry.

"So be it. It's quite risky to be inside these walls at all. Besides, this is the only chance we have to get close to the radio. Since that damned Werner came, the door to the guardroom is, as you know, constantly watched."

Hans Blass received enthusiastic and well-deserved applause for his performance. When he withdrew with a bow, Bober, the master of ceremonies, was quickly back onstage again.

"I'm happy to see and hear that the honored audience knows how to value a good performance. And now the three troubadours, Max, Moritz, and Harry, will entertain you. First they will sing about the immortal 'Valentine,' and that can only be done in French. Hans Blass will accompany them. Go ahead, troubadours."

Under different circumstances I suppose I would have suffered badly from stage fright, because the singing voice nature gave me is nothing to write home about, and I did not know a word of French when Max began to cram the words to "Valentine" into my head. But in this situation I forgot such trivial matters completely. Just when we began to sing, Pick and Stein slipped into the guardroom. I thought I could hear the door squeak and I was convinced that the SS men had heard it too.

I waited for them to rush up from their benches and run toward the guardroom, but they did not. They listened and watched the three of us, looking pleased. We sang a resounding version of "Valentine" and were applauded with the curtain up. While we cleared our throats and took a rest until the next number, Hans played a swinging Viennese waltz as only a person from Vienna can do it. It was then that it happened.

We saw Wild West whisper something to young Psoch, who got up and crossed the floor—to the guardroom.

"Now all hell is about to break loose," whispered Max.

But Bober, the strategist, had included plans for just such an incident in his calculations. On his signal, Hans produced a loud, piercing, discordant note in the middle of the languishing waltz. Then he tapped one of the keys and pretended that it had gotten stuck, smiled apologetically at the audience, and continued to play. But it was too late for the two in the guardroom to get back without being noticed. We stood as if on glowing coals when Psoch disappeared into the guardroom. Every minute we expected to see him come back, dragging the offenders. And then he came out—alone. Could it really be possible that Pick and Stein had managed to hide? Yes, it had to be true, because nothing suggested that Psoch was the least bit upset. He went calmly over to Wild West, handed him a package of cigarettes, and sat down again in his place.

We three troubadours sang "Ferdinand" with such unbridled enthusiasm and strength that it ought to have created suspicion. Fortunately it did not. On the contrary, Krüger and company clapped enthusiastically when we slipped behind the blanket.

"That went really well," said Bober, just as he came back onstage to resume his duties as the master of ceremonies.

"And now, gentlemen, we will present a small skit. Text and decorations by our famous dollar expert, Tovarisch. Raise the blanket, men."

The two men, who were responsible for the technical department, each pulled his half of the blanket aside with a practiced, elegant tug.

What the audience saw now was a dollar bill, more than six feet long and more than three feet high. The colors, numbers, and drawings were perfect. Behind it Hans Blass began to play an improvised prelude to *"Es geht alles vorüber"* ("Everything Will Pass"). Suddenly both ovals of the bill were opened like windows, and the faces of the Berliner Norbert Levi and the cosmopolitan Max appeared. They sang:

> *Es geht alles vorüber,*
> *es geht alles vorbei,*
> *nach jedem Dezember*
> *Kommt immer ein Mai.*
> *Es geht alles vorüber,*
> *es geht alles vorbei,*
> *es kommt ja ein schöner Mai*
> *und dann sind wir frei.*

(Everything will pass, May follows each December, everything will pass, December will be followed by the beautiful month of May, and we will be free then.)

Krüger clapped and smiled broadly, and Werner and staff had no choice but to play along. None of us had dared to believe this skit would ever become reality.

Max stuck his head out through the oval and looked at Norbert. "Good evening, sir."

"But good God, are you British? I didn't think there were any of you left."

"Oh yes, Winston and I and a few others were able to survive all those terrible 'Vs,' you know. But this morning they messed up our cave so badly that I decided to catch the last plane across the Channel. I thought of going to Berlin, but then my stupid pilot crossed the path of one of those popping bonbons, although it was fully lit up. Fortunately I had

Chamberlain's umbrella with me; it was Winston who asked me to hand it to the chief of the National Museum in Berlin. When I saw what was happening, I opened it and jumped out. It would probably last throughout my lifetime too, I said to myself. But where did I actually land?"

"In Block 19, man."

"Block 19?"

"Don't put on an act. Don't tell me that you're an Englishman and don't know about Block 19?"

"What are you saying? That I, insignificant as I am, have really landed in the world's renowned pound factory? Good Lord, this is something to tell Winston about when I get back to our protectorate. Only yesterday he said to me: 'Everyone has his own money to administer, John, but so help me, there are no money administrators like those in Block 19. There were only amateurs by comparison in the Bank of England, when it existed.'"

Now the oval openings were closed as efficiently as they had been opened. And then the curtain fell.

The applause was thunderous.

Stein and Pick took this opportunity to sneak back into the room.

"It's all set," said Bober, who stood near the peephole. "Put on the beard, Norbert, and the glasses too. Table and stool in place! Now I'm going back onstage to announce the next skit. When I say 'Blanket up,' everything has to be in place. Hey, by God, this is fun!"

One minute later the curtain was raised. Director Norbert Levi, sporting a beard and a pair of glasses, sat at a table covered with documents. He barely had time to look up from the papers before Mr. John came in to see him, bowing.

"Who the hell are you? What do you want?"

"I apologize for disturbing you. I am the last Londoner."

"The ghost of the last, you mean. All right, what do you want? Hurry up, ghost."

"Well, is it really true that it's here you manufacture those extraordinary pound notes?"

"Yes, of all denominations, from five to fifty."

"Maybe you also produce something else?"

"Certainly. All types of important documents, Russian identification cards and English stamps. Stamp collectors all over the world will fight over those stamps, as we have placed a Star of David on the royal crown, and along its sides you'll find the hammer and sickle. But you have to use a magnifying glass to see it. Also we will soon begin the manufacture of fifty-dollar bills en masse. I swear old Uncle Sam is going to be so bloated with dollar bills that he will burst."

"I am completely overwhelmed, Herr Director. You obviously produce all kinds of things here."

"Yes, we make everything for the *chaserim*."

The prisoners in the room howled with laughter. Krüger and company laughed too. They, like young Kristiansen at Berg, had no idea that *chaserim* was Yiddish and meant "pigs."

Mr. John, alias Max, proudly pulled an egg from his pocket and held it between two fingers. "But this is something you can't produce here."

Director Levi looked sympathetically at the other man over his glasses.

"Oh, is that what you think?" He stuck one hand down between his thighs and cackled like a chicken about to lay an egg. "What do you call this?" he asked, and showed him a big egg.

Krüger laughed so hard his chair shook.

Afterwards the performers stepped and yodeled and played a real accordion and an invisible saxophone. Max, Harry, and I were sent onstage once more to sing "Better and Better Every Day." I sang the refrain in Norwegian and the others took care of the rest in Dutch. The fact that I was completely out of my element did not bother me at all. Finally, Bober gathered the whole ensemble for the finale, and we sang our own version of *"Es geht alles vorüber"* in different voices.

Bober was onstage again when the rest of us withdrew.

"Dear friends of all ranks, now there's only one thing left to do, and that is to thank you for wanting to come here and listen to us. I hope you enjoyed yourselves, because we did. And so we count on it that all of you will do us the honor next time we're in these parts. But gentlemen, the cashier's report of this evening's proceeds has forced us to stipulate that, unfortunately, free tickets are out of the question next time, not even for the orchestra seats. Everything is expensive today, and traveling conditions are extremely problematic for my colleagues and me. Of course, it's not necessary to mention this difficulty in a gathering such as this. Good-bye, gentlemen!"

It was so much like Krüger that we were stunned.

But kind Uncle Krüger did not take offense. He was one big smile when he got up. "Gentlemen, please allow me to thank you for the brilliant entertainment you have provided for us this evening," he said. "I really hope that you will repeat it soon, and it will be a great pleasure for me to attend. I promise you that your cash register will not be quite empty next time. I suppose money cannot tempt pound billionaires like you, but there are other things too. Good-bye, gentlemen."

While we worked hard to clean up the room, Pick and Stein's "catch" went from ear to ear. Because of the incident with Psoch, they had not been able to hear much of the British broadcast, but it was more than enough to establish that the Germans had been forced to retreat on all fronts. Hitler had already lost the war that he, in his delusions of grandeur, thought would make him the sole ruler of Europe. The V-1 bombs were causing major damage in England, but they would never affect the outcome of the war.

"It's only a question of months now," predicted Bober.

The questions rained down on the evening's heroes when we got back to the dormitory. How the hell had they managed to hide from Psoch?

"Tell them," said Pick.

"Well," began Stein. "It was a bit nerve-wracking. We had just found the right station when Hans started his terrible squeal. We knew that it was important to act fast, and I daresay we did. Pick opened the window while I adjusted the radio. It was not enough just to close it; the setting had to be right too. We heard Psoch's steps just as we jumped out the window. The same second we slid it shut, he turned the door handle. What we were most afraid of while we were huddled against the wall was that he would discover that the hook of the window was unclasped and lock us out in the exercise yard. Luckily he did not, and as soon as he had left the room, we were back inside and turning on the radio. Most of the news was over by then, but we heard this much: It's only a question of time until Germany is overrun by Allied soldiers."

"Come here, Stein!" called Bober. He was sitting at one of the tables with a small map of Europe in front of him. He had snitched it from Marok's belongings before they were sent to Berlin.

Italiener crossed the floor, humming. He stopped in front of Rozjen.

"Why so serious? Are you not happy that Hitler and all of his trash are going to hell?"

"Of course I am, little one. But I'm thinking about what happened in Auschwitz one day when I was in a kommando that worked near the gas chambers. Several trucks with women went by. They knew that we couldn't help them, so they called out, 'Avenge us.'"

"You may be sure of that, Rozjen," said Italiener seriously. "They will be avenged."

"We're not going to avenge anybody," said Cytrin, who sat next to Rozjen. "We're not going to get out of here alive, not any of us." He got up and gesticulated with his arms. "None of us will get out of here alive!" he shouted hysterically.

Rozjen and Italiener made him sit down again on the stool.

"Don't look on the dark side," said Rozjen, and put his hand on Cytrin's shoulder. "We must keep up hope, and you'll see that we'll pull through somehow."

"Oh, sure. I'm too old to believe in miracles."

"I thought that I was too. But then one happened when I stood, so to speak, with one leg in the gas chamber."

"A fluke."

"Miracle or fluke, it's one and the same. What's important here is that I was actually saved when I had given up hope long ago. The same thing happened to the others who came here together with me. We who are here have a far better chance of pulling through than many other prisoners do. We are the hens who lay the golden eggs. You can be sure that they're not going to get rid of us before they absolutely have to. Much can happen before then."

Little by little Cytrin calmed down.

Chapter 21

"Nachtstern." Psoch waved to me with the one hand he had left.

"Parcel," said Luka when I got up.

"Don't forget you promised me a Norwegian cigarette," said Max, who sat opposite me.

I went over to Psoch, and he asked me to come with him. *What does this mean?* I thought, when he headed for the exit door. I had permanently fallen out of Werner's good graces, so I was prepared for just about anything.

"There's a parcel for you," snarled Psoch when we got outside to the exercise yard.

I was completely confused while I followed him to the gate in the board fence. I had always picked up my parcels in the guardroom previously.

Two men stood outside the gate. One of them had a package under his arm.

"Good morning." Both of them greeted me in German. "We're Norwegians, and we have a parcel for you. Sign your name on this receipt."

I thanked them and signed.

"By the way, how many packages did you receive this month?" asked the man who gave me the package.

I did not know what I should answer. Actually, I had received two parcels, but Werner had taken one away from me. Of course I could not mention this while Psoch was listening.

"Two," I answered, and thought that I had played it safe.

"What? Only two? But we have sent you five packages this month. We even got receipts for them. A fine mess this is. We will go straight to the commandant and report this."

I was totally speechless. Not because I had found out that Werner and his gang had stolen my packages without showing them to me at all; I was wide-eyed with astonishment that a prisoner dared say something like this in the presence of a German without getting a beating. Psoch did not say a word.

Very apprehensively I went into the guardroom with the package.

Werner examined the contents carefully. When he had finished he said to my great surprise: "Collect your things and take them with you."

But then Psoch came and gave his report.

I had reached the door with the parcel under my arm.

"Come here, man."

I knew then that there would be hell to pay.

"So you claim that we steal your packages?"

I did not answer.

"Why did you say that you had only received two packages this month?"

"Herr Oberscharführer, that is all I received."

Werner jumped up from the stool and gave me a cuff on the ear that made my head rattle. "You are not even going to get a taste of this package. Instead, you will get half an hour of punishment drills after work, which Psoch will look after; he is an expert in the field. Understood?"

"Yes."

"Leave."

Empty-handed and thoroughly enraged, I went back to work.

Luka glanced at me.

"It did not go well today either, I understand."

"Worse than last time," I said, and told him what had happened.

Luka shrugged his shoulders.

"Well, this is how it is with thieves. Once they give a poor wretch the evil eye, they never leave him in peace. I should know it. In Buchenwald they were after me night and day. One time they chased me out to an ice-cold pond. They threw stones at me until I was up to my neck in icy slush. I simply had to stand there until I was blue all over my body. When I was finally allowed to crawl ashore I was more dead than alive. There was some straw on the beach, so I put some of it down my trousers to warm up. I should never have done that. They were furious and threw me into the pond once more.

"Shortly after this incident they put Kurzweil and me into a hospital as guinea pigs. First we were injected with all kinds of bacteria, and then they came with the patent medicines. We were five guinea pigs in all. Kurzweil and I pulled through; the other three ended up in the oven. But just before I landed in hospital I had a great experience. I was in a stone quarry unit. Stein and Pick were there too, by the way. The foreman always thought that I carried only small stones. 'I will teach you how to work,' he said one day, and put me between the handles of a heavily loaded wheelbarrow. He himself took hold of the other two handles. God only knows where I got the strength from that day, but I totally exhausted the foreman."

"And I had so much looked forward to a Norwegian cigarette," sighed Max.

"Shift change!"

When the others went to eat I stayed behind and waited for the punishment-drill expert, Psoch. He did not let me wait long. It was not hard to see that he was looking forward to giving me his full treatment. To begin with he made me run in a circle until I was almost out of breath. Then he began in earnest with: "Lie down! Get up! Lie down! Hop! Lie down! Get up! Lie down!"

I threw myself down, I jumped and did knee-bends while I inwardly cursed Psoch in every language I had ever learned. I sent the most passionate prayers to heaven and hell that lightning should strike the one-armed devil with the dog whip. Both the cursing and the praying were futile. After one *Lie down!*, I blacked out and remained flat on the ground. When Psoch was unable to get me back on my feet with his shouts of *Get up!*, he positioned himself a few feet in front of me and waved with the whip.

"Just come here—only here."

As I moved forward on my elbows, he moved backward. Eventually I could no longer lift up my head.

He nagged and threatened and ordered me to move again. With what little breath I had left, I panted a dangerous "No," come what may.

"Are you pretending?"

I did not even answer . . . did not even look up.

The flogging I expected did not come.

"Get inside, you damned dog!"

It took me a long time to crawl into the mess hall. Luka and Max met me at the door and helped me into my bunk. The sores on my body cut and stung, and my heart was beating furiously in my chest.

Suddenly I noticed that Psoch stood in the doorway, watching me.

"I was good to you just now, but I think you're pretending. Wait till this afternoon and I'll take you outside once more."

Immediately after he left, Levin came and listened to my heart. "Just lie still and you'll be okay. I'll find out from Werner whether you can be spared the punishment drills this afternoon."

"You can tell him from me that they won't get me out of bed alive today."

I meant it.

They did not come to get me.

I lay there and dreamt about revenge. Before the radios were confiscated at home I had heard that it was said in London that all Norwegian Nazis would be sent to Bjørnøya (Bear Island in northern Norway) at the end of the war. Should I survive this hell, I would make sure that Werner and Psoch would also end up there. I myself would apply for a job as a guard. They would run and jump until they were blue in the face. I pictured it so vividly that I forgot to lie still. My muscles and tendons were dreadfully sore and I moaned out loud.

Max, Luka, and Tovarisch came to see me to find out how I was.

"Oh hell, did he ever play havoc with you," said Max.

"So help me, you can be glad you weren't kicked to death," said Tovarisch, to console me. "I have never seen a prisoner survive a flat 'no' to a German military man."

"Are you crazy?" said Luka. "No one gets kicked to death in a sanatorium like this."

"How are you doing with the dollars?" I asked, to change the subject.

Tovarisch strutted.

"It's going well, man. It won't be long and you'll see a fifty-dollar bill that beats everything in the industry. It will be my life's masterpiece. Krüger is more and more enthusiastic each time he drops in on me. He talks and treats me to cigarettes and is so pleasant that it's not to be believed. I'll never be able to figure out that man, really I won't."

"Take it easy, Tovarisch," said Luka. "No one can."

A prisoner staggered past us with both hands in front of his face. When he crawled up to his bunk we saw that it was streaked with blood.

"Gosh," said Max compassionately.

"He only got what he deserved," said Luka. "For a long time, he's clung to one of the young boys like a vine. Last night he crawled into the boy's bunk and tried to rape him. Werner probably got wind of that story and has made the man pay for it."

"The sex drive, the sex drive," said Max. "In Auschwitz we didn't know about such miseries. There, body and mind were filled with a single strong desire—for food. Food, food, food."

The poor, whipped wretch lay in his bunk groaning, his hands covering his face.

Levin came into the dormitory.

"Everything is okay, Moritz. Werner agreed to let you off this afternoon. But now I'll tell you the latest news. Stein has been appointed foreman. Kurzweil is going to start working in the bookbinding shop, together with Güting. It appears that big orders for Gestapo protocols have been received. Bookbinder Kurzweil walks around shining like a sun, but Stein does not. He tried as best he could to wriggle out of this risky job, but of course he couldn't."

"I'm going to miss Kurzweil and his endless refrain," said Luka.

⌐⌐∾⌐⌐

Werner waved with his hand à la Krüger.

"Just sit, just sit."

We looked at each other in surprise. What had happened to the man since we had seen him last? He had had an eight-day leave, and it had been a peaceful time for us. We only wished that his leave had been considerably extended.

Werner continued into the dormitory, humming.

"I know," said Harry. "The man has got himself married."

"Nonsense," scoffed Schnapper. "No woman wants such a bore."

"Oh yes," I said, and told them about the picture and the book I had seen when cleaning Werner's place.

"She's welcome to him," mumbled Schnapper. "There probably aren't many men to choose from for German women now."

Just then Werner came back from inspecting the dormitory. He began to look at our closets.

"It's not just that," whispered Schnapper enthusiastically. "Don't you see that the fellow has a new silver stripe in addition to his two stars? He's been promoted to Hauptscharführer. That was some wedding present for a man like him."

Werner inspected one cupboard after another. When he came to the one Pick and Stein shared, we saw him frown.

"Pick and Stein, come here."

The two men stepped forward.

Werner stuck his forefinger into a corner of the cupboard.

"What is this?" he asked, holding the finger in front of the offenders' faces.

None of them answered.

"What is this?" he roared, once again the old Werner.

"Dust, Herr Oberscharführer."

"Exactly. One of you is a Stubendienst and the other a foreman, and you have the worst closets of all. But maybe you think that personages such as yourselves can forget about regulations. Besides, I am Hauptscharführer now. Understood?"

"Yes, Herr Ob—Hauptscharführer."

"Good. And now you can come with me to the exercise yard for a while. Exercise is the best medicine for apathy."

"They didn't get these punishment drills because of the cupboard, but because they didn't notice the silver stripe," said Schnapper when the three had left.

All those who found a scratch in the window paint of course looked out to watch the punishment.

When they came out to the exercise yard, Werner signaled with his hand. "Run!"

Pick and Stein started out. In the beginning they kept the usual speed, but somehow, tentatively, they ran slower and slower. To our surprise Werner pretended not to notice.

"Jump," ordered Werner when the men had loafed around for a while.

The offenders jumped, but their knee angle was many times wider than permitted.

"Such bold devils," Schnapper said with a chuckle.

Werner went over to the two. "Stop. This is impossible." He placed himself in front of the two men and assumed the perfect jumping position. "This is how it should be done," he said, and then he began to jump.

Pick and Stein stood with their hands on their backs and watched him.

When Werner had jumped a fair distance, he straightened up and looked back. "What in hottest hell?" he said.

Pick and Stein clicked their heels. "You won, Herr Hauptscharführer."

"Oh no!" Schnapper lamented.

Werner's face showed the most contradictory feelings. Then he smiled so broadly and boyishly that we could hardly believe our own eyes.

"Get inside, you damned thieves," he ordered, gesticulating with both hands.

That was the first and the last time we saw that the Jew hater and Nazi career robot Kurt Werner had a human trait.

Chapter 22

THE COMMOTION BEGAN IMMEDIATELY AFTER WE SAT DOWN TO WORK in the morning.

"Look at Stein," said Luka. "Now something is really wrong."

Stein nervously moved the bundles of notes that he had taken out of the hand press. All notes were pressed after they had been pinpricked and crumpled.

"Gosh," said Glantzer, "the poor man looks really confused. I could swear that there's something wrong with one of the bundles."

"If there are notes missing, he'll surely find them in another bundle. It's happened before."

Stein looked through the bundles several times. Watching him, it was obvious to us that he did not find what he was looking for. He walked to the middle of the floor.

"Hello, men. Did anyone here take something out of the press?"

No one answered. Everyone looked at him curiously.

"What a question," mumbled Luka.

"Well," said Stein seriously, "then I have to report that twenty-one five-pound notes have disappeared."

What he said was so appalling that we all just stared after him as he headed for the guardroom.

"Now there's going to be a hullabaloo here," said Luka after a little while.

Stein, Werner, and Wild West came out from the guardroom. All three looked upset. They stopped in the middle of the floor.

"Everybody come here," said Werner. "I advise you to answer my questions truthfully. Did anyone take the notes that are missing from one of the bundles that were in the press over there?"

"No," we said in unison.

"Has anyone been near the press since the notes were put in?"

"No."

"Is it possible that one of you has accidentally mixed in the notes with your own? No? Well, twenty-one five-pound notes have disappeared. If they aren't found, I feel sorry for all of you. You know the punishment for sabotage."

"Herr Hauptscharführer?"

"Is there something you want to say about this matter?" asked Werner.

"I just remembered that I saw Güting near the press just before we finished work yesterday. He seemed to be busy with some bindings. Maybe he accidentally took some of the notes with him."

"Get Güting," said Werner to Stein.

Stein left and returned with Güting a few minutes later. Güting looked at us, surprised.

"Güting, you were here yesterday afternoon, right?"

"Yes, Herr Hauptscharführer, I used the hand press for about half an hour."

"That's right. What did you do with the notes that were in it?"

"I removed them while I used the press. When I was finished, I put them back."

"You wouldn't have accidentally taken some of the notes with you to the bookbinding shop?"

"No, Herr Hauptscharführer."

"How would you know? Did you check your bindings already?"

Güting became a bit confused but composed himself quickly. "If some of the notes had gotten lost in between the files, I would've discovered them yesterday. But I made sure that all the notes were there when I put them back."

Werner walked across the floor. Then he turned around.

"Everyone back to work. Stein, pick out ten men and go through whatever papers there are here."

Luka, Glantzer, and I hurried back to our table. None of us had any desire to play detective.

"The notes were probably misplaced, and they'll find them somewhere," muttered Glantzer.

"Maybe," remarked Luka.

"Maybe?" Glantzer was irritable. "Don't start with your foolish notions. Who in hell do you think is interested in stealing those pieces of paper? For what purpose? To dry his rear end or bribe the guards, or what?"

"We'll see."

Stein and his ten assistants searched through all the notes and papers in the room.

"Did you find the needle in the haystack?" Luka asked when it was our table's turn.

Stein shook his head. "No, and I don't expect to either," he said.

"So, you don't believe that the notes are here?"

"No more than you do."

The notes were not found.

Sometime later we saw Güting go into the guardroom, together with Apfelbaum.

"The net is closing in on the suspect," said Luka, as if reading a detective novel.

Glantzer shook his head. "He can't be so raving mad that he'd steal a bundle of notes."

Psoch appeared in the door of the guardroom. "Stein, Pick, and Ehrlich, come here!"

"Oh boy, now . . . ," Glantzer let slip.

Even Luka blinked his eyes.

While Stein went into the dayroom to get Pick, little Ehrlich—he did not weigh more than seventy pounds when he came to us from Buchenwald—stood there, calm and cool, and waited for them.

The three men spent no more than three minutes in the guardroom. But it was easy to see that those few minutes had been less than fun.

Luka carefully waved to Stein.

Stein pretended for a while to look at one of Luka's notes. Then he whispered fiercely: "That damned rat Güting has snitched on us that we listened to London that night. Pick and I confessed that we had done it. The devil only knows what will happen with this mess."

"That wretch. But all of us participated. What did they want with little Ehrlich?"

"The rat informed on him too. He maintained that Ehrlich said he wished that Psoch and the other cripples were also missing their heads."

"Good God, all of us said that. Did Ehrlich confess?"

"Trust me, he did not. He did not say a word. He only went over to that rat Güting and slapped his face. By God, it was one of the most impressive things I have seen since I came here."

"It's okay," said Werner. "You can go. We'll get back to the radio affair." Güting had not come out of the guardroom when we went to eat.

There was much discussion, wild guessing, and nervousness at the dinner table.

"It was that thief Güting who took the notes to get us into trouble," Schnapper said firmly. "He believed that he was safe in his bookbinding shop, the dog, and thought that no one would remember he was here using the press yesterday. I hope they will be able to squeeze the truth out of him in the guardroom."

"One should not judge in advance," said Springer, looking at Schnapper reproachfully.

Schnapper was about to answer, but Cytrin beat him to it. "What? Are you sitting there defending the man? The dog has done nothing but cause us trouble, grief, and misery. But this time he will get what he deserves, no matter how slippery he is." Cytrin tossed his spoon into his dish so the food splattered. Then he got up from the table and left the room.

I tried not to see or hear what took place around me. I did not succeed.

"Nachtstern, come into the print shop," Apfelbaum called from the doorway.

I could feel how the fellows stared after me when I left.

Güting stood in the middle of the floor with only his shirt on. His face was battered and swollen and his right wrist was bandaged. Next to him stood Psoch and Apfelbaum with a dog whip each. Werner and Wild West were there too. And Cytrin. He turned to me, upset.

"Now you'll have to answer for yourself. Did Güting not say to you once that no one but he would get away from here alive?"

"That's a lie," yelled Güting.

"Now, Nachtstern," Werner spoke slowly. "Don't you hear Güting say that you are a liar? Did he say it, or is it something you have imagined?"

Now I knew that it was either Güting or me.

"That's what Güting said to me the first day I was here."

"You damned liar!" shouted Güting desperately.

Cytrin rushed over to Güting, waving his forefinger at him. "Was it a lie you said, you dirty sewer rat? You, who would send your own mother to hell if you saw fit. You said it, and it's you and no one else who stole these notes. You thought you'd get us into trouble, but this time you yourself will have to accept the consequences of your malice."

"You are lying," hissed the dwarf, who resembled a lemming on two legs.

Werner had gone over to the inspection table.

"Come here, Güting. Come, and I will show you something."

Psoch and Apfelbaum followed Güting across the floor.

Werner pointed to a little box on the table. "Have a look at this. What do you think this is?"

The half-naked dwarf jumped to get away, but Psoch and Apfelbaum were prepared.

"Hold on to him; we don't want any more wrist operations today. Do you understand where these ashes come from, Güting? You are right; we found them in the oven. The one next to the press."

"I didn't do it," said Güting stubbornly.

Werner took the whip from Apfelbaum and struck.

I left without waiting for an order. I could not stand staying there any longer. None of the SS men noticed that I had left the room. They were too busy admiring Werner's skill with the whip.

A few minutes later Cytrin came into the mess hall.

"Now we've gotten rid of the devil," he said, excited. "They're driving him to Berlin, and I think they will finish him quickly there."

"Did he confess?" asked Schnapper.

"No, he adamantly denied it, although he gave himself away time and time again. In the guardroom he rushed to the door when he realized that he was finished. So help me, he managed to cut his wrist before they caught him in the exercise yard. They patched him up and continued the interrogation." Cytrin turned to me: "You saw how he gave himself away when he saw the ashes."

"What kind of ashes are you talking about?" Bober looked anxiously at Cytrin.

Cytrin told them everything he had heard and seen in the print shop.

"In the end they tied his hands and feet and locked him up in the air-raid shelter. To hell with the slippery rat."

"But he's a human being too," said Springer sadly.

"I'll be damned if he is," objected Cytrin angrily. "If he had stayed here a while longer, he would surely have set fire to the whole place; he had it in for us."

"Time's up!" called Stein.

In truth it was probably only Springer who worried about Güting's fate. The rest of us dreaded the consequences of his slander. To listen to the news from England was after all a deadly sin, even for the Germans. That day Stein and Pick were worst off. They should have been like little Ehrlich. Even if Werner had not believed them, he might have pretended that he did. He would have been hard put to admit to Krüger that something like this could happen in a place where he was in charge.

"If this is reported to Berlin, we'll be in trouble," Glantzer said loudly to himself.

"Take it easy, Glantzer," said Luka. "Werner will never say a word about the radio affair. It would be the same as to admit that he as well as the other SS men neglected their duties in the worst way."

"But what if Güting continues to blabber about it during the interrogations in Berlin?"

Luka shrugged his emaciated shoulders. "Then Werner would call the allegation a complete lie. Besides, no one can make me believe that Werner or anyone else plans to send Güting to Berlin. It's simply ridiculous to think that they would make such a fuss for a poor prisoner who is also a Jew. Of course, Krüger will find out about the matter, and you can bet your life he'll make sure it doesn't get any further."

Both Werner and Wild West showed up several times in the print shop, but neither of them referred to the matter of the radio. We actually began to believe that they had decided to pretend they had forgotten the whole affair.

"I don't like it," said Stein once, when he stopped at our table. "Both Werner and Wild West treat Pick and me as if nothing happened. But I wonder what Werner talked to Bober about for so long just now."

"I can well imagine what that was about," said Luka. "Güting must have said that it was Bober who not only hatched the plan but also pulled the strings while he showed off as master of ceremonies. If Werner talked to Bober, you can be sure he knows the score. This time it's we who say 'one for all and all for one.'"

"Do you really think the fellows will hold out, Luka? Do you think they can?"

"Not all, but enough so that Werner will never dare to risk having the experiment be unsuccessful, if you understand what I mean."

Stein was obviously relieved when he left our table.

We anxiously kept an eye on the hands of the large clock on the wall. No more than ten minutes was left of the working day.

Then Wild West arrived in his finery, with polished boots and white gloves.

"Pack up!"

"Punishment drills," whispered Luka triumphantly.

He was right.

Wild West was standing on a stool, waiting for us when we came outside to the exercise yard.

"Run! Faster! You made your bed, now lie in it." While we panted and ran he stood and fanned his face with his gloves. "Lie down! Get up! Hop! I have lots of time, men! Lie down! Get up! You made your bed, now lie in it."

He continued this way as long as we managed to stay on our feet. But neither that day nor later did we hear one word about the radio affair.

The following day Krüger came over personally and told us that Güting's life had ended on the gallows, following a hearing and sentencing in Berlin.

"I don't doubt for a minute that they have hanged him," said Luka after Krüger left. "But what he said about a hearing and Berlin is way off."

———

"My word!" swore the high-ranking SS officer, impressed, when Krüger opened the door to the "treasury." "Here you have more pound notes than the Bank of England itself." Krüger bowed and smiled proudly.

"Good God," said Glantzer when the old man and his distinguished guest had disappeared into the storeroom. "I think it's Himmler himself who is out and about. Did you see the man's eyes, Luka? They looked as though they were glowing."

One day several truckloads of a new type of box arrived. The boxes were overflowing with identity cards from all over Europe. Following Werner's order, Stein chose forty men to work with them. The work consisted of removing the photographs from the cards. It was not a pleasant job, because we knew what had happened to the owners of the cards.

"Can you understand what this is supposed to be good for?" said Max as he reached for another card from the box. "Is it possible that they intend to put different photos on the cards in order to sail under false colors when the war is over? Oh my, what a gorgeous girl," he let slip when he opened up a new card. "And these eternally damned brutes have murdered such a beauty in cold blood!" Max's voice trembled.

"They are up to some tricks with this," said his friend Harry, changing the subject. "You'll see how the superhumans are going to humiliate themselves and become subhumans when the war is over. "'Here you are; here's my identification card. I am Polish . . . French . . . Belgian,' and so on. Judging from these mountains of cards, there will hardly be a German left to hang."

We worked with the identification cards for eight days. On one of the last days something happened that we had long expected. One of the prisoners, Wilde, found a card that had belonged to a close relative of his. He became completely hysterical, and after a break outside, he refused to go back to work. Of course this would be considered sabotage, so we tried to talk some sense into him. Any upheaval would benefit neither him nor us—on the contrary. And what had happened to his relative was just as irreparable as it was sad. We said all this and more to him, but he would not be budged.

"They can do with me whatever they want," he said hysterically. "I'm not going back to those terrible boxes, and neither should you."

The situation was becoming dangerous. There were several others besides him who were on the verge of hysterics. Then Felix Tragholz went over to Wilde.

"You are talking about a close relative, Wilde. Two days ago I found the cards that belonged to three of my siblings. For a moment I thought of doing what you want to do now. But I didn't do it. I imagined I could hear them say: 'Felix, don't be foolish. You have a slight chance to pull through—take good care of it. You won't be able to give us back our lives, and we don't want it to be our fault that you lose yours.'" He took Wilde by the arm. "Come, let us go inside and continue together with the others. Maybe our time will come."

Wilde went with him.

That evening new people came to the block for the last time—eighteen emaciated Hungarians who had been gathered by the tireless Krüger from various concentration camps. Glantzer did all he could to help his countrymen settle in. The amount of cigarettes and food he managed to scrounge and forage for the exhausted newcomers was unbelievable.

"Did you empty the entire stockpile?" asked Luka when Glantzer came over to us. "Had I my top hat here, I would ask you to conjure up a rabbit. Are the three sitting over there brothers?"

Glantzer nodded.

"Yes. They ended up in three different concentration camps and knew nothing about each other's whereabouts until they met in the quarantine block here in Sachsenhausen. The two next to them are father and son. They also met in the quarantine block."

"Life is strange," said Luka.

Chapter 23

IT WAS THE FIRST OCCASION ON WHICH QUIET AND CALM KURT LEVINSKY showed any sign of nervousness. He took a walk across the room and came back to the table where we were playing chess.

"No, I don't like the atmosphere nowadays," he repeated. "Don't you sense that there's a crisis in the air?"

"You're just imagining it, old man," said Schnapper. "The air is neither better nor worse than it has been. Sit down, you're spoiling the view."

"Imagining it? Do you think I've spent twelve years in concentration camps for nothing? Trust me—I've learned to read the signs."

"Okay, okay," Schnapper flared up nervously. "Read your signs all the hell you want, but keep it to yourself. We're playing chess here."

It was not only Schnapper whose nerves were on edge at the time; we all felt the same way. We expected, any day, to find out that the print shop would be closed down. Lately the printing had been done at such excessive speed that the storeroom containing the notes was full to capacity. We also knew that the Russians and Americans were on German soil. Even if the Germans thought they could manage to stop the enemy, we had to figure that they would consider it wise to wipe out all traces that would reveal the slightest thing about the activity in our block.

"Chess is an excellent diversion," said Levinsky slowly. "I just think it's about time we took stock of the situation."

"Of course," grumbled Schnapper angrily. "Maybe you think we should establish a counterfeiters' trade union and demand better conditions. I'm sure you'll be willing to accept the role of representative and lead negotiations with Werner. I'm afraid you'll be away a long time. No, you old camp veteran, the only chance we have is a sudden end to the war."

"I don't understand what they're going to do with the pound notes now," said Shurak. "Not to mention the idiotic stamps with the Star of David and the sickle and hammer."

Bober, who had not said a word until now, turned to Shurak. "Was it *understand* you said? Why should little Shurak from Radow be the first to understand a German?"

"Move," said Tovarisch.

"Checkmate." Bober made one of those incredible moves he came up with once in a while. "But to change the subject, Tovarisch, how are you doing with your dollar bill?"

"Between you and me, it will be ready any day now."

"Will it look good?"

"What do you think? I've produced many good things with worse resources than I have here. It would also be fun to know that one has created something really special before everything goes up in smoke. You're a devil on the chessboard, Bober."

"This dollar bill might become very important for all of us," said Bober.

"Then it should not be long in coming" was Levinsky's gloomy comment.

⁓

Apfelbaum and Psoch were sitting at the inspection table. Apfelbaum poked fun at his one-armed colleague.

"It's a long time since you got a package from home, Psoch."

Psoch started to say something, but stopped.

"Those were great parcels you used to get," continued Apfelbaum, blowing grayish-yellow smoke into the air. "For that matter, I never got to taste the delicacies. It was only Werner who had the honor."

Oberscharführer Jansen came over to the two and sat down. Suddenly he turned to Psoch: "Do you know what 'L-S-R' means?"

"*Luftschutzraum* [air-raid shelter], I guess," said Psoch innocently.

"Oh no; it means *Lerne schnell russisch* [learn Russian quickly] . . . at any rate, in East Prussia, where you come from."

Apfelbaum laughed out loud and slapped his thighs. "That's a good one. It's obvious you have to learn Russian, Psoch. You're a Russian now, you know."

Psoch jumped up from the chair.

Just then Werner came out from the guardroom. Psoch threw his arm around him and sobbed like a kid. Werner stroked his hair.

"Take it easy, my boy. We're winning the war."

Psoch leapt a few steps across the floor. Then he clicked his heels and raised his hand: "Heil Hitler!" he gasped.

"I'll remember and enjoy this scene as long as I live," said Luka when Werner had returned to the guardroom.

"Same here."

"They must be quite discouraged and indifferent to behave like this in front of us. But if Psoch snitches on Apfelbaum and Jansen, you can bet your life that Werner will yell at them."

Stein came into the dayroom, seemingly shaken.

"Now it looks bad. It seems they're thinking of closing down the whole thing."

The room became as silent as the grave.

"Where did you hear this?" asked Bober, somewhat later.

"From Werner. It's an order from Berlin, he says. He was flushed with malice."

"I have expected this for a long time," mumbled Levinsky to himself.

"First I want to hear Krüger tell us," said Tovarisch. "He left for Berlin yesterday with a test print of the dollar bill."

"Are you completely finished with it? Does it look good?"

"You should have seen Krüger. He embraced me and carried on like a maniac. I can tell you this, men—if anyone has produced a better fifty-dollar bill than mine, he has not been discovered."

Schnapper cleared his throat. "I could swear that that confounded Werner said this to Stein just to scare us. It would be just like him."

"I've been imprisoned in camps since 1933 and managed to stay alive for twelve years. I don't intend to let them take my life now, just like that. They will not get me to the gas chamber alive."

"Me neither," said Krebs, who usually did not join in our conversations. "I'd like nothing better than to set fire to the whole mess hall tonight."

"Stop such childishness," Bober interrupted him coldly. "It's sad to hear an old prisoner like you coming up with such hysterical nonsense. Who the hell would enjoy it if you set the place on fire? I have no intention either of letting them take me without putting up a fight, but I'm not going to be reckless. First, let's see if there's something to what Werner says. Anything can happen now. Even miracles."

"To hell with you and your miracles," snarled Krebs, and went to his bunk.

Bober looked after him contemptuously.

We froze on our stools when we heard a car come through the gate in the board fence.

Was it Krüger finally coming? We had not seen him since the day he went to Berlin with the copy of the fifty-dollar note, the straw all of us clung to. To be sure, we had not gotten any confirmation of Werner's disturbing remarks to Stein, but on the other hand, we knew the Germans did not tend to attach importance to such minor details.

"It's Krüger," whispered Glantzer, moistening his lips. "I recognize the sound of the car engine."

There was no doubt it was Krüger's car. But so what? First of all, there was no guarantee that he himself was in the car, and secondly, we did not know what instructions he had for us, if indeed he had any. We were only a gang of prisoners, and of course, he himself had to obey the orders of the men in Berlin.

We did not talk together, just listened, with our nerves on edge. We were startled each time someone came to the door of the guardroom, but it was always only one of the regular SS men.

"Where is he?" muttered Glantzer. "This doesn't look good."

"It doesn't have to be a bad sign that he takes his time coming in here," whispered Luka. "And if it was really he who came before, I actually take it as a good sign. There's Stein. He looks as though he knows something."

There was a glimmer in Stein's eyes.

"Was it Krüger who came before?" asked Glantzer anxiously before Stein was able to open his mouth.

Stein nodded. "Yes, and I don't think the situation is as black as Werner says. Something else must be brewing, because Uncle Krüger and Tovarisch are walking arm in arm outside in the exercise yard, smoking and talking like the best of friends. One would think they were two classmates reminiscing."

"The dollar bill," said Luka.

Ten minutes after Stein left, Krüger came in. "Good day, gentlemen," he greeted us, and smiled his "uncle smile" to the right and to the left. "I have news for you which I hope you will appreciate. Our superiors in Berlin have decided to move the project to a safer place. It was I who took the liberty of suggesting it. Our work is too important to risk a bomb putting a stop to it. I want to know that both my capable coworkers and our irreplaceable machines are safe. It will be tiring work to move everything, but I am sure that you will all do your best so that we can leave as soon as possible. Finally, I want to remind you once again that those who are diligent and devoted will always find that they have a loyal protector in me—but only those . . . Good luck, gentlemen."

———

Tovarisch did not hide the fact that he was enjoying himself immensely as he stood up on a stool.

"If you don't nag and talk all at once, you'll get the whole story. Krüger came straight into my workshop from the car. 'My dear Tovarisch,' he said, 'your masterpiece created the biggest stir in Berlin. That is an understatement,' he added. You should have seen his face. I thought he would throw his arms around me. Well, fellows, we're going to print dollars until Wall Street has to go into the shoelace business. There you have the whole story in a nutshell. As you know, I am a modest man, but I have a feeling that my dollar bill came at the eleventh hour. Whatever Werner said to Stein was most probably not just bluff." Tovarisch jumped down from the stool.

"What was it you and your agent talked about so long outside in the exercise yard?" asked Bober.

"Technical details and personal experiences in different areas, my friend."

Bober put his arm around Tovarisch's shoulder. "I have a tidbit in my cupboard—it's for you, the uncrowned king of the counterfeiters. You not only perform miracles, but you yourself are a miracle. Come with me."

It was almost impossible to recognize the dayroom. It was as if a fresh gust of wind had left its mark on a black fogbank. Even Cytrin lifted his hands from his knees and treated Italiener to a cigar.

"Thank you, you old pessimist," said Italiener as he sat down next to him. "There, you see—as long as there is life, there is hope."

"Hmmph," grumbled Cytrin, but it was not the usual angry grunt.

Hoffgaard and I emptied our closets. Both of us had received a parcel a few days ago. Of course Tovarisch occupied the place of honor at the party.

We packed against time to get ready at the stipulated hour.

Luka and I were nailing down the cover of one of the note-boxes. Each box, of which there were huge stacks, weighed about 220 pounds. Other boxes were filled with English stamps, decorated with sickle and hammer and the Star of David, and still others with false passports and various types of documents. There were also the huge boxes containing the precious paper. Of course, those who worked with the heavy instruments and machines had the hardest job.

Luka straightened his back and drew his hand across his sweaty forehead.

"Even as we speak I think I'm dreaming about this insane undertaking. What in hell do they want with all these notes; can you tell me that?"

"Krüger has told us more than once. First, they are going to ruin the archenemy on the other side of the Channel, and then it will be the turn of 'God's own country.'"

Luka waved his hammer angrily. "If you can't be serious, you might as well keep your mouth shut."

"I'm only repeating what Krüger predicts and surely believes; he's obviously not the only one who believes this, either."

Max, who worked next to us, poked at Luka. "Just be happy as long as they have this mad idea. They even think that they're going to win the war, despite the fact that half the country is occupied and the other half is in ruins."

"Look," said Luka. "Where are they taking poor Sukenik?"

The young tubercular journalist from Bialystok came through the room flanked by two SS men. He had been sick in bed these last few months. Now he raised his hand.

"Take care, fellows, and thank you for your company. I won't be coming back."

"Don't be silly," said one of the guards. "We've told you that you're going to the hospital to recover."

Sukenik shrugged his bone-thin shoulders almost patronizingly. "So close and yet so far. Think of me once in a while, boys."

The guards pushed him through the door.

"He knew where he was headed," mumbled Luka.

Max shook his head.

"I just don't understand how they can tell a man here the absurdity that he is going to the hospital. Why didn't they just give him an injection like they usually do?"

"It's Werner who's behind it. He wants to show us that it's not beyond him to put a man against the wall and to finish him with a shot in the back of the neck."

Chapter 24

LUKA PRESSED HIS FACE TO THE OPENING BETWEEN THE IRON BARS. THE train was standing at a small station just outside Prague. The Czech capital lay on a slope below us.

"Do you see the factory here, just on your right, Max? I have passed it many times." Luka clenched his fists around the iron bars as if he wanted to tear them down. "And my first girl lived on the other side in the white house. Maybe she still lives there. Oh no, she probably got married a long time ago. She was wonderful, Max, the most wonderful of them all. We cannot see my home from here; it's down there in the middle of the city." Luka's animated voice became rough.

"Get away from the opening," yelled one of the guards.

Luka did not pay attention to the order. We had to use force to tear him away from the iron bars.

It was the third day of our journey to Mauthausen, fifty men in each cattle car. We did not even have the whole car to ourselves. Our guards had taken possession of a wide strip of floor between the sliding doors. We were hungry and dirty. Most of us had finished the sixteen slices of bread we were given as provisions before we left Sachsenhausen. We spent the first night at the railway station in Oranienburg, and when we finally left, it took four hours to travel the eighteen miles to the pile of rubble that was Berlin. All along this route the Germans were working like mad to repair the bomb damage. It had been like this everywhere we passed.

We stopped for a while in Dresden. The city had obviously received the same treatment as Berlin. The railway station was a chaotic scene of twisted iron beams and scattered tracks. "For my wife and children," said someone who hailed from the city.

The train started to move.

Stein stood at the opening and cried when we passed a small village ten minutes later. It was his hometown.

We squeezed down to the floor and tried to sleep. Even Italiener and Hoffgaard had become silent.

At the other end of the car someone began to sing:

> *As long as in the heart within*
> *a Jewish soul still yearns*
> *and toward the end of the east*
> *an eye still watches toward Zion.*

> *Our hope is not yet lost*
> *the hope of two thousand years*
> *to be a free man in our own land*
> *the land of Zion: Jerusalem.*

(An older version of "Hatikvah," the Israeli National Anthem)

We arrived at the little town of Mauthausen on the Danube in the evening. The eighty-mile-long journey had taken five days and nights. Thus, the average speed had been between four and six miles an hour.

The doors were pushed aside.

"*Raus!*" Werner was in his element now.

It was a dark February night and pouring with rain. The Mauthausen concentration camp was located four miles from the town, and it was uphill all the way. We had to support the oldest of the men.

Exhausted and ready to collapse from hunger, we staggered into the block that waited for us. It was isolated from the other barracks with a wall and a double electric fence. We threw ourselves down on the floor as we came in and lay there gasping for breath with our eyes closed.

Luka was the first who sat up.

"Men," he said a little while later. "Sit up and look around this palace. I thought I'd seen the worst when it comes to barracks, but I only see it now. There's not even a stool here, not a bed or a table. Damn it, get up and take a look. The walls and windows are full of bullet holes, and there's blood everywhere. The smell of blood and corpses fills the air—don't you notice it?"

"Halt maul!" Werner stood in the doorway. "So, you think there is a smell of blood, Luka? That could be right, my man. Some Russians stayed here, and the idiots thought they could escape. Look out of the windows and you will understand why they did not succeed. Those who did not croak in the electric fences got what they had coming to them from the three machine gunners in the watchtowers, who guard this block closely night and day. So now you know what happens to those who are stupid enough to try to get away from here on their own. Tonight you will get mattresses to sleep on. Tomorrow we will get down to putting this block in order. The cars at the railway station must be unloaded too." Banging the door shut, he left.

"Devil," Luka hissed after him.

The mattresses we got were rotten with mold and dampness.

"We'll never get away from here alive," moaned Cytrin, who was lying near the wall.

Italiener raised himself up on his elbows. He sighed with fatigue and lay down without saying anything. Then Bober got up.

"Listen, men, we have gone through so much that we cannot let that damned shit Werner scare us with his talk. You can be sure that he does not dare to go any further than Krüger and Berlin permit him. Besides, it's obvious that the printing of the notes is to continue, and this, gentlemen, cannot be done without us. Let's go to sleep and see what the morning will bring."

"Compared to this pigsty, Sachsenhausen and Block 19 was a luxury hotel," said Luka.

We froze on the clammy mattresses. There was little sleep.

The breakfast we got the following morning consisted of a loaf of bread divided between six men. One third of the bread was so moldy that we had to cut it away.

"You have nothing to complain about," Psoch consoled us. "The Russians who sleep in a tent here get one loaf of bread for sixteen men."

❦

I was in the group that was sent down to the railway station to unload the machines and everything else we had brought with us. The prisoners in the camp looked at us as if we were strange animals when we passed them. They had, of course, never seen prisoners with long hair. When we left through the gate we saw a man chained to the wall, arms above his head. He still stood there when we returned in the evening. The torture chains on the wall were never empty during the five weeks we were in Mauthausen.

It was a terrible grind to empty the eight railway cars. The boxes of notes and paper were sent up to our block. We did not have room for the machines, so we had to haul them to a large hay barn near the station.

"What do you think about this, Tovarisch?" asked Bober during the noon break. "After all, you know Mauthausen from before."

Tovarisch slurped the last drop of the water-thin soup the camp kitchen had sent down to us for lunch.

"It will never be possible to set up a print shop here. I could have told them that before. But it's their business. For us, it's time that is important."

"Look at the poor wretches," exclaimed Glantzer, who was looking in the direction of the road.

A long column of Musselmänner staggered toward us, ragged and filthy human wreckage that could barely stand up. They were lined up in a tangled mass in front of the station building. When we came back from the hay barn in the evening, at least a hundred of them lay on top of each other in the mud. Some Germans tore their clothes off them and threw the dead or half-dead poor wretches this way and that onto trucks. One of the Germans said with a sneer that these prisoners had walked more than twenty miles on the country road. Their destination was the gas chamber and crematorium in Mauthausen.

Tovarisch was right. It was impossible to set up a print shop in Mauthausen. All the barracks were overcrowded with prisoners evacuated from other camps, and the crematorium ovens were not able to keep up with the gas chambers. But wherever Krüger was at that time, he was fighting passionately for his beloved counterfeit operation.

One day orders arrived from Berlin that we were to move to another camp with the machines and everything else.

❦

And now we stood packed together in two open railway cars on our way to Redl-Zipf, about fifty-five miles away. A cold rain shower had drenched us just before we were crammed into the baggage cars. When the guards secured the rail in the back, we stood there like a glued-together, shivering mass. And this was how we had been standing for more than twenty-four hours now. Those who fell asleep or fainted were not at any risk of collapsing, as there was simply no room for it.

When we arrived in Linz, the city had just been visited by American bombers. On the roof of the destroyed station building stood a tank that had been hurled up there by the air pressure of a bomb. At Wels, an important junction, hundreds of locomotives and other railway material were scattered around, and only one of the many tracks was passable.

We arrived in Redl-Zipf at night. Only at dawn the next morning were we allowed to leave the cars. We reeked as if we had been spit out of a sewer, and our faces were covered with filth.

Werner was surprised that all of us were alive.

Redl-Zipf was a small camp with no more than three barracks and a few hundred prisoners. The entire guard crew consisted of twelve older soldiers and a camp commandant, all Austrians.

"This is not an ordinary concentration camp," Schnapper the sleuth was able to tell us the first day. "It's a work camp, and most of the prisoners are Spaniards. By God, we have been unusually lucky now. The Spaniards move about almost as they please. They forage food from the farmers outside the camp and live like little lords. You'll see we'll be okay here, men."

"Not as long as that bastard Werner is in charge," said Levinsky. "You can be sure that he'll give us a hard time here too."

It was as Levinsky had predicted. The first thing Werner did was to put up a barbed-wire fence around the two blocks he had confiscated. The Spaniards simply had to crowd together in the third. Using every trick in the book, we managed to place our counterfeit equipment in the two barracks. But there was no room for the sorting of the notes. Berlin took care of that matter too. The Germans had blasted away a section of the mountain just outside the camp and had built an enormous workshop in the cavern. One of the huge halls was cleared of machines and turned over to us as a sorting room. Tables and chairs were supplied for the forty of us who worked with the sorting. The lighting was excellent, but after having worked twelve to fourteen hours a day in the artificial air, our heads felt like lumps of lead.

～

We were on our way home from the sorting hall one day when suddenly Luka bent down and picked something up. It was a whole cigarette. A little later both Glantzer and I each found one at the roadside. Here and there the men squatted down.

"It's the Spaniards who put them here for us," said Luka, moved. "Good God, how wonderful it is to have an experience like this."

"At first I thought Werner had laid a trap for us." Glantzer blew his nose into his fingers. "I didn't think there were such people left in the world."

This experience meant an incredible amount for all of us in the two isolated barracks.

"But didn't the SS guards see you pick up the cigarettes?" asked Schnapper when we told him about the big event.

"I'm sure they did," replied Luka. "But haven't you noticed that most of them have changed considerably lately? They know very well that defeat is unavoidable, and they probably hope that their good deeds in the eleventh hour will benefit them."

"There is something in what you're saying," admitted Schnapper. "But if I get through this, they can be sure they'll get a piece of my mind."

There was only one man who still remained the same—Werner. His behavior toward us worsened steadily. One day an extra food bucket stood outside our gate, a gift from the Spaniards. Werner refused outright to let us accept the gift. We were not supposed to have any more food than he decided we should have. We became weaker and more emaciated with each passing day. The thin soup we got was full of caterpillars. Obviously it was Werner's intention to make us into Musselmänner.

"That Krüger, that Krüger," said Schnapper one evening when our sorting unit came back to the camp. "Would you believe he picked up three half-dead printers in one or another camp and sent them here? They are so weak they can barely stand on their feet. Either the man is stark raving mad, or he's an angel who goes around saving doomed Jewish wretches who are printers by profession."

"So do you think this means they'll be safe here with us?" asked Luka ironically.

One of the three newcomers died on the following day.

Chapter 25

"WE'RE CLOSING DOWN," WERNER SAID IN AN ICE-COLD VOICE WITH AN undertone of malice. "All notes with the slightest inaccuracy are to be burned, quickly but thoroughly. You know the punishment for sabotage."

We just looked at each other when he was gone. Everyone knew what this meant. Now what had gnawed at us all along had happened. *We're closing down.*

We burned notes for five days, with our nerves stretched to the breaking point. Werner hovered over us like an evil spirit. He went through the ashes with the long club he had acquired.

"If I find so much as a single piece of paper in the ashes, I will shoot you on the spot."

Then something happened that caused a wild spark of hope to flare up within us. The last day we burned notes, the air-raid warning sounded in the camp for the first time. Two American fighter planes thundered past above our heads.

I could not help thinking of Sukenik's words: *So close and yet so far.* Nonetheless, the Americans had to be close by.

"Moritz," said Max, who sat next to me.

"Yes."

"It sounds idiotic, but I have exactly the same impulse to sing 'Valentine' and 'Ferdinand' as I had that time in the gas chamber line in Auschwitz. I think it's a good omen."

"Maybe, Max."

Bober and I were talking together when Luka came over to us with a strange expression on his face.

"What's the matter with you?" Bober asked, scrutinizing Luka's face. "Did you hear any bad news?"

"Yes and no."

"Yes and no—what kind of nonsense is that? Out with what you've heard. Damn it, speak up."

"Three days ago, orders came from Berlin that all of us should be shot. Not one of us would be alive now if the Spaniards had not interfered."

"The Spaniards? How?"

"They somehow found out about this and reported it to the leaders of the resistance movement in the area. The day after the orders to liquidate us arrived from Berlin, the camp commandant here got a threatening warning from them. The result was that he refused to carry out the Germans' orders. Of course he knows that total collapse is bound to occur any day now. But he is supposed to be a nice man who has always treated the prisoners here well."

Bober struck his palm with his fist. "And you call such news 'yes and no'? It could not be better, man. Now it's important for us to stick together in earnest. Why do you think Werner has not acted on his own? You can bet your life he knows of the order."

"When all is said and done, it's the camp commandant who's the chief here."

"Do you think Werner would've cared about that in the least, if he had otherwise felt safe? No; it's simply that he doesn't dare begin to liquidate us. First of all, we have not turned into harmless Musselmänner yet, and secondly, I don't believe he could get his people to participate in mass murder now. They know as well as anyone that defeat is imminent. By the way, who told you all this?"

"One of the guards. I promised I wouldn't reveal his name."

"There, you see? Now it's more important than ever to keep our eyes and ears open."

"Achtung!"

We did not believe our own eyes when we saw Krüger come in, tired and exhausted.

"Good day, gentlemen. Well, it looks like it's all over now." He went over to Tovarisch and patted his shoulder. "I'm sorry that we did not succeed in bringing the dollar paper here. We could have produced some amazing bills. Well, what's not supposed to happen is not going to happen. Soon you will be free, and I wish you all the best for the future. I have issued orders that you will be moved to a place where you can be safe until you are liberated. We will meet there. Rely on me, gentlemen. Good-bye."

"Angel or arch devil?" muttered Luka.

"I guess we'll soon see," said Bober.

"Hurry! Hurry!" Werner nagged hysterically and waved his wooden club. "We have only this vehicle, and everyone must leave today."

Eventually sixty-five of us stood crowded together on the huge truck bed, with a guard in each corner and two on the roof of the driver's cab. The latter were armed with machine guns. Werner sat next to the driver. And then we left. We stood too close together to be able to wave to our comrades. They knew that if the truck was not marked with a small red cross when it returned, they should refuse to get on it.

The driver used the horn constantly. The road was overcrowded with refugees. People drove, carried, and hauled whatever they had been able to take with them. Along the roadside lay ragged, exhausted, and dejected soldiers, resting. All of them had thrown away their weapons.

The first signs we drove past said To Mauthausen. I glanced at Max who stood next to me.

He nodded determinedly. "If Werner intends to drive us to the gas chambers in Mauthausen, we'll attack them just before we arrive. It's better to get shot. I hope everyone will act according to the plan when we give the signal. Some of us should be able to pull through."

GMUNDEN said the sign we raced past a little later. When we arrived in the town, the truck stopped. Werner stuck his head out of the window in the driver's cab and signaled to a traffic soldier. We could hear the words *Mauthausen* and *Americans*.

"Bravo," Max started to say.

"Shut up," grumbled the closest guard.

We were headed uphill toward the Austrian Alps.

"Back to life," said Max in a low voice. "If only this desperate driver doesn't drive us into some abyss. Good heavens, what an engine this truck must have!"

The truck maneuvered around loops and curves until it creaked. If the side rails had given way, all of us in the truck bed would have been thrown off. Despite the uncertainty and the crazy speed, I could not help but admire the splendor of the nature that unfolded around us. The landscape alternated between deep-black crevices and idyllic valleys. And high up on mighty mountaintops the sun illuminated the snow.

Three hours after we had left Redl-Zipf we arrived at Ebensee concentration camp. When it turned out there were no separate barracks there in which we could be held in isolation, we were locked up in an SS bathhouse just outside the camp.

❦

Max got up restlessly from the cement floor we sat on. "Where the hell are the others? They should have been here by now. It's surely been six hours since Werner and his people left."

"Hush." Glantzer, who sat near the wall closest to the road, shook his fist at us. "I hear a vehicle. It must be them."

It was our comrades, but not all of them. The truck we came with had had engine trouble on the way down. The new vehicle Werner had acquired only had room for thirty-odd men.

"They are coming later," said Lauber. "Werner is already on his way down again. Were you able to mark the truck you came in with a cross, Max?"

Max nodded. "I was, but it didn't help much, since it didn't get there. You risked it just the same then?"

"Luka spoke to one of the guards before we decided. He said that you were here."

"Where is Luka?"

"He was not let go this time. Werner probably saw to it that he pumped the man. Anyhow, something happened before we drove out of the camp. Psoch ran around waving with his arm like mad. We could not hear what he said because of the engine noise. Have you found out what they want with us here? All the note-boxes have been taken away, but the machines are still in Redl-Zipf, where they will probably remain, because the sky above the camp was teeming with American planes. Do you have any food?"

We had not been given a crumb to eat since we arrived.

"Oberscharführer Jansen and two more of our guards are coming," shouted Italiener. He stood on a bench and looked out through the barred window. "They are in an impressive-looking passenger vehicle. It looks like they have lots of luggage with them too."

Oberscharführer Jansen gesticulated hysterically with his fist when he entered the bathhouse. "No, not one of you devils is allowed out. You have got a small keg of soup, and you have to manage with that. If anyone tries to get out, he's the one who will suffer the most. In Redl-Zipf two idiots tried to run away. One of them is dead, and the other one hovers between life and death in the hospital. Just try it, and you'll see—the same thing will happen. I have six men outside, and they have been ordered to shoot without warning."

"Who could it be, I wonder?" said Glantzer when Jansen had left.

"So, this is why Psoch ran around yelling," remarked Lauber.

"Jansen is only bluffing," commented Max excitedly. "He ought to tell that nonsense about one of our group being in the hospital somewhere else. I could swear that the men pulled through, whoever they are. The Americans are probably very close to Redl-Zipf."

One of the enlisted SS guards came into the bathhouse. "You can come outside and get some fresh air," he said.

We almost had a fight getting out of the stinking room, where we sat on top of each other. Then Jansen came running.

"What the hell does this mean? Who let them out?"

"I did," said the guard.

"You? Who gave you permission?"

"I took the liberty."

Jansen blushed deeply with fury and pulled out his pistol. "Get into the bathhouse right away, or else I'll make sure that each and every one of you is sent to the gas chambers this minute. There are plenty of them in this camp."

We went inside again.

"The man is desperate," said Max. "Now it's important to keep cool."

❧

It was the fourth day we had spent in the bathhouse. Max and I stood at the barred window and watched the road. Werner and the last group of prisoners had not yet arrived.

"You'll see that the Americans have captured both Werner and our comrades."

"If so, I wish we had been left until the end," said Max. Suddenly he clutched my arm and pointed toward the officers' barracks that were located on an elevation 100 to 130 feet away.

"Now they are starting to burn papers."

The Germans were carrying piles of protocols and other papers to a fire they had lit.

"This is so strange that I can hardly dare to believe it's true," said Max in a low voice. "Less than a week ago we were burning notes the same way. And now it's their turn. Look, now they're beginning to leave too."

One car after another left with the officers and their luggage. Some of the men had put on civilian clothes; others had removed the SS emblems from their uniforms while they drove down to the main road. Women were at the wheel in several of the cars. Suddenly Jansen stood in the doorway. He had also removed the SS symbols from his uniform collar.

"You are allowed into the camp with the other prisoners. You will be liberated soon. But don't tell anybody that you have made counterfeit money. Come along."

We saw nothing of the two enlisted SS soldiers outside. It was only Jansen and the Wehrmacht soldiers who marched with us toward the camp. When we got to the gate they had all disappeared.

We stood inside the gate, completely confused. Thousands of prisoners ran around sobbing and laughing and shouting in many different languages. Even those who did not have the strength to stand on their feet participated in the rejoicing. But there were also many who staggered around, unable to comprehend the wonderful thing that had happened. Also, for many of the 16,000 prisoners in this camp, the rescue was too late; they were too weak from hunger and maltreatment to be saved.

Everywhere we went we were surrounded by curious men who wanted to know how it happened that our hair was long. I found three Norwegians in the camp. One of them told me that there were two more Norwegians in camp, but they were so ill they would most probably not survive.

"Luka!"

"Moritz!"

We threw our arms around each other.

"When did you arrive?"

"Half an hour ago, on foot, my man."

"Did you really walk here from Redl-Zipf?"

"We simply had to; it was impossible to get a ride. The slave-driver Werner forced us with his own and nine other pistols to trudge uphill toward these alpine mountaintops. Anyhow, the seven soldiers from the Wehrmacht soon ran away. When we were midway, we met a truck with a mountain of note-boxes on the truck bed. The driver shouted to Werner and the other guards that the Americans were nearby. Five minutes later Werner was alone with us. So help me, the situation was becoming comical. There was Werner barking and waving with the pistol. We refused to walk faster than it suited us. Kurzweil and two others ran off into the woods, but bad luck led them straight into the arms of a troop of Germans who handed them over to Werner. He foamed at the mouth with rage and waved his pistol ominously under the noses of the runaways. But of course he did not dare to shoot. He knew that as soon as he fired a shot, we would attack him.

"He lasted a long time, but just before we arrived at this camp, he too disappeared. He must have lost his mind, because the last thing he said to us was that what we had been occupied with these last years had to remain a deep secret. We roared with laughter at this nonsense and continued walking. Dear God, I still don't believe it's true, that we've been rescued. Is it really true that you and I are standing here talking together as free men, Moritz?"

"I don't dare to answer yes, Luka. I don't dare to believe anything until the Americans are here. Maybe not even then. It will probably take time until we get used to this miracle. Listen, Luka, did anyone try to escape in Redl-Zipf?"

"Levi and Bier. They not only tried, but they succeeded! I hope they managed to get to the Americans. They were able to escape thanks to the

Germans' simplistic respect for regulations. Psoch had his pistol case on his right hip despite the fact that he only has his left arm. When Bier and Levi ran away from him, he dillydallied so long before he got ahold of his pistol that they managed to disappear into the woods."

Luka left to look for people from his country. I myself went to the SS bathhouse. Among the luggage Jansen had put into one of the rooms, I found the book I had seen in Werner's apartment in Sachsenhausen. I stuck it into my pocket and left.

Outside the bathhouse I met a prisoner who carried a large bundle. He nodded to me.

"If you feel like eating a better dinner, comrade, come home with me."

"Home? Where is that?"

"I moved into the commandant's villa. Just come with me."

I went with him. He and three other prisoners had actually taken possession of the villa. I was wide-eyed as I watched the fellow open up his bundle and pile chickens and rabbits on the kitchen bench.

"Where in the world did you get all this?"

"Bought it, of course, from a farmer nearby."

"But where did you get the money?"

"Money?" he scoffed. "Why would I need money when my friend the camp commandant was kind enough to leave things behind that I can barter for delicious food?"

While the men prepared the food I became dizzy simply from the aroma. The feast that followed was magical. Be careful now, I said to myself with each heavenly mouthful I took. But it was inhumanly difficult to be careful. Suddenly we stared at each other. The sound of shots came from the camp. We jumped up and ran over to the window. There was not one person near the camp gate.

"Just stay here," said the host. "I'll go and investigate; I'll be back soon."

He came back no more than fifteen minutes later. "They've gone completely crazy in there. They've broken into the warehouses and got ahold of alcohol and weapons. The idiots are staggering around, shooting at random. You must stay here tonight, Norwegian. It's dangerous in the camp now."

That night I slept on a spring mattress in the camp commandant's bed. The following day the Americans arrived.

⌒—⌒

Max, Luka, and I lay in the sun on a grassy hill outside the camp as we smoked one American cigarette after another.

"I don't understand why they let us sit in the bathhouse instead of killing us," said Max.

"Werner wanted to have us all together before murdering us," Luka said slowly. "He wanted to be sure that not a single one of us was left. We were not intended for the gas chamber. We were supposed to be lured or threatened into an undermined tunnel close by and blown up. I heard this from one of the old prisoners here. A Hungarian in the Wehrmacht told him just before he ran away."

"We would never have gone into the tunnel. Did he really imagine that we would obey such an order?"

"He was supposed to fool us by telling us that the Americans were on their way here to bomb the camp."

"Can you think of anything more naive than a German in uniform?"

Hoffgaard came running. "Tomorrow you and I are leaving, Moritz. We're flying to Copenhagen via Brussels."

⌒—⌒

The ship steamed along the Oslo fjord. The June sun glimmered in shiny windows on both sides of the world's most beautiful fjord. Squawking snow-white seagulls circled above the ship, and sunburned boys and girls paddled colorful canoes on the clear summer water. I hid behind a lifeboat and cried.

Two Interviews with Moritz Nachtstern

A journalist who met Moritz Nachtstern at Bæreia Convalescent Home for war invalids described him as follows:

His head is bent, he stares at the floor, and his fingers are twisted around each other with a hard grip. I ask him if he wants to tell me about what happened to him during the war. He lifts his head; his eyes are sad. He would really like to tell, but he is not up to it, not today. Maybe another time. But if I would really like to know, he can get a scrapbook. He turns its pages quickly—somewhat agitated. His eyes keep roaming around the room all the time without resting on anything—it's as if they look beyond time and place and reflect something that happened long ago and in another place. "There," he says, hands me the book, and is gone.

From a newspaper interview in 1959:

He is tanned and agile and looks energetic and completely healthy, but on his left arm his prison number is burned into his skin. He has gone through unfathomable suffering, which has marked him for life. After the war he was hospitalized for four years altogether; he saw the best nerve specialists in the country, but no one can help him. He has given up hope of becoming completely healthy. But is he bitter?

"We do not get anywhere with revenge. When things were at their worst I swore that I would kill each and every German when the time came. That time will never come. My son Jan, who is eight years old, asks me sometimes if it's true that I was in prison because I made false money. He does not understand what it was about. My daughter Sidsel, who is thirteen years old, has just read my book and

cries and asks for my reassurance that it will never happen again. When both of them have become adults they will understand. Then they will realize that there is something called lust for power among human beings. Until we put an end to that, the world will not be a good place. Do not misunderstand; I am doing well and am satisfied with what little I have, and will not take anything with me to my grave. It's more important to make as much as possible of the time we have."

CREDITS

Moritz Nachtstern (1902–69), a typographer, was one of the 532 Norwegian Jews deported to Germany on the SS *Donau* in 1942. From March 1943 until February 1945 he was a prisoner in Sachsenhausen concentration camp.

Norwegian journalist **Ragnar Arntzen** edited the memoir for publication in 1949.

Moritz Nachtstern's daughter **Sidsel Nachtstern** contributes a moving foreword to the book.

Translator **Margrit Rosenberg Stenge** was born in Cologne, Germany. She escaped to Oslo, Norway, with her parents in 1939, where they survived the war hiding in a small mountain village. After the war Margrit finished her studies, specializing in languages. In the 1950s she moved to Canada with her husband where they settled in Montreal. On a visit to Norway in 1996, she was given a book by a Holocaust survivor. After reading it, she decided to translate it. Since then she has translated a number of books about the Holocaust.

Bjarte Bruland is a historian specializing in the Holocaust in Norway. From 1996 to 1997 he was a member of the Commission appointed by the Norwegian government to investigate what happened to Jewish property during and after the Second World War. He works as chief curator at the Oslo Jewish Museum on a permanent exhibition about Jewish culture and history in Norway.

Lawrence Malkin is the author of *Krueger's Men: The Secret Nazi Counterfeit Plot and the Prisoners of Block 19,* which has been translated into seven languages. He is also the author of *The National Debt.* In his long career as a journalist, Lawrence was the European correspondent of

Time magazine and the *International Herald Tribune*'s correspondent in New York. His articles and reviews have appeared in many magazines including *The Atlantic Monthly, Fortune, Horizon,* and *The Quarterly Journal of Military History.*

GLOSSARY

Hauptscharführer SS Head Squad Leader, equivalent to U.S. Master Sergeant or British Sergeant Major

Himmelkommando Heaven unit; those going directly to the gas chambers

Kapo A prisoner appointed to be foreman by the SS

Kommando Work detail

Musselmänner Living corpses; those who were so weakened and emaciated by their starvation in the camps that they appeared to be literally walking skeletons

Oberscharführer SS Senior Squad Leader, junior to Hauptscharführer

Sicherheitsdienst SS Security Service

Sitzenkommando Sitting detail, in which prisoners were forced to sit in one position for hours on end

Sonderkommando A special unit working in gas chambers and crematoriums

Stubendienst Room supervisor, a prisoner

Stubendienstassistent Room supervisor's assistant

Sturmbannführer SS Storm Unit Leader, equivalent to Major

Unterscharführer SS Junior Squad Leader, junior to Oberscharführer

Index

accordions, 71–72, 110, 183–84
airplane crashes, 155
air raids, 153–54, 177, 227
American dollar bills (counterfeit
    notes), xxvi, 188, 197, 212,
    213–14, 215, 216
Apfelbaum (German guard), 176–
    77, 203, 205–6, 212
arbeit macht frei, 25, 28
arrests
    of German guards, 129–32, 137
    of Jews, xiv, xvi–xvii, 2–3, 17
Aryan race, xii
Auschwitz (city), 28–29
Auschwitz Album, xviii
Auschwitz concentration camp.
    See also Birkenau (Auschwitz
    II) concentration camp;
    Monowitz/Buna (Auschwitz
    III) concentration camp
    arrival process, xviii–xix, 25–27
    death statistics, 48
    deportation to, xvi, xvii–xviii,
    13–21
    description, 25
    gas chambers, xviii, xx, 165–66
    infirmary visits, 42–45
    prisoner statistics, 25
    purpose, xix–xx

quarantine block conditions,
    40–43, 45–47
transportation to, 39–40

Bald Heads' card club, 118
bandage incident, 73–74
Banditenschatz, Der (The Bandit
    Treasure), xxxi
Bank of England, xxvi, xxvii–xxix
barbed wire, 23, 33
Bæreia Convalescent Home,
    xxiii, 237
Bauer (German guard), 146,
    151, 153
Bazna, Elyesa (*aka* Cicero), xxviii
beatings, 31, 32, 38, 41, 46, 58, 77,
    175, 197
Beckmann, Helmuth "Wild West"
    firebombs, 178–79
    introductions, 139–40
    punishment drills, 181, 208
    Red Cross parcels, 142
    supervision and new guards,
    146–47
    Werner and, 159–61
Behak, Nils, 4
Belzec concentration camp, xix
Berg concentration camp,
    xv–xvi, 7–13

243

Berlin (Germany), 51–52, 182
Beyond (Galsworthy), 175
Bier (counterfeiter), 234–35
Birkenau (Auschwitz II)
    concentration camp, xx–xxi,
    21–23, 57–58, 78–79
Bjørnøya (Norway), 196–97
Blass, Hans, 183–84, 186
Blaustein, Max, 51, 52, 59, 62, 149
Bober, Max
    cabaret performance, 183–89
    closing print shop rumors,
        213–14
    dollar bill, 212
    engraving workshop, 83
    equipment damage, 85–86
    execution orders, 228
    Norwegian song printing, 84
    optimism, 221
    phone calls from women, 75–76
    posters, 146–47
    practical jokes, 89–92, 99–100,
        179–80
    radio access and broadcasts,
        147–49, 207
Bodd, Bernhard, 10–11, 18
Bøhm, Harry, xvii
boils, 27, 42, 43–44
bombings, 154–55, 177–78
books, 175, 235
border shootings, xiv, 1
bread stealing, 41, 68–69
Bredtveit Prison, 5
Britain, xxvii–xxviii, xxx

Buchenwald concentration camp,
    64, 141, 195
Buna concentration camp. *See*
    Monowitz/Buna (Auschwitz
    III) concentration camp
Burger, Adolf, xxxi

cabaret performances, 172, 183–89
card games and clubs, 75, 77, 118
cement sacks, 38–39
chaserim, 10–11, 188
chess, 75, 77
Churchill, Winston, xxx
Cicero (spy), xxviii
citizenship laws, xiii
clothes, xix, 23, 25–26, 26, 42,
    47, 61
concentration camps, xix. *See also
    names of specific camps*
counterfeiters. *See also specific
    names of counterfeiters*
    apprenticeship, 63–70
    engraving workshop, 83–87
    equipment transportation from
        Berlin, 182
    execution orders, 228, 236
    group statistics and ethnic
        origins, xxiii, 40, 63, 169
    health, 98
    memoirs and books by, xxxi
    optimism of, 77, 109, 110, 117,
        134, 136, 141–42, 149, 190
    pessimism of, 149, 190–91,
        216, 221

print shop regulations, 60–62
professions of, 54, 93, 105, 133, 165–66, 180
selection process, xxvii, xxi–xxii, 39, 165–66, 169, 225
sorting division, 107–8, 224
work conditions, 71–79, 173
work efficiency balance, xxii, xxvii
counterfeit notes. *See* American dollar bills; English pounds
counterfeit operations, xxx. *See also* counterfeiters; Operation Bernhard
crematoria, 27
Cytrin, Felix
  dagger theft, 162–63
  engraving workshop, 83–84, 107
  gun shot, 87
  Güting, 84–85, 204–6
  parcels, 102–3
  pessimism, 149, 190–91, 216, 221
  radio announcement jokes, 89–92
  sitting detail, 87

dagger thefts, 161, 162–63
"damned shithead," 75
death kommando
  counterfeit operation as, xxii, 62, 70, 85
  optimism and, 77, 109, 117, 134, 149

deportation, xvi, xvii, 13–21
disciplinary punishment, 125
ditch digging, 11
dogs, 11–12
dollar bills (counterfeit notes), xxvi, 188, 197, 212, 213–14, 215, 216
Donau aus Bremen (ship), xvii–xviii, xx, 15–20
dysentery, 36, 42–43

Ebensee concentration camp, xxii, 230–36
Edel, Peter, xxxi
Ehrlich (counterfeiter), 203–4
Eichmann, Adolf, xvi, xviii
Endlösung der Judenfrage, xii–xiii
English pounds (counterfeit notes)
  British cover-up, xxix
  British government ban on, xxvii
  circulation of, xxvi, xxvii–xxix
  destruction of, xxvi, 227
  Jewish underground use of, xxix
  missing, 201–6
  paper splinters, 176
  production methods, 64
  production statistics, xxv
  public displays of, xxix
  recovery expeditions, xxx–xxxi
  secret markings, 176, 177
  sorting, 107–9
Epstein, Leib, 60, 167, 168
escape attempts, 34

evacuation, xxii–xxiii, 217, 219–24, 227–36

extermination. *See also* death kommando
  counterfeiters and execution orders, 228, 236
  cremations, 27
  gas chamber, xx, 22–23, 42, 78–79, 165
  Nazi policies of, xii–xiii
  river beatings, 57–58
  shootings, 33, 47
  work philosophy, xx

Fälscher, Die (The Counterfeiters) (film), xxxi
Final Solution of the Jewish question, xii–xiii
firebombs, 177–78
food. *See also* Red Cross parcels
  at Auschwitz, 27–28, 45–46, 197
  at Redl-Zipf, 225, 231
  at Sachsenhausen, 54–55, 56, 66, 140
  stealing, 30, 31–32, 41, 58, 68–69
fortune tellers, 169

Galsworthy, John, 175
games, 75, 77, 126–28
gas chambers, xx, 22–23, 42, 78–79, 165
Glantzer, Isaak
  card clubs, 118

communication style and bets, 58–59
  counterfeit notes, explanation of, 176–77
  on death, 161, 170
  evacuation and Ebensee camp, 230, 232
  firebombs, 178
  Kahn incident, 111, 113
  Kreb's theft and punishment, 163
  Marok and Weber's arrest and punishment, 129–30, 132
  missing notes, 203
  and promise of women, 119
  radio broadcasts, 148
  Red Cross parcels, 98–99
  in sorting division, 108
  transport through Berlin, 52
Goebbels, Josef, xxvi
gold fillings and bridges, xix, 38, 144–45
Gordon, Arne, xix
Gordon, Bernard, xix, 11, 19–20
Gordon, Doris, xix, 19
Gordon, Edith, xix, 18–19
Gordon, Leo, xix
Grini prison camp, 2, 6
Groen, Max
  cabaret performance, 183–89
  on counterfeit plans, 217
  death of, xxxi
  evacuation and Ebensee camp, 229–30

identification cards, 209
interview with, xxxi
optimism, 172, 227
post-punishment drill
    assistance, 196, 197
Red Cross parcel, 193
selection of, 165–66
Grossmann, Klaus, xvii
guilt, xxii, xxiii, 153
gun shots and shootings, 33, 47,
    87, 97
Güting, Herman
as assistant and private orderly,
    121, 140, 161
death of, 208
description, 61, 66–67, 84–85,
    140–41
gold bridges, 144–45
hair clipping, 116
harassment, 69, 93–94
meeting, 55, 59
missing notes, 202, 204–6
parcel, 100, 102
photographs in SS uniform, 76

hair clipping, 26, 114–16
half-Jews, xiii
hangings, 38, 113, 208
Harry (counterfeiter), 167, 172,
    183, 188, 209
Harten, Jaac van, xxix
"Hatikvah" (Israeli National
    Anthem), 220
Himmelkommando, xx, 22

Himmler, Heinrich, xix–xx,
    xxii, xxvii
Hird, The, xiii
Hitler, Adolf, xii– xiii, 175
Hoffgaard, Sven, 133–36, 141,
    156–57, 171, 216, 236
Hoffman (German guard), 146,
    151, 153
homosexuality, 111–13, 117,
    178, 197
Høss, Rudolf, xix
Hungarians, 210

identification cards, 209–10
identification papers, xiii, xiv
infirmaries, 35–37, 42–45
"Internationale" (song), 71–72, 110
Italiener, Leib
air raids, 154
arrival, 105, 106
avenging Jewish women, 190
bed inspections and bets,
    157–58
optimism, 105, 110, 141,
    149, 216
practical jokes, 155–56

Jackie (counterfeiter), 111–13, 117
Jansen (German guard), 212–13,
    231, 232, 233
Jelo, David, xxi, 29
Jewish underground, xxix
Jews, definitions of, xiii
"J" markings, xiii, 23, 25

job security, 146
jokes, practical, 74–75, 89–92,
    99–100, 155–56, 179–80
Josel (counterfeiter)
    assistant and private orderly
        appointments, 81, 121
    bread stealing, 41
    games, 127
    language examinations, 74
    Marok wedding band, 56
    practical jokes, 99
    singing Norwegian songs,
        100–101
    sleeping incidents, 67, 81–82

Kaddish (prayer), 174–75
Kahn (counterfeiter), 111–13, 117,
    119–20
Krakowski, Avraham, xxxi
Krebs, Leo
    as barracks head, 55, 67
    Beckmann and behavior of, 142
    bets, 158–59
    bread stealing from, 68–69
    closing print shop rumors, 214
    dagger theft and appointment
        removal, 161, 162–63
    engraving workshop, 83
    fight with Marok, 97
    games, 125–28
    harassment, 93, 121–23
    Kahn punishment, 113, 119–20
    photographs in SS uniforms,
        75–76

practical jokes, 90–91, 99–100
punishment drills, 67
Red Cross parcels, 101–2, 123–
    25, 142–43
Werner and, 159–60
Kristiansen (Berg guard), 8, 9,
    10–11, 12
Krüger, Bernhard
    British internment of, xxix
    cabaret performance
        attendance, 183–89
    counterfeiter selection process,
        xxvii, 165–66, 225
    as counterfeit operation
        commander, xxii
    death of, xxxi
    dollar bill notes, 213–15, 216
    evacuation plan, 229
    expansion announcement,
        145–46
    firebomb response, 179
    gold bridge incident, 144–45
    Güting's death
        announcement, 208
    hearings and trials, xxiii, xxx
    Kahn incident reprimand,
        118–19
    Marok and Weber's arrest,
        131–32, 137
    money pick up, 97, 171
    paper specialist arrival, 94
    print shop evacuation, 215–16
    prisoner treatment, xxvii, xxx,
        54, 60

production priorities, 145
reward promises, 82, 89, 118–19
SS officer tours, 208–9
Toplitzsee note recovery and,
    xxx–xxxi
Krupp, Bernhard, 36, 39, 142
Kurzweil, Hans
    air raids, 153
    bookbinding, 198
    evacuation, 234
    as foreman, 65
    job change and parcels, 107–8
    Marok and Weber's arrest,
        129–30, 131
    medical experiments, 195
    officer impersonation practical
        jokes, 100
    radio announcement joke, 90–92

language examinations, 74–75
Lauber (counterfeiter),
    144–45, 231
letters, 95–96, 98–99
Levi, Norbert, 186–88, 234–35
Levin, Arthur, 161, 170–71, 172
Levinsky, Kurt, 211, 213, 224
Levy, Yaakov, xxix
liberation, xxiii, 233, 236
Løgård, Leo, xii, xv, 1–2, 11,
    16–17, 31
luck, 141–42
Luka, Richard
    background and selection as
        counterfeiter, 64–65

on being kicked to death, 197
bomb death *vs.* gas chamber, 161
card clubs, 118
cigarettes on side of road,
    224–25
Danish bank employee theory,
    135–36
evacuation and Ebensee camp,
    231, 233–35, 236
execution orders, 228, 236
German defeat prediction, 225
guard recreation, 71
Güting description, 66–67
Hungarian newcomers, 210
Kahn's glasses, 111
Krebs, 67, 123, 124–25, 128
Krebs and Werner, 159–60
Krüger, 82, 132
language examinations, 74
Marok and Weber's arrest,
    129–30
Marok cigarettes, 68
at Mauthausen, 221, 222
missing notes, 203
Prague, transportation
    through, 219
print shop move, 217, 219
promise of women, 119,
    120, 172
radio access, 207
Red Cross parcels, 99, 101, 144,
    172, 194–95
in sorting division, 108
SS men arrivals, 151

storytelling, 75
survival theories, 77, 82

machine guns, 97
marksmanship practice, 33
Marok, Herbert
  arrest and punishment,
    129–32, 137
  Danish bank employee, 135–36
  description, 55, 56
  games, 125–28
  gold bridges, 144–45
  inspection, 68
  Kahn-Jackie incident, 112–13
  Krebs and, 67
  language examinations, 74–75
  letter writing, 95–96
  machine gun shootings, 97
  motorbikes, 110
  Polish-Russian newcomers, 106
  print shop arrival and
    regulations, 59–62
  punishment drills, 65
  recreation, 71, 72, 75–76,
    97, 121
  Red Cross parcels, 101–3,
    123–25
  Springer's doctor visit, 117–18
Marthinsen, Karl Alfred, xiv
Mauthausen concentration camp,
  xxii, xxiii, 220–23
Max (counterfeiter). See Groen,
  Max
medical experiments, 195

Meir, Golda, xxix
Meiran, Ellinor, xv, 4
Meiran, Jakob, xv, 4
memoirs, prisoner, xxxi
mittens, 25–26
Monowitz/Buna (Auschwitz III)
    concentration camp
  conditions, 29–35, 37–38,
    41–42, 95
  death statistics and causes,
    xxi, 35
  infirmary visit, 35–37
  march to, 28
Morgenthau, Henry, Jr., xxx
motorbikes, 110
Museum of Tolerance, xxix
Musselmänner, xxi, 37, 165,
    222–23
Myerson, Goldie, xxix

Nachemsohn, Henry, xxi–xxii,
    27, 39
Nachtstern, Moritz. See also
    related topics
  arrest and interrogation, xv, 2–3
  birth and childhood, xii
  death of, x, xxiii
  early employment, 152–53
  early years, xii
  interviews, 237–38
  manuscript writing and
    publication, xi–xii,
    xxiii–xxiv, xxv
  post-war hospitalization, 237

post-war life, vii–viii, xxiii

post-war psychological effects, ix, xxi–xxii, xxiii

survival statistics and, xi

weight loss, 61

Nachtstern, Rachel, viii–ix, xxv

Narvik (Norwegian prisoner), 41

Nasjonal Samling (National Unification Party), xiii, xiv

Nazism, xii–xiii

Norway, xi, xiii–xvii, 1–3, 17

numbers, prisoner, xxi–xxii, 27, 237

Operation Bernhard. *See also* counterfeiters; English pounds (counterfeit notes)

American dollar bill notes, 188, 197, 212, 213–14, 215, 216

closing and evacuation, xxii–xxvi, 213, 217, 219–24, 227–36

as death kommando, xxii, 62, 70, 85

early planning and implementation, xxvi–xxvii

location, xxii, 53–54, 60, 61

print shop regulations, 60–62

prisoner protection, xxiii

production statistics, xxv

purpose and procedure, xxii, xxv–xxviii, 62

optimism, 77, 109, 110, 117, 134, 136, 141–42, 149, 190

Oslo (Norway), xvi–xvii, 14

Oslo Gang, 15

Palestine, 149

paper, print, 63, 177

parachutists, 155

Peppiatt, Sir Kenneth, xxvii

Perez (counterfeiter), 57, 77–78

Pick, Alfred

assistant appointments, 161

cupboard inspection, 198–99

medical experiments, 195

missing notes, 203–4

punishment drills, 199–200

radio access, 184, 187, 189–90, 204, 207

stone quarry detail, 195

pigs, 10–11, 188

pillows as decorations, 31

pinholes, 64

Poland, xix, 46

Polish prisoners, 41, 46

ponds, 195

potato stealing, 30, 31–32, 58

prayers, 174–75

property confiscation laws, xv

Psoch (German guard)

cabaret performance and guardroom, 185, 189–90

evacuation, 231, 232, 235

German defeat, 212–13

Güting and missing notes, 203, 205–6

at Mauthausen, 222

punishment drills, 195–96

Red Cross parcels, 193–94
punishment drills, 28, 67, 73–75,
    97, 106, 174, 181, 195–96,
    198–200, 208

quarter-Jews, xiii
questionnaires, xiv
Quisling, Vidkun, xiii, xv

radio announcement jokes, 90
radio broadcasts, 147–48, 181,
    189–90, 204, 207
Red Cross parcels
    as counterfeiter selection reason,
        135–36
    disciplinary punishment,
        122–25
    intact, 171
    letter writing and receiving,
        98–99
    receipts vs. receiving, 193–95
    safeguarding methods, 143–44
    sharing with prisoners, 103, 216
    stealing vs. giving, 101–3,
        142–43
    treatment due to, 100–101,
        107, 121
Redl-Zipf concentration camp,
    223–28, 231
Reussen (counterfeiter), 169
revenge, xxiii, 196–97, 237
Rød, Knut, xvii
Røgeberg, Olav, 170
Roosevelt, Franklin D., xxx

Rozjen, Boris, 190–91

Sachnowitz, Herman, 32
Sachsenhausen concentration
    camp
    arrival, 54–56
    Block 2 (Norwegian block),
        170–71
    Block 18, 146, 161, 169
    Block 19, xxii, 53–54, 60, 61
    description, 52–54
    evacuation from, xxii–xxiii,
        217, 219–24
    quarantine conditions,
        56–58, 166
    transportation to, xxii, 48–49,
        51–52
sand shoveling, 118
Schellenberg, Walter, xxvi–xxvii
Schinkenklopfen (game), 126–28
Schnapper (counterfeiter)
    bets, 58–59
    card clubs, 118
    on death, 170
    end of war, 211–12
    food criticism, 66
    games, 126–28
    hair clipping comments, 116
    hair-free head, 59
    missing notes, 204
    practical jokes on, 155–56
    and promise of women, 119
    radio announcement jokes, 100
    radio broadcasts, 148–49

revenge, 75
Sachsenhausen quarantine, 53–60
transportation to Sachsenhausen, 51–53
Werner's promotion, 198
Schwend, Friedrich, xxix, xxviii
secret markings, 176, 177
sex
    German guards and, 71–72, 97
    homosexuality, 111–13, 117, 178, 197
    promise of women, 119, 120, 121, 172
shoes, wooden, 33
Shotland, Isak, 35
showers, 22, 26, 40, 72–73
Shurak (counterfeiter), 53, 56, 85, 105, 156, 212
Sitzenkommando, 87
Sobibor concentration camp, xix
sock mending units, 42
"Solveig's Song" (song), 101
Sonderkommando, 42
soot jokes, 155–56
Soros, George, xxviii–xxix
sorting divisions, 107–9, 224
Spaniards, 224, 225, 228
splinters, 177
Springer, Arthur
    arrival, 93–96
    attitude and personality, 116, 117, 141, 204, 206
    doctor visits and torture, 117–18

games, 126–27
sleeping incident and torture, 109–10
stamps, 188, 212, 217
Star of David, 25, 188, 212, 217
Steen, Asbjørm, 2, 95, 98
Stein, Oskar
    closing print shop rumors, 213
    cupboard inspection, 198–99
    foreman appointment, 198
    hometown, 220
    medical experiments, 195
    missing notes, 201–3
    punishment drills, 199–200
    radio access, 184, 187, 189–90, 204, 207
Steinbeck, John, xxx
Steinmann, Lillegutt, 39
Steinsapir, Rubin, 18
Stensbak A/S, 152–53
stone quarry work, 195
Sukenik, Izaak, 217–18
survivor statistics, xi, 17

tattooing, xxi–xxii, 27
Terboven, Josef, xiv
Todorov, Tzvetan, xx
Toplitzsee lake, xxvi, xxx–xxxi
Tovarisch (counterfeiter)
    arrival and profession, 180
    cabaret stage design, 185–86
    closing print shop, 213
    dollar bill notes, 197, 212, 215, 216, 229

new print shop location, 222
Tragholz, Felix, 210
train transportation, xvi, xviii, 6,
  13–14, 20–21, 220, 223
Treblinka concentration camp, xix
Tubler (counterfeiter), 77, 79
typhus, 27

Ukrainian prisoners, 41, 46
underground armies, xxix
U.S. Secret Service, xxix

"Valentine" (song), 167–68,
  184–85
Vernichtung durch Arbeit, xx

Wagner, Wilhelm, xiv, xvii
Wally (Monowitz camp head),
  29, 30–31
watchmakers, 57
water hoses, 73
Weber, Heinz
  arrest and punishment,
    129–33, 137
  hair clipping punishment,
    114–16
  introductions, 65
  radio announcement joke, 90
  recreation, 71–72, 97, 121
  Springer and heat, 109–10
  SS uniform photographs, 75–76
Werner, Kurt
  air raids, 153
  apartment of, 175–76

appointment
  announcements, 161
  Beckmann and, 160–61
  bets, 157–58
  closing print shop rumors,
    213, 214
  description, 173
  evacuation, 227, 229–31, 234
  execution orders, 228
  firebombs, 178
  inspections, 157–58, 198
  introductions and arrival, 146,
    151–52
  Krebs and, 159–60
  at Mauthausen, 221
  missing notes, 201–2, 205–6
  parcels, 193–94
  production increase, 173
  promotions, 198
  punishment drills, 198–99
  at Redl-Zipf workshop,
    224, 225
Wiesenthal, Simon, xxix
Wilde (counterfeiter), 209–10
women
  for counterfeiters, 119, 120,
    121, 172
  and German guards, 71–72, 97
work philosophy, xx–xxi, 25, 27, 28
Work Will Set You Free (arbeit
  macht frei), 25, 27, 28

Zimmerman, Perez, 57, 77–78
Zyklon B, xx